WBCN AND THE AMERICAN REVOLUTION

How a Radio Station
Defined Politics, Counterculture,
and Rock and Roll

Bill Lichtenstein

The MIT Press
Cambridge, Massachusetts
London, England

© 2021 LCMedia Productions, Inc.

All rights reserved. No part of this book may be reproduced in any form by any electronic or mechanical means (including photocopying, recording, or information storage and retrieval) without permission in writing from the publisher.

This book was set in Neue Haas Grotesk by the MIT Press. Printed and bound in the United States of America.

Library of Congress Cataloging-in-Publication Data

Names: Lichtenstein, Bill, 1956- author. Title: WBCN and the American revolution : how a radio station defined politics, counterculture, and rock and roll / Bill Lichtenstein. Description: Cambridge : The MIT Press, 2022. | Includes index. Identifiers: LCCN 2021011596 | ISBN 9780262046251 (hardcover)

Subjects: LCSH: WBCN (Radio station : Boston, Mass.)--History. | Music radio stations--Massachusetts--Boston--History. | Counterculture--United States--History--20th century. | United States--Intellectual life--20th century. | United States--Social conditions--1960-1980.

Classification: LCC PN1991.67.M86 L53 2022 | DDC 384.54/53--dc23

LC record available at https://lccn.loc.gov/2021011596

10 9 8 7 6 5 4 3 2 1

publication supported by a grant from
The Community Foundation for Greater New Haven
as part of the **Urban Haven Project**

For Bernice and Eddie
and for Rose

Contents

Foreword by Charles Laquidara ix
Foreword by Ty Burr xi
Foreword by Louis Menand xiii
Preface xv

1   Boston 1967: Before the Revolution 1
2   The Boston Tea Party 13
3   Ugly Radio Is Dead 35
4   A New Kind of Radio 53
5   1968: The Year That Everything Changed and That Changed Everything 61
6   WBCN and the American Revolution 77
7   Campus Unrest 91
8   Peace Is in the Air 111
9   WBCN: The Hub of the Community and the Soundtrack of the City 127
10   WBCN News and Public Affairs 149
11   The News Dissector 161
12   The Second Wave 179
13   *The Lavender Hour:* Gender Freedom in the Air 197
14   *Lock-Up* 207
15   We've Got to Get Rid of Nixon 213
16   Rock and Roll Future 233
17   Fifty Stories above Boston 257
18   Nixon's Resignation and the End of the Revolution 265
19   Lessons Learned 277

Acknowledgments 282
Index 285

Foreword
Charles Laquidara, WBCN announcer

Given the sorry state of corporate radio today, I doubt the magic of a radio station will ever again be as representative of the spirit of an era as WBCN was. On any given autumn or summer day, you could walk five miles from the financial district of downtown Boston to Ball Square in Somerville without a radio and hear a medley of eclectic sounds — from the Firesign Theatre to Jimi Hendrix to Bob Dylan, Muddy Waters, Joan Baez, Captain Beefheart, and Frank Zappa — without missing a note.

BCN was playing everywhere — beaming from apartment house windows, college dorms, car radios, portable radios, storefront speakers, malls, factories, and shipping plants. In the late 1960s to the mid-1970s, the term *ubiquitous* would not be an understatement referring to WBCN-FM in Boston. It was the best of times during the worst of times, and BCN was the messenger.

Foreword

Ty Burr, Pulitzer Prize–nominated film critic, *Boston Globe*

It was like a jungle drum sending out messages only the kids could hear. A secret society of the airwaves. A sonic wavelength for music, anger, and activism pitched too high for anyone over thirty.

If you were young and growing up in the Boston area from the late 1960s through the early 1980s, WBCN was a radio station, but it was lot more than that. You heard bands and albums and songs no other station would touch, from prog rock to punk. You felt as if you were best friends with DJs like Charles Laquidara, Norm Winer, and the deathless Maxanne Sartori. They spun what they wanted as long as it was good. The Grateful Dead got played on WBCN and nowhere else, and Van Morrison's *Astral Weeks*; a decade later, the station was breaking the Police and U2. A kid named Bruce Springsteen showed up one day to play before anyone knew who he was.

Perhaps most critically, the little FM station that could was a lifeline for the youth of New England to the counterculture that was pushing back increasingly hard against the Nixon administration and the Vietnam War. The station pioneered the field of alternate news coverage through on-air reporter Danny Schechter "the News Dissector" and commentator Andrew Kopkind; they broke stories, exposed corruption, and reported on rallies and protests both locally and nationally.

There was nothing else like it. For someone like myself, growing up in Boston and loving that dirty water from birth, WBCN came as a shock after a childhood of AM Top 40 radio: good-natured loudmouths like Dale Dorman at WRKO and Arnie "Woo-Woo" Ginsburg at WMEX. The WBCN jocks were cool — older brothers and sisters who'd let you borrow their records and hip you to what was really happening in the wider world. Listening to the station was a generational glue and a secret password; if you met someone new and they mentioned BCN, you were in good company.

It was too good to last — it always is — but the miracle is that the glory days of WBCN continued as long as they did. Bill Lichtenstein started at the station as a volunteer in 1970, when he was fourteen, and worked his way up to weekend DJ and newscaster and then into a career as an investigative reporter and documentary filmmaker. His 2019 film *WBCN and The American Revolution* is a grand wayback machine for all of us who were there, and it led to this book you are holding, a repository of precious memories and memorabilia. A half century later, as America rises up once more in a spirit of resistance, it's good to be reminded of the roots of our rebellion and the soundtrack that went with it.

Foreword

Louis Menand, professor of English at Harvard University and Pulitzer Prize–winning author

I was seventeen years old in 1969. I have a pretty oversized superego (as we used to call it back in the sixties, when we were all Freudians), so there was not much danger that I would drop out of school, march around carrying a Vietcong flag, or burn my draft card. But I was fascinated by, and sympathetic to, people who did those things. I had an instinctive sense of generational solidarity.

To me, there is no question that what drove that sense of solidarity for most of us was the music. I went to a very small, very expensive, and very conservative all-boys boarding school north of Boston, where most of my classmates were the kids of Park Avenue Republicans. Daily attendance at chapel was required, and we had to wear jackets and ties to class and at meals. I was a scholarship student and considered a troublemaker because I wore antiwar buttons and let my hair grow an inch below my collar. The headmaster ordered me to get it cut.

We were, in other words, the dialectical antithesis of the counterculture. But we listened to the same music that everyone else our age was listening to. After Latin class, back in our rooms, we played air guitar to Hendrix and Neil Young, not as well as Bradley Cooper, maybe, but with the same commitment. The music was a huge part of our lives. I don't think we listened to the radio at school; many of the students had LP collections and incredibly expensive stereo systems. But when I was home – my parents were not rich; we lived in Lexington – I listened to WBCN. What the music gave us was not politics, exactly, but attitude.

I don't remember how I learned that students had occupied a building in Harvard Yard. That was on April 9, 1969, the spring semester of my senior year. I must have heard about it from my father, who was the director of a college prep program called Upward Bound at MIT. I was eager to see what was happening at Harvard. I knew about the student occupations at Columbia University in the spring of 1968, and I had watched on television, with my parents, the demonstrations at the Democratic National Convention in Chicago that summer. As a graduating senior, I had to do some sort of senior project, so I borrowed a Super 8 camera from the school (state of the art in affordable handheld movie cameras in 1969) and a reel-to-reel tape recorder and, with a couple of friends, took a taxi to Cambridge. That is how I got the footage and the audio used in Bill Lichtenstein's documentary.

At 5 a.m. the following morning, police stormed the building, University Hall, dragged out the demonstrators (not all of whom were Harvard students), and arrested more than 250. Some seventy-five were injured. Needless to say, I wish I had been there, but they had closed the Yard as we were leaving that afternoon, and the police raid was timed so that no one could film it. The decision to send in the cops was hard to believe because it was the very same mistake Columbia had made, one year before, when it had police remove students from Hamilton Hall, which was itself the same mistake U.C. Berkeley had made four years before that when it had police remove demonstrators occupying Sproul Hall. They all had the same results: bad publicity for the schools (it took Columbia years to recover: I went to graduate school there in 1974, when there was zero student activism, and the place was still hung over) and the forced resignation of the universities' presidents. This book reveals that the administration was motivated by fear that confidential files would fall into radical hands – which they did, making the raid even more counter-productive.

In response to the police action, Harvard students went on strike, and a rally was staged in the football stadium, Soldiers Field, across the river. We came down to film that, too, but the event was disappointing, and the movement fizzled out. It had some effects, though, notably the termination of Harvard's ROTC program, which had been one of the students' demands. (My father, who was very antiwar, ended up arranging with Harvard's new president, Derek Bok, for Harvard students to do their ROTC training at MIT.)

As it turned out, I came along at the tail end of the so-called sixties generation. The last blast of campus activism was in the spring of 1970, when the United States "invaded" Cambodia — the unrest that led to the Kent State shootings. The movement that grew up around the protests against the war persisted to the resignation of Richard Nixon, in 1974, but on campus, the air was beginning to leak out of the revolutionary balloon. I entered Berkeley in the fall of 1970, and the only political activity, apart from some residual Progressive Labor Party antics, was a parade of soap-box orators in Sproul Plaza performing largely for the tourists. I liked to hang out and listen to them, but I kept up with my schoolwork. After two quarters, I left. But although we stopped flashing peace signs, we all still listened to the radio and the music that has now become classic rock. And it really is. When I went home for vacation, the car radio was always set at 104.1 on the FM dial — WBCN.

Preface

On a summer evening in 1968, I was watching the local evening news on my family's television in our living room in Brookline, Massachusetts. As a twelve-year-old, I was aware, largely through the colorful photo-rich cover stories in *Life* magazine, of the psychedelic, LSD-fueled youth revolution that had exploded in San Francisco the summer before in the city's Haight-Ashbury district as part of the "Summer of Love" and concurrently in New York City's East Village.

But in Greater Boston, even with its more than a hundred colleges and universities and hundreds of thousands of college students, the youth revolution that would soon upend the world had yet to arrive.

And then, suddenly, it did.

In the summer of 1968, "the hippies," as they were called, appeared on the Boston Common. There were thousands of young people — dressed in rainbow colors, barefoot with long hair, playing guitars and Frisbee — and they took up residence on the Common, the plot of land that had traditionally been the backyard for the Boston bluebloods who lived on exclusive Beacon Hill.

Like the story of the Pied Piper, the presence of the hippies sent out a clarion call to young people throughout the city and suburbs. As for me, I remember getting up and leaving my family's living room after seeing the hippies on the local TV news that early summer evening and taking the train from Brookline to the Boston Common to see the hippies and the scene for myself.

Soon after, in November 1970, I was a ninth-grader in an alternative educational program in Newton, where students were given the chance to work at a volunteer job one day a week.

Being a devoted fan of radio — albeit Top 40, which was the only radio available at the time that played rock and roll — I called what was then a newly launched underground radio station in Boston, WBCN-FM, and asked if they needed help. My timing couldn't have been better as they had recently started a "Listener Line" staffed by volunteers to handle the flood of calls the station was receiving to answer questions about everything from how to help a roommate on a bad LSD trip or how to respond to a draft notice to how to find a cross-country ride or help finding a lost cat or dog, or maybe just to request a song.

I began answering the station's Listener Line, and soon after I was asked to cover demonstrations for the news department. I helped develop a distinctive sound for news reports that combined highly edited sound bites (often clips of Richard Nixon or other politicians) intercut with music and comedy into audio montages in a style that would become a signature of the radio station. Soon after, I was given my own weekly four-hour radio show. It left me with a keen sense of belief in the power of media — especially radio — to create and fuel political, social, and cultural change and perhaps most important, to give a voice to those who didn't have one and to serve as the connection between all of us. It launched a fifty-year career in media that included working as an investigative producer for a network news magazine and then starting my own company to produce public television and radio programs and documentary films to help create social change, winning print and broadcast honors along the way, including a Peabody Award.

Over the years, I thought about WBCN and the powerful impact it had, and by 2006, in the wake of the 9/11 attacks and during the war in Iraq, I began work on a documentary film that would tell the story of the early days of the radio station. It was a way of remembering and demonstrating the impact media could have and the importance of each of us bringing whatever talents we have to bear with regard to matters of social importance. The film would become *WBCN and The American Revolution*. There were no archives of audio from the era at the radio station or elsewhere, and so in 2006, even before the word *crowdsourcing* was first used, we reached out to the public, and people responded by providing us with hundreds of hours of tapes of WBCN that were recorded off the air, including live broadcasts, concerts, and news reports. The same happened with photographs and other visuals, which were shared with us by leading photojournalists of the period, notably Peter Simon and Jeff Albertson, along with dozens of others. In all, more than forty interviews were done for the documentary film and those stories and accounts are used throughout this book.

It seemed clear from early on in the production of the documentary that a book was called for to provide readers with the additional details and images that expand the remarkable story of the station and the amazing times.

With everything going on in the world today, the story of WBCN is as relevant – and timely – now as it was then. Enjoy!

Bill Lichtenstein, filmmaker, *WBCN and The American Revolution*

Bill Lichtenstein (author) at age sixteen on the air at WBCN-FM, 1973. *Source: Don Sanford.*

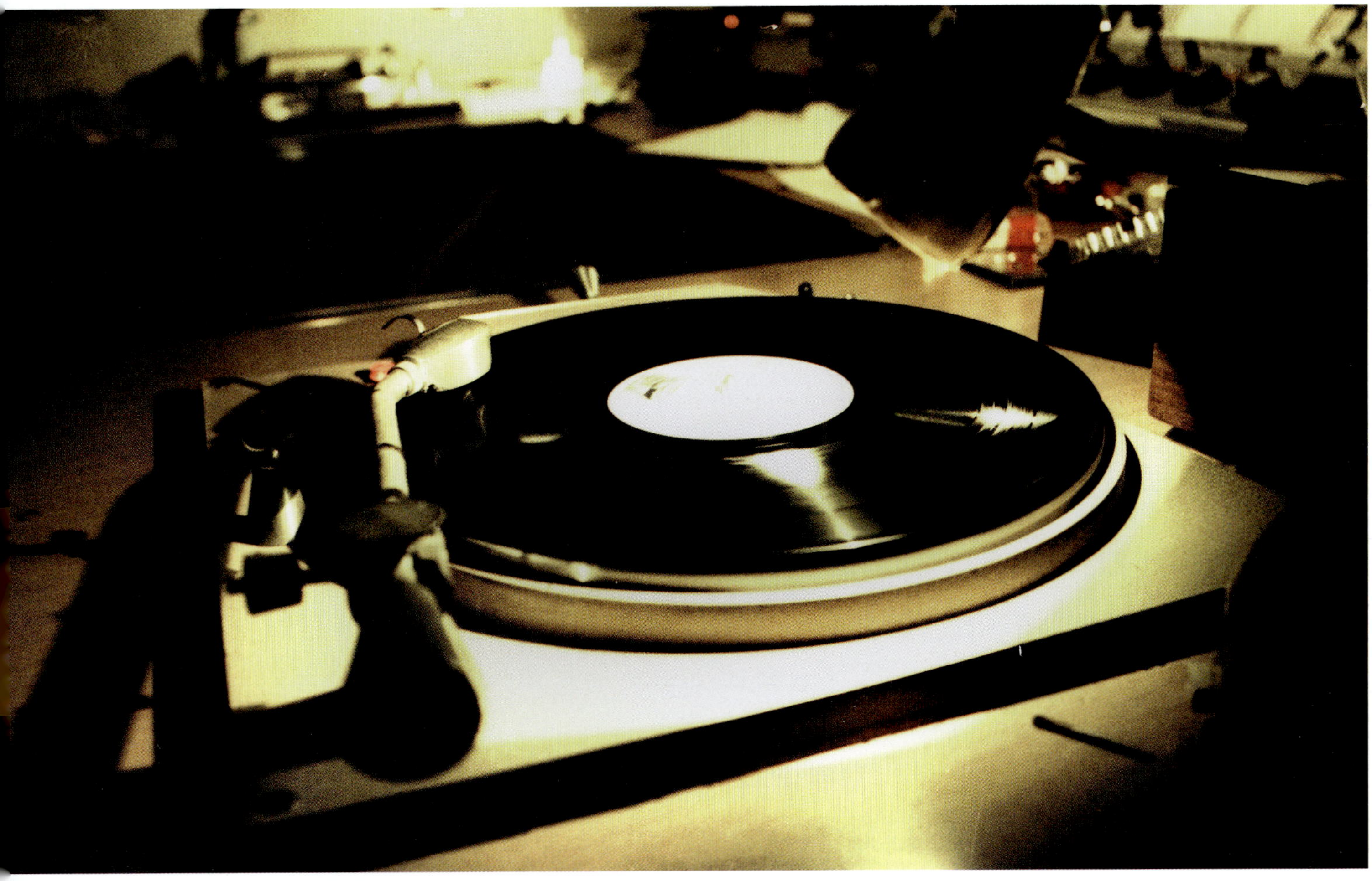

...phony Hall; Neiel Youn..., Dec. 6, Music Hall, and Janis Joplin, Dec. 21, Music Hall; Pete Seeger, Jan. 22, Symphony Hall; Tom Rush, Jan. 29, Symphony Hall.

AT BOSTON TEA PARTY: Small Faces with Rod Stewart, Ball 'n' Jack, Oct. 5–7; Mungo Jerry plus second group, Oct. 8–10; John Mayall, Oct. 12; Frank Zappa & Mothers of Invention, Oct. 18; Lee Michaels, Haystack Balboa, Oct. 22–24; Leon Russell, Elvin Bishop, Nov. 5–7; Grateful Dead, Nov. 25–28, and Poco, Dec. 3–5.

AT STONEHENGE, IPSWICH: Tim Hardin, Oct. 13–15; Allman Brothers, Oct. 20–22; Paul Butterfield Blues Band, Oct. 27–29; James Cotton Blues Band, Nov. 10–12.

AT STARLIGHT LOUNGE, RTE. 1, PEABODY: Junior Walker & the All Stars, Nov. 10–14.

BOSTON UNIVERSITY

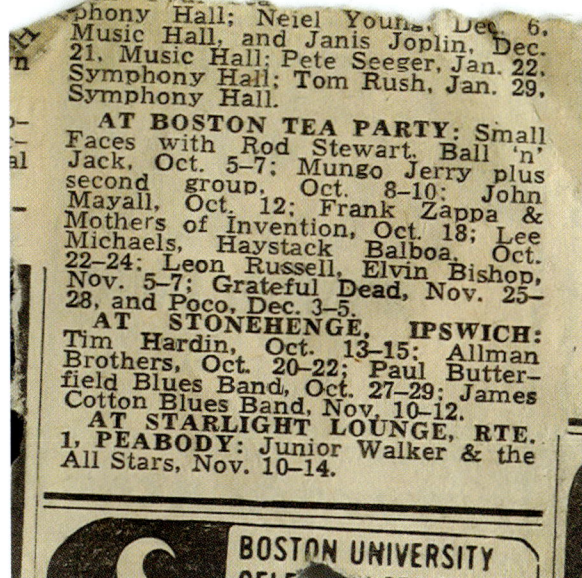

Turntable in the main air studio at WBCN-FM, 1972. *Source: Peter Simon Collection, Special Collections and University Archives, UMass Amherst Libraries.*

Local concert listings, October 1970. *Source: WBCN and The American Revolution Documentary Collection. Special Collections and University Archives, UMass Amherst Libraries.*

Boston 1967:
Before the Revolution

1

Boston 1967: Before the Revolution

1

The story starts in Boston, Massachusetts, in 1967.

When compared to the eye-popping, psychedelic countercultural explosions that are taking place both in San Francisco (where 100,000 young people, many with flowers in their hair, descend on the city's Haight-Ashbury district for a "Summer of Love" featuring music, sex, and LSD) and in New York City's East Village (where tens of thousands of kids flock to celebrate new forms of music, art, and states of mind), Boston seems to be an unremarkably dull and dreary place.

Despite the Greater Boston area being home to more than a hundred colleges and universities and hundreds of thousands of college students, there is little obvious evidence that a transformative youth cultural revolution is about to explode.

In fact, any hints of a youth revolution, particularly one that would significantly challenge authority or the status quo, are quickly and publicly frowned upon and repressed by buttoned-down, staid-in-their-ways Bostonians, who affectionately call their city "the Hub" (derived from Oliver Wendell Holmes's 1858 tongue-in-cheek reference to Boston as "the hub of the solar system").

But just below the surface, signs of the counterculture can be seen and heard brewing, and it will soon find a home in Boston. Consider these early harbingers of a youth revolution in the making:

Boston skyline, 1960s. *Source: Nick DeWolf Photo Archive.*

Don Levy is co-owner of Krackerjacks, a "psychedelic clothing store" on Massachusetts Avenue in Harvard Square, Cambridge, just across from Harvard Yard, which, at the time, is the only clothing store in Boston where young people can buy military surplus army topcoats and navy bell-bottom jeans, soon to become the uniform of the evolving counterculture.

Levy begins selling small round lapel buttons with clever sayings on them such as "F*ck Censorship," "Fornication Makes Friends," and "Draft Beer, Not Students." The store is quickly visited by the Cambridge Police Department in response to a complaint by Cambridge City Councilman Thomas H. D. Mahoney, who charges that the buttons being sold are "blasphemous, vulgar, and, in some cases, obscene" and generally a bad influence on the city's young people.

Despite the police demand, Levy refuses to remove or to stop selling the buttons, instead covering them from view with a cloth, and he asks his customers to support the matter of free expression by signing a petition in opposition to this button crackdown. Signatories to the petition include singer/songwriter Jonathan Richman (later of the Modern Lovers), who at age fifteen signs the petition with a note calling the attempted button banning "an example of lingering Victorianism." According to Levy,

> I opened Krackerjacks in 1966 in Cambridge, and we really were the beginning of the change in menswear in the industry: we were making the trends. The overall look of the store was theatrical and lively, nothing like where men had purchased clothes before, like the Harvard Co-op or Brooks Brothers. We were the only place in town that sold bell-bottoms. The people behind the counter who were selling blue jeans were young and flowery. We were open every night. I don't think there were many stores at that time that were open at night. We played great music in the store to keep people entertained. So this was a new form of retailing.
>
> We sold buttons that made all kinds of statements about sex and drugs, banning the bomb, banning the bra, soixante-neuf (69 in French), let's get naked and smoke, support your local police bribe a cop today, etc. Anything that could be put into words that were against the police and against the city and the government was what people were looking to wear.
>
> There were complaints about us selling these buttons by the Cambridge City Council. At the same time, I had draped an American flag over a mannequin in the window, and they felt that it was not respectful and I should take it out. The police actually came and made me take down the flag. Then they told me I was not allowed to sell the buttons. I said, "What do you mean? This is the freedom of America." The cop said, "Well, you can't sell them, and we're going to issue you a court summons."
>
> So I started a petition, and I let my customers know that the city was after me for selling these buttons. I got four hundred to five hundred signatures.... People felt that this was an American right.
>
> In court, I was told, "Well, what we'd like you to do is to cover up the buttons that are really obscene and put a piece of fabric over them." And so people over eighteen could lift up this and see these obscene buttons, but the general population wouldn't see it. The intent was to put a gag on freedom of speech.

Don Levy at his groundbreaking clothing store Krackerjacks in Harvard Square, Cambridge.
Source: Don Levy Papers, Special Collections and University Archives, UMass Amherst Libraries.

A Bull Market
'The Buttons' Battle Back

By WILLIAM J. FRIPP
Staff Reporter

Cambridge efforts to ban allegedly obscene buttons have sparked a button bull market.

College and high school students apparently miffed at the attempt to surpress the controversial badges, are swarming to Harvard Square to buy them.

The proprietors of Truc and Krackerjacks — Cambridge's most mod emporiums — both report record sales this week.

"We've sold about $60 worth in just a couple of days," said Krackerjacks owner Donald Levy. And Cyrus I. Harvey, owner of Truc, reports "fantastic" sales.

Both agree that the button surge is a student reaction to the low-key campaign by the Cambridge police to cut down on the sale of buttons they consider to be obscene or vulgar.

The buttons were attacked last week by Cambridge City Councilor Thomas H. D. Mahoney, who said they were "blasphemous, vulgar, and, in some cases, obscene." At Mahoney's urging, the council passed a resolution asking the police to have merchants ban the buttons voluntarily.

Many of the buttons refer rather boldly to sex, drugs and religion. The majority are fairly innocuous messages, such as "Support Your Local Poet," "Defrock John Birch Cops," "Bomb Hanoi," "Stop the War in Viet Nam," and "Frodo Lives."

The 25-cent buttons are produced by the Big Store and Underground, Uplift, Unlimited, both New York firms. Along with hopsack pants and World War I army jackets, they are in vogue with teenyboppers and hippies from coast to coast.

Levy and Harvey agree that so far policemen's efforts to suppress the buttons have been soft-sell. Police have come by both stores a couple of times and asked that certain buttons be dropped.

Harvey has generally cooperated. "Their demands weren't excessive. Besides, I've always exercised censorship here." (He also owns the Brattle Theatre.)

'When the younger generation wishes to express itself, it has a lot of difficulty getting a hearing. These buttons are one way to express their opinions . . .'

"What's the point of fighting the thing? After all, they're just buttons."

Harvey agrees that some of the buttons are obscene, and has removed these. However, a few of the buttons police suggested removing are still on display.

But Krackerjacks owner Levy is putting up stiffer resistance. As yet he has not taken down any buttons, and will probably not until he hears from his lawyer, he said.

"I am opposed to any form of censorship, and I think it's nebulous whether any of these buttons can be considered por ography."

Levy and Harvey both stressed that there are more blatantly insidious influences around the Square than buttons, including girlie magazines and the problem of "stealing, cheating and drug addiction."

And they pointed out that in Berkley and New York—where the buttons are reportedly much more obscene—there have been no attempts at suppression.

According to Harvey, by far the most popular buttons are anti-President Johnson and anti-Vietnam War and those dealing with Frodo and Gandalf—characters from the popular Tolkien "Ring" trilogy.

"Even the young teenyboppers who come in are violently opposed to the President and the war. This is one way they can express themselves," Harvey said.

Harvey tossed out a letter written by three Cambridge eighth graders opposing the button ban, which read in part:

"When those of the younger generation wish to express themselves, they have a lot of difficulty in getting a hearing. These buttons are one of the few ways they have to express their opinions and we hate to think that Professor Mahoney seriously intends to infringe on their rights of free expression."

Boston Globe coverage of the button ban, March 4, 1967.
Source: Don Levy Papers.

Not long after, Harvard Square is also the scene of another police censorship action when the Cambridge Police shut down the first night of a $6-a-person videotape showing at the Orson Welles Cinema, a film art house, of the bawdy Broadway hit *Oh! Calcutta!* Theater staff were arrested, and the police confiscated movie equipment and cash. According to the *Harvard Crimson*: "Police arrested nine persons, including one Harvard student and teaching fellow Peter A. Jaszi '68, and seized projection equipment, tape sound track, tickets, posters, and $1,400 in cash . . . on two counts of 'immoral and obscene entertainment.'"

"There were some lines you could get a kick out of it if it wasn't so filthy," Cambridge detective sergeant Duncan S. McNeil, who coordinated the raid, told the *Harvard Crimson*. "I've attended stag shows, and there wasn't much more in those than in this," added Detective McNeil.

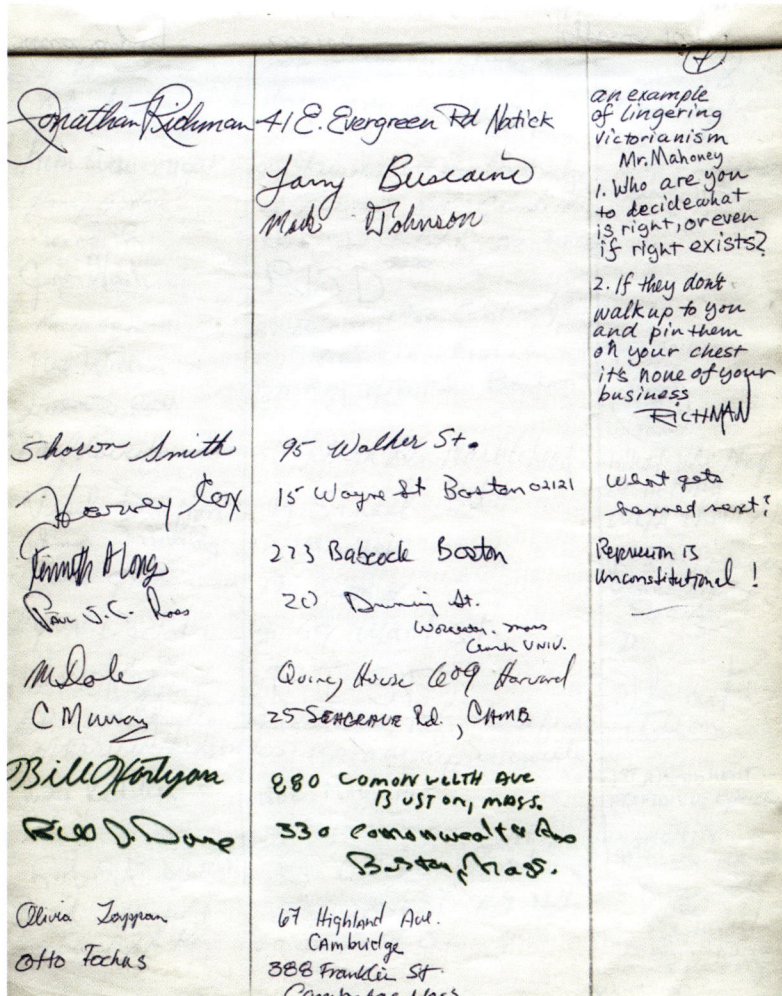

Petition opposing "button ban" signed by Jonathan Richman, 1967.
Source: Don Levy Papers, Special Collections and University Archives, UMass Amherst Libraries.

Boston 1967

Staff of the Orson Welles Cinema, Cambridge, circa 1970. *Source: WBCN and The American Revolution Documentary Collection, Special Collections and University Archives, UMass Amherst Libraries.*

Be-in on Boston Common, 1967. *Source: Peter Simon Collection, Special Collections and University Archives, UMass Amherst Libraries.*

And similarly, the early rumblings of a youth and countercultural revolution can be felt across the Charles River on the Boston Common as young people assemble for a modest gathering billed as a "Love-In," which, according to the *Boston Globe*, draws a small crowd of 150 young people—most with short hair, many wearing pressed white shirts and jackets—who "gave away chocolates, bubble gum, bracelets, balloons, daffodils and pinks" as interested onlookers looked on. The Love-In on Boston Common is filmed and broadcast by an experimental WGBH-TV show, *What's Happening Mr. Silver?* which, via television, brings the nascent youth counterculture into living rooms across Boston, as David Silver, a twenty-two-year old instructor who teaches Shakespeare at Tufts University, travels throughout the city to find out what is happening:

David Silver (TV host): Hello. Why are you here?

Woman attending Love-In: Because I like Love-Ins.

Silver: Is it possible to love everybody?

Woman: Yes.

Silver: How come? How come people haven't loved everybody for two thousand years?

Woman: Because they've been mixed up!

Compared to the youth revolution that is rocking the world—from New York to San Francisco as well as from Paris to Mexico City, where students are rioting in the streets—the Boston version appears polite, well-mannered, and neatly dressed in Brooks Brothers tweed. However, it all changes shortly thereafter during the summer of 1968. Without warning, thousands of young people—most with long hair and carrying backpacks, Frisbees, and musical instruments from guitars to sitars—migrate like a wave to Boston and find a home on Boston Common. They lay out their sleeping bags and gather to play music, smoke marijuana, and discuss with each other the state of America and the world. And they do not go unnoticed.

Scene from "The Love Revolution" episode of *What's Happening Mr. Silver?*, 1967. *Source: WGBH Educational Foundation.*

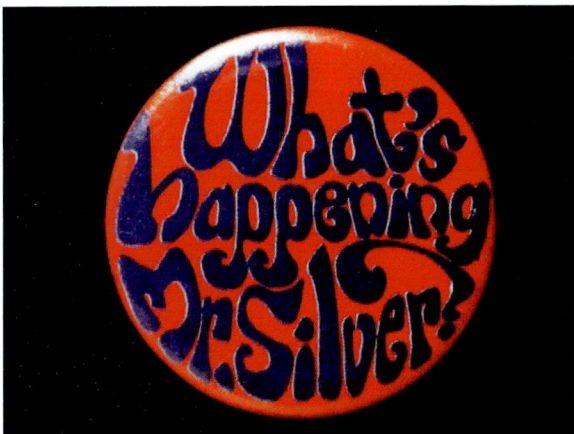

Button from the *What's Happening Mr. Silver?* television program. *Source: WBCN and The American Revolution Documentary Collection. Special Collections and University Archives, UMass Amherst Libraries.*

Boston Common is the public space that has been at the heart of the city for more than three hundred years. It also serves as the front yard for wealthy Bostonians living on prestigious Beacon Hill, who are dismayed to see their beloved park and gathering spot turned into an unsanitary encampment for tens of thousands of long-haired, unbathed young people who call themselves hippies.

As Mitchell Kertzman, then a student at Brandeis University, says:

> To put Boston in 1968 in context, I think you have to start with 1967 and the Summer of Love in San Francisco. It was quite organic in San Francisco. Young people came from all over the country, attracted by peace, love, understanding, with a sprinkling – or perhaps more than a sprinkling – of free love and drugs. Sitting in Boston, that seemed very far away. Then, suddenly, the Boston Common became the center of counterculture life in Boston in 1968. To the extent that we didn't have a Haight-Ashbury community [as in San Francisco], we did have the Boston Common, which was where the hippies congregated.

Boston Common serves as the front yard for the Massachusetts State House and the residents of Beacon Hill. *Source: Spencer Grant Collection, Boston Public Library.*

Chapter 1

The news media is quick to react, dispatching TV camera crews and reporters like John Henning to offer on-the-scene reports on the "hippie invasion" on Boston Common. As Henning tells his Channel 5 TV audience: "By the score, the hippies have been descending on the Boston Common.... The very presence and activity of this community has caused crossfire and conflict from other groups inside the community of Boston—namely, the police department, local businessmen, and members of the Boston City Council."

"People were camping out, sleeping in sleeping bags and in tents. That was quite benign for a while and almost pleasant," recalls Mitchell Kertzman. "It had a good feeling, and it continued that way until—not surprisingly—the residents of Beacon Hill, who had the Common as their front yard, ultimately didn't enjoy having hippies camping there. The City of Boston wanted the hippies off Boston Common."

One city official assigned to deal with the hippies was Barney Frank (later a sixteen-term U.S. congressman), who following his graduation from Harvard took a job as chief assistant to Kevin White, the newly elected mayor of Boston:

> I was working for Kevin White. [I] had jurisdiction over things involving the Left. We were three months into his mayoralty when Dr. [Martin Luther] King was murdered. [Mayor White] did an excellent job establishing for the first time a good relationship with the Black community. Previous Boston mayors had really not done that.
>
> In 1968, we got the hippies and in particularly runaways—underaged teenagers—coming to Boston. What the mayor authorized me to do was to preserve some order in a humane way—not to criminalize these kids but to try and control things. We tried to move them to shelters and set up an operation where parents could contact their kids.... With the counterculture and hippies initially, Boston was not in the forefront. It was behind San Francisco and New York. But as a center of the antiwar movement, it would become as active as anywhere. That was because the students were a larger percentage of the population in Boston than of any other city.

City officials quickly mobilize to contain and counter this hippie invasion. Hearings are held at the Boston City Council, where angry local residents and elected officials loudly complain that the hippies are "using Boston Common as a lavatory" and are "full of bugs and parasites."

"If you show them a bar of soap, they run for the hills," says Boston City Councilor Christopher Iannella, emphasizing, "this is not the same city of Boston that we grew up in."

With the support of local politicians like Boston City Councilor Joseph F. Timilty, a curfew is passed, with Timilty urging the city to get tough with the young people: "Boston Common was set up originally for the benefit of all of the people of Boston.... Today, a colony of unwashed, unshaven people have managed to infest that area and desecrate that community by their 'love-ins,' their 'sit-ins,' their 'smoke-ins,' and a few other 'ins' that I dare not describe here today. It's a different type of pollution, 'people pollution,' 'hippie pollution,' the 'flower people.' All I am asking is for the police department to enforce the regulations."

The police respond, and after Mayor Kevin White institutes a nightly curfew for Boston Common, more than two hundred young people are beaten by the police with their nightsticks and many are arrested. And just like that, the generational lines are drawn in Boston.

Young people on Boston Common, summer 1968. *Source: Nick DeWolf Photo Archive.*

Young people on Boston Common, June 20, 1968. *Source: Brearley Collection, Boston Public Library.*

Dancer on Boston Common, circa summer 1968. *Source: Nick DeWolf Photo Archive.*

But nothing sparks the change or fuels the youth revolution to come in Boston as does the arrival of a thirty-year-old tort lawyer from Kansas City by the name of Ronald Ray Riepen who comes to town to study for a graduate degree at Harvard Law School. Soon after, in 1967, Riepen opens the Boston Tea Party, the first rock hall on the East Coast, following the opening of the Fillmore Auditorium in San Francisco. A year later, Riepen starts an underground radio station, WBCN-FM, followed by the *Cambridge Phoenix* newspaper, of which he becomes part owner. A cultural revolution is in the air in Boston.

Boston police enforce a curfew on Boston Common, summer 1968.
Source: Nick DeWolf Photo Archive.

Boston police making an arrest for the violation of a curfew on Boston Common, summer 1968.
Source: Brearley Collection, Boston Public Library.

Left
Hare Krishna followers on Boston Common at Park and Tremont Streets, May 1968.
Source: Nick DeWolf Photo Archive.

2

The Boston Tea Party

The Boston Tea Party

2

In the summer of 1966, Kansas City tort attorney Ronald Ray Riepen, known to friends as Ray, arrives in Cambridge to begin his postgraduate studies at Harvard Law School. Riepen has grown tired of the practice of law and thinks a master's degree from Harvard Law might give him an entrée into teaching.

While studying at Harvard Law School, Ray Riepen is asked to do a favor by Jessie Benton, the daughter of the American realist painter Thomas Hart Benton, whom Ray knows from Kansas City. Riepen has previously worked on Jessie Benton's divorce from a local commune leader named Mel Lyman, who has become both famous and infamous in Boston in the mid-1960s as an early king of all media or at least all underground media. Lyman's involvements include being a member of the Jim Kweskin Jug Band (which features singer Maria Muldaur) and publishing a biweekly underground newspaper called *Avatar* that often runs afoul of the authorities for its flagrant use of profanity in print. Lyman also has a collaboration with the pioneering filmmaker Jonas Mekas, who later becomes known as "the godfather of American avant-garde cinema." Mekas is an associate of New York artist and director Andy Warhol, and Mekas bankrolls Lyman's first book, *Autobiography of a World Saviour*.

Jessie Benton tells Riepen that she is working with Mekas and Warhol to expand their New York–based film center, the Film-Makers' Cooperative, and that the Ford Foundation has agreed to bankroll a second location for the film organization in Boston, where the group has been holding screenings. She asks Riepen if he can help by negotiating and signing the lease for a building they have found to serve as the Boston home of the film cooperative.

Ray meets with the landlord and signs the lease for the space, a century-old Unitarian Meeting House in the South End of Boston with a giant Star of David on the front. Riepen advances $5,000 of his own money for the lease deposit and is, therefore, not expecting the call he gets shortly thereafter from Jessie Benton, who tells him that the deal has fallen through. As a result, there is not going to be a Boston branch of the Film-Makers' Cooperative, and the Ford Foundation is not going to pay for the cost of the lease, including the deposit.

Riepen recalls suddenly finding himself as a law student stuck with a lease on a former house of worship in the South End of Boston. "I quickly had to figure out what I was going to do – besides file for bankruptcy!" he recalls.

Riepen says it occurs to him that "with hundreds of thousands of students in Boston, the best chance I had to pay the rent on this thing was to play rock music there and have a rock club."

Ronald Ray Riepen posing in front of a mural at the Boston Tea Party, January 1971. *Source: Jeff Albertson Photograph Collection, Special Collections and University Archives, UMass Amherst Libraries.*

Below
Building at 53 Berkeley Street, Boston, which serves as the first home of the Boston Tea Party. *Source: South End Historical Society.*

Flier for a screening at the Boston Film-Makers' Cinematheque, April 18–20, 1967, featuring a film by Andy Warhol. *Source: WBCN and The American Revolution Documentary Collection. Special Collections and University Archives, UMass Amherst Libraries.*

Below
Entrance to 53 Berkeley Street, Boston. *Source: Steve Nelson Archives.*

Because the space has no liquor license and because Riepen wants to convey a sense of propriety to the Boston city establishment from whom he needs permits to operate, he calls the club the "Boston Tea Party." "I thought it was just a fabulous name, and it also had the advantage of having *tea* in the title, which was another name for a very popular recreational drug that was going through the city like wildfire," Riepen recalls.

Steve Nelson, who becomes the first manager of the Boston Tea Party, remembers the dance hall/rock club: "It was an old temple-like building. You'd walk up these wooden stairs to a landing with a coat room. Then up another flight and you'd enter this gigantic open room that had a stage. Across the top of the stage, it said 'Praise Ye the Lord,' because in the 1930s the building was used as a Calvary Temple and that inscription was still there. So there were these religious overtones."

Led Zeppelin performs at the Boston Tea Party under the "Praise Ye the Lord" inscription, 1969.
Source: Steven C. Borack.

The Boston Tea Party would be the first rock hall on the East Coast, preceding Bill Graham's Fillmore East in New York City by more than a year.

"The Tea Party put up posters and handbills around town every week to advertise who was performing there," recalls Nelson. "Some of the posters were really artistic. But they were not necessary, as there was a cultural wave happening and people just started showing up at the Tea Party no matter who was playing. In the beginning, it was mostly local bands, but later more established acts came and performed. Regardless, tickets were just $3.00."

Over the next four years, crowds of young people show up to see emerging rock artists destined to become superstars, including the Who, Cream, the Yardbirds, Led Zeppelin, the Velvet Underground, Traffic, Van Morrison, Fleetwood Mac, Jeff Beck, Rod Stewart, Elton John, the Allman Brothers, the Kinks, Chuck Berry, Bo Diddley, Santana, Joe Cocker, the Grateful Dead, Frank Zappa, Pink Floyd, and such jazz and blues greats as B. B. King, Muddy Waters, John Lee Hooker, Buddy Guy, Rahsaan Roland Kirk, and Miles Davis.

"Initially, it was known as a hippie hangout," recalls Nelson, "but as it gained popularity, the crowds diversified as all kinds of musicians came."

"Ray was good at finding talent — bands that these days you would say, 'My God, Led Zeppelin, really?'" recalls Tommy Hadges, a student at Tufts who later becomes an original announcer at WBCN. "Yes, yes really."

"Led Zeppelin made their first U.S. tour in January of '69," recalls Steve Nelson. "They actually had only about an hour's worth of music in their set. The audience was just going crazy. Led Zeppelin started just improvising, and they went on to play for four hours. Their manager, a guy named Peter Grant, was quoted afterwards as saying, 'Wow, I knew we made it when I saw the reaction of people at the Tea Party.'"

"We were all hippies. We all had long hair, and Ray didn't," recalls Mitchell Kertzman. "Ray was a straight guy. You would not have picked out Ray to be the owner of the Tea Party and the guy that hired all these hippies and musicians. He still looked like a lawyer."

Boston Tea Party schedule for May 1969. Artist: Eric Engstrom. *Source: David Bieber Archives.*

Top
Joe Cocker performs at the Boston Tea Party, 1969. *Source: Steven C. Borack.*

Left
Ray Davies performing with the Kinks at the Boston Tea Party, October 23, 1969. *Source: Peter Simon Collection, Special Collections and University Archives, UMass Amherst Libraries.*

Below
Johnny Winter performs at the Boston Tea Party, June 1969. *Source: Bob Margolin.*

Jeff Beck (right) with Rod Stewart at the Boston Tea Party, May 1969. *Source: Steven C. Borack.*

Elton John (left) in the dressing room at the Boston Tea Party with unknown visitor. Al Kooper (sitting on floor), October 1970. *Source: Jeff Albertson Photograph Collection, Special Collections and University Archives, UMass Amherst Libraries.*

Chapter 2

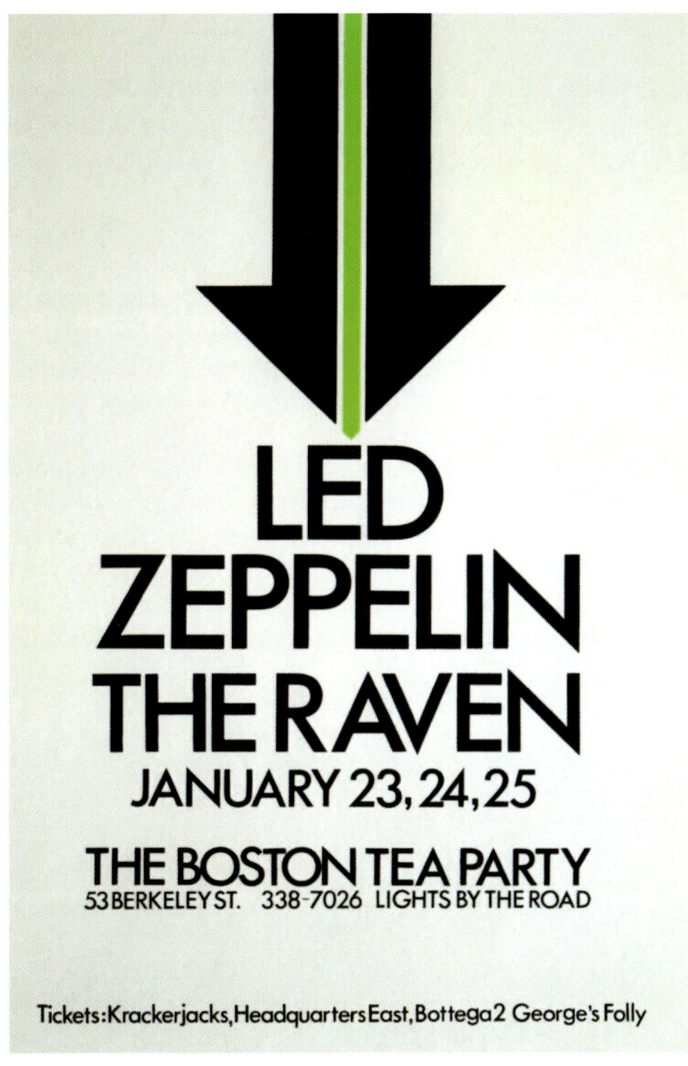

Top
Poster for Led Zeppelin at the Boston Tea Party, January 1969, artist Bob Driscoll. *Source: WBCN and The American Revolution Documentary Collection, Special Collections and University Archives, UMass Amherst Libraries.*

Top right
Led Zeppelin performs at the Boston Tea Party, 1969. *Source: WBCN and The American Revolution Documentary Collection. Special Collections and University Archives, UMass Amherst Libraries.*

Right
Led Zeppelin contract to perform at the Boston Tea Party in May 1969. *Source: WBCN and The American Revolution Documentary Collection. Special Collections and University Archives, UMass Amherst Libraries.*

The Boston Tea Party

"Ray was kind of an interesting character. Here he is, still very much the Kansas City lawyer, still wearing the suits and ties, and the slicked down hair. He had a way of sitting back from it all and enjoying it, hanging out with the musicians. I think that he quickly realized that he was really onto something," says Steve Nelson.

As Riepen recalls:

> My mother [who was visiting from Kansas City] called me one day after the club became successful. She said, "Well, Ronald, my friends are calling me and telling me that they're reading about you in *Newsweek* and the *New York Times* and that you have opened some kind of a rock and roll club in Boston. And I thought you went back there to start an academic career. What is this?" She came to Boston to investigate what had happened to me.
>
> I took her down to the Tea Party, and Country Joe and the Fish were playing. They were playing without shirts, the back projection on the liquid overhead projector was going, the sound was about 140 DB, we didn't have any air conditioning, and the place was packed. So we walked up to the door, and when I opened it this cacophonous roar came out along with all the sweat and heat. She looked at me and said, "Well, Ronald, I won't go in there." And that was the kind of place the Tea Party was! It had a good vibe to it. It was just a great funky place. We had the real thing.

Ray Riepen at the Boston Tea Party. *Source: Wilson Bilkovich (CC BY-SA 2.0).*

Often the musical pairings were eyebrow raising. Rahsaan Roland Kirk opened for the Who. The Grateful Dead were paired with the Bonzo Dog Band. Roots-rockers the Allman Brothers opened for the urban-psychedelic Velvet Underground.

In addition to British rockers, the Tea Party featured the great blues artists who until that point were largely relegated to playing segregated clubs for Black audiences.

"There were some great blues musicians who performed there: Muddy Waters, Howlin' Wolf, John Lee Hooker, B. B. King, and others . . . In 1967 and 1968, to have a band of racially mixed players or to have a racially mixed audience, in a lot of parts of Boston, it would raise eyebrows. It was controversial and was not tolerated," says Steve Nelson.

"There was a whole transition period that was starting to happen with these traditional blues players that were performing before a white audience for the first time. People never saw anything like that," says Charles Daniels (also known as "the Master Blaster"), who served as MC at the Tea Party, welcoming the audience and introducing bands.

"To see people like Muddy Waters for the first time was just mind-boggling," adds Andy Beaubien, then a student at University of Rhode Island who would go on to become a WBCN announcer.

Playing the Tea Party represents a breakthrough for these musicians as well, according to WBCN announcer Eric Jackson:

> [At the Boston Tea Party] these musicians were able to reach an audience they had never been able to reach before. Whereas, before they probably played for 90% or more Black audiences in small clubs. Now, they were playing in a much larger club to a larger and younger audience.
>
> You know, those blues guys — they've been playing and hitting the Billboard charts since the early fifties. Well now they are finding an audience who may not have been born in the 1950s, so it was a whole different world for them too.

During the last weekend of May 1967, the Velvet Underground played the Tea Party. "It turns out that this was a really, really important gig," says Tea Party Manager Steve Nelson, "because up until that time they had been part of Andy Warhol's Exploding Plastic Inevitable, with the whip dancers, and the multimedia. This was the first time they had walked away from that. This was the first gig that they ever had where it was just the four band members playing as a rock band. The Velvet Underground said it was their favorite place to play in the country."

"Boston was the whole thing as far as we were concerned," said Lou Reed, during an interview with WBCN's Steven Segal. "It was the first time we played in public and didn't have all those things thrown at us — 'leather freaks,' 'druggies,' they're this, they're that. It was the first time anybody just listened to the music, which blew our minds collectively. Our first time here, we just couldn't believe it. We couldn't believe it. And it's been that way ever since. I never believe it when I'm in Boston. It's just a really nice scene."

Meanwhile, the atmosphere at the Tea Party is geared to the widespread taking of mind-altering drugs, from marijuana to psychedelics, to enhance the experience.

One person inspired by the psychedelic scene at the Boston Tea Party was a young George Clinton, the musician and producer who later creates the Parliament-Funkadelic (P-Funk). Clinton has said that the Boston Tea Party, LSD, and Led Zeppelin opened the "gate" to P-Funk.

Clinton told the *Boston Herald* that when he arrived in Boston in 1967, he preferred what the *Herald* called "suit and tie R&B," but that changed after Clinton took LSD and went to see Led Zeppelin at the Boston Tea Party.

Ticket for the Who and Rahsaan Roland Kirk at the Boston Tea Party, May 1969. *Source: WBCN and The American Revolution Documentary Collection. Special Collections and University Archives, UMass Amherst Libraries.*

Muddy Waters performs at the Boston Tea Party, April 4, 1968. *Source: Jeff Albertson Photograph Collection, Special Collections and University Archives, UMass Amherst Libraries.*

Right
Boston Tea Party MC Charles "Master Blaster" Daniels, circa 1974. *Source: Ron Pownall.*

The Boston Tea Party

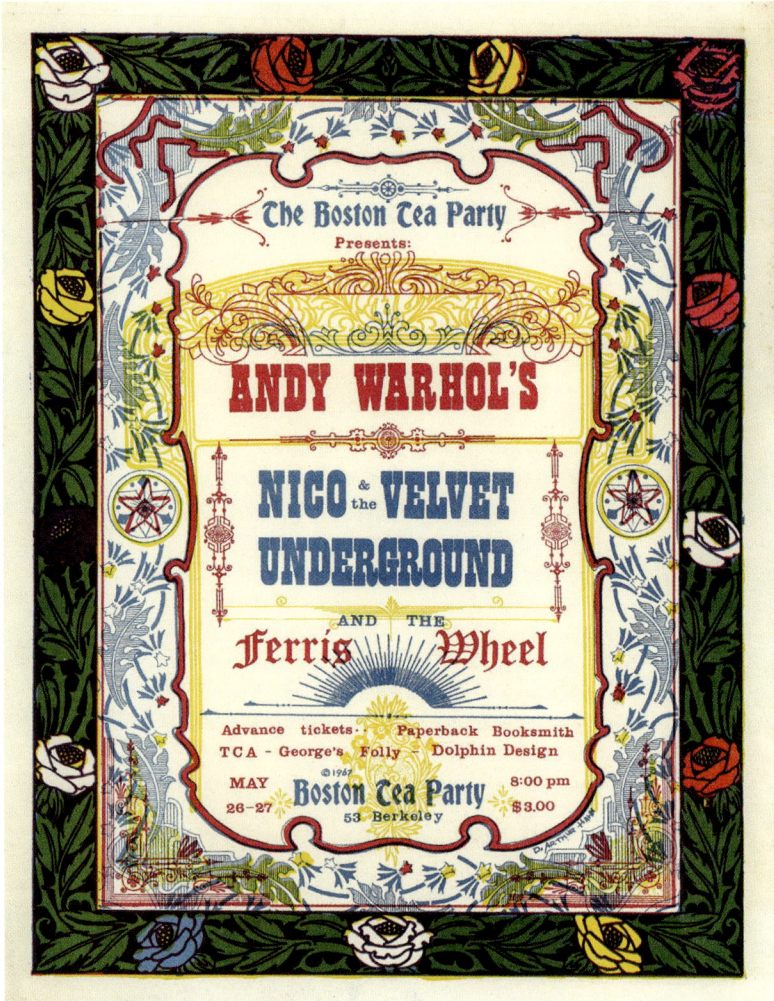

Poster for a Velvet Underground performance at the Boston Tea Party, May 26–27, 1967. *Source: WBCN and The American Revolution Documentary Collection. Special Collections and University Archives, UMass Amherst Libraries.*

The Velvet Underground (left to right: Sterling Morrison, Lou Reed, Maureen Tucker, Doug Yule) photographed on the banks of the Charles River, May 1967. *Source: Jeff Albertson Photograph Collection, Special Collections and University Archives, UMass Amherst Libraries.*

Right
Lou Reed photographed in the studio by Henri ter Hall, circa 1970. *Source: Steve Nelson Archives.*

Chapter 2

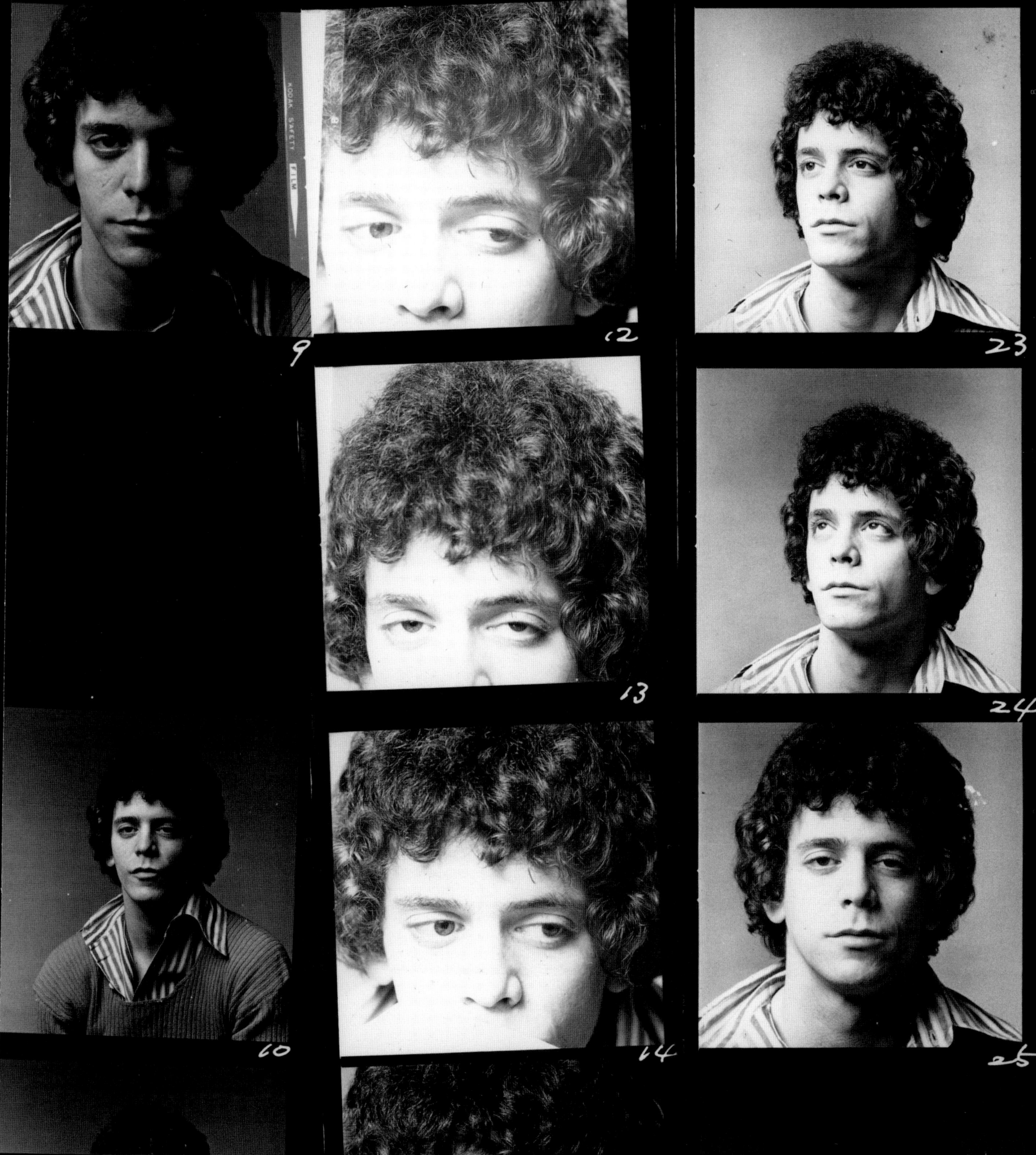

"Zeppelin, Jethro Tull, Vanilla Fudge, King Crimson: we saw them all, or we played shows with them," Clinton said. "We got turned out on acid and these British bands. We had to have funk in our music, but we were also moving through the Vietnam War, the Beatles and Sly Stone, and psychedelia. We came through all this as it fed into our music."

"The audience was mostly stoned, and there was a psychedelic light show geared around that," explains Steve Nelson. The light show at the Tea Party featured original films that were made by an art student named Ken Brown in a process he innovated and would call psychedelic cinema — a hybrid of animation and visual images that Brown shot and edited in his Super 8 camera.

According to Brown:

> Psychedelic cinema was the name I gave to the technique I developed of shooting with a Super 8 film camera that produced these fast-paced films with images and animation.
>
> I bought a Super 8 camera in 1966. I was just curious about it, and I also took a film course at Boston University night school. They showed a lot of movies, but I wasn't really interested in films. I lived on Beacon Hill, and I started walking all over Cambridge and Boston just shooting with the camera.
>
> Part of the evolution of my work involved a quirk of fate. Early on, the camera I had that shot 8mm film was lost, or it got stolen, which was fortunate since I then got a Super 8 camera made by Fujica. It was one of the only ones that allowed you to wind back the film once you shot it, so you could do double and triple exposures, fade in and out, and do cross dissolves in the camera.

Ken Brown develops a psychedelic cinema style of filmmaking in 1967, and his films are shown as part of the light shows at the Boston Tea Party as well as at other music venues. *Source: Boston Phoenix Collection, Northeastern University Library.*

Image from a psychedelic cinema film produced by Ken Brown. *Source: Ken Brown.*

Chapter 2

> I became immersed in experimenting with what you could do with it. I would shoot things around me — traffic lights, headlights, and then rewind the film and shoot again. I would cut up images I would find in magazines on the streets of Boston and use those. I dabbled with animation, live footage, nature footage, mixed with city lights, and slow sequence dissolves.
>
> From 1967 through 1970, my films were shown at the Boston Tea Party as the visual backdrops to the bands. The beauty of the films was the synchronicity of audio and image, and often it would be miraculous how they went together so well. That was my weekly job, and it was the best job a kid could possibly have.

Another filmmaker who visited the Tea Party was Andy Warhol, as part of a publicity stunt engineered by Riepen. As Riepen recalls:

> After eight months of the Tea Party's success, another club opened across town by a promoter who decided that the Tea Party had a monopoly and they were going to put us out of business with a club called the Crosstown Bus. They had a lot more money and big connections in New York. They hired the Doors to perform and paid them more for one night than I might pay groups over four or five months. And by the time the date came, the Doors had the number one single in America with "Light My Fire." We were pretty disheartened because they had a $200,000 sound system and advertising on television. We'd never taken any ads on television. We just had handbills, and that was it.
>
> So we thought, well, we've shown people the way, but we're not going to survive this. We're going to be buried under this money. And then I got the idea. Andy Warhol owed me a lot of favors because I was booking the Velvet Underground, and no one else in America was playing them. So I called Andy Warhol up, and I said, "Listen, I want you to come up here and shoot a movie. And I don't care whether you got film in the camera or not. I want you to bring Nico and all those well-adjusted young people you hang around with at the Factory. This new club's opening up — and they're opening up with the Doors, for gosh sakes!"
>
> And so he did. He agreed to do it and they all came up.
>
> I printed up these hand bills that said "Be Part of What's Happening!! Come to the Boston Tea Party This Weekend to Capture the People on Film as They Explode to the Sights and Sounds of the Velvet Underground. Be a Part of Boston's First Authentic Underground Movie. Andy Warhol, Velvet Underground, Boston Tea Party, AND YOU!!!"
>
> So opening night, of course, the Doors sold out, and the Crosstown Bus owner's financial backer was up from New York, and they said "Let's drive by and see how the Tea Party is doing tonight." And it was raining. And so they got in their limo and drove over to the Tea Party. And from Clarendon Street Station four blocks down to the Boston Tea Party, there was a line of people from the suburbs standing in the rain waiting get in on this Andy Warhol movie. And the club's backer evidently said, "You're not going to beat those guys." And that was it. They closed six or eight weeks after they opened.

Bands booked to play the Boston Tea Party on Friday and Saturday nights cap off their weekends by performing free, live concerts on Cambridge Common on Sunday afternoons. The Allman Brothers, J. Geils Band, It's a Beautiful Day, James Taylor, and others play to the crowds for free as the outdoor performances become a weekly gathering spot for young people.

Left
Poster for the Doors performance at the Crosstown Bus, Brighton, August 10–11, 1967. *Source: WBCN and The American Revolution Documentary Collection. Special Collections and University Archives, UMass Amherst Libraries.*

Jim Morrison singing with the Doors at the Crosstown Bus, Brighton, August 10, 1967. *Source: Peter Simon Collection, Special Collections and University Archives, UMass Amherst Libraries.*

Left
Advertising fliers offer the opportunity to "Be a Part of What's Happening" by attending Velvet Underground concert at the Boston Tea Party to be filmed by Andy Warhol in order to "be a part of Boston's first authentic underground movie," August 12, 1967. *Source: Type Punch Matrix.*

Harvard Square subway station. *Source: Courtesy of the MIT Museum.*

A Sunday afternoon free concert on Cambridge Common with It's a Beautiful Day performing. *Source: Dan Beach.*

The Boston Tea Party

Top
The J. Geils Blues Band performing at a free Sunday concert on Cambridge Common (left: guitarist J. Geils, right: bass player Danny Klein). *Source: Benjamin Lowengard.*

Left
Leda Frank-Andrews dances at a Sunday Cambridge Common concert. *Source: Nick DeWolf Photo Archive.*

Smoking paraphernalia for sale at Cambridge Common concerts. *Source: Nick DeWolf Photo Archive.*

An ice cream truck selling rolling papers. *Source: Nick DeWolf Photo Archive.*

Left
Playing recorders on Cambridge Common during the Sunday concerts. *Source: Nick DeWolf Photo Archive.*

Musician John Cate recalls a Sunday visit to Cambridge Common:

It was a Sunday in May in 1969, and we were off to Harvard Square for the weekly free concerts on the Cambridge Common. These were dreamy times. We – the youth of America – had found a common voice in music, politics, sex, and in mind-expanding psychedelic drugs, meditation, and self-awareness. It was in this moment in time that we came together – some of us from the wealthy 'burbs, and some from Dorchester – we were united in that spirit of peace, love, and music. We had found each other.

My crew took the Green Line from Newton – the Riverside Line – to Park Street Station, where we connected to the Red Line that took us to Cambridge, over the Longfellow Bridge, the so-called Salt-and-Pepper Bridge because its architectural features resembled salt and pepper shakers. Up we went into the blue sky and the bustle of youth on the traffic island by Nini's Corner and Out of Town Tickets. We would stop at Truc, the head shop, for rolling papers or another string of beads before we walked the last few blocks to the Cambridge Common, and the smell of strawberry incense hit us like magic.

As we got near the Common, we could hear the sound system getting tweaked out and that smell – the smell of incense and pot – fantastic. We were home, with our people. The crowd thickened, and Leda and Marla were there with their posse of dancers in their long skirts and lace tops, beautiful and flowing, and, yes, there were flowers in their hair. Wow. As we got closer to the monument at the center of the common, there were several hundred seated just beyond the "stage," a patch of dirt marked off for the musicians.

You could feel that this Sunday was a special day. There was just something about it. Here came the joints – one, then another. Yes. Leda and the girls danced by. Everyone was smiling. The show was about to begin. And then impresario Bob Gordon got up and, after welcoming us all, said, "Ladies and gentlemen, from Macon, Georgia, THE ALLMAN BROTHERS BAND!"

And what happened next was something anyone who was there will never forget. The band ripped into "Don't Want You No More" with two drummers, two lead guitarists, and that organ – that ripping Hammond B-3. The incredible sound of the wall of amplifiers with the instruments all blended together was unbelievable – like a freight train – and holy shit we were bowled over, then STOP. And it was that VOICE – Gregg Allman – as they slammed into "It's Not My Cross to Bear." The set included all the songs from the first album and most of the tracks from *Live at the Fillmore East*, which was a couple of years away at that point.

The concerts ended in the early seventies, like so many things and feelings of the time. But the impressions lived on in the music and in the spirit of those of us who had a glimpse of that utopia. Now Gregg has gone the way of his brother Duane. May we pass the beautiful feelings of those times along in some way to our future generations who need them now, more than ever.

Ugly Radio Is Dead

3

Ugly Radio Is Dead

3

As late as the beginning of 1968, the only place rock music is heard on the radio in Boston is on Top 40 AM stations, which include WMEX (whose announcers are known as the Good Guys), WBZ, and the newcomer, WRKO.

"You'd turn on the radio, and they would play the same forty songs over and over again. And that's why they called it Top 40," explains Mitchell Kertzman, then a Brandeis student and later one of WBCN's original announcers.

"At the time we didn't notice that it was the same songs every thirty minutes or so because it was kinetic, and it was active, and it was loud," says Steven Segal, another one of the early WBCN announcers.

Richard Barna, an early WBCN announcer, says the disc jockeys for Top 40 stations were professionals who had built up this "super high-energy, false-happiness approach to radio."

"There were eighteen minutes of commercials every hour," says Barna. "They had highly produced jingles and an announcing style that I would characterize as putting a coat hanger in your mouth and yelling – with a smile."

Ron Della Chiesa, a classical music radio host, recalls Top 40 radio and music of the era, saying, "In Italian, they have a great phase, and the opera singers use it – 'senza coglioni.' It means 'without balls,' literally. And you know something is sort of white bread – it lacks feeling, it lacks passion – and I think that was a lot of what was being broadcast."

By the spring of 1968, Ray Riepen sees the lines of young people around the block, waiting to get into the Boston Tea Party for musical artists and bands whose music cannot be heard anywhere on the radio. "I thought in a town with over a hundred colleges and hundreds of thousands of college kids, it might be a good idea to play on the radio the music they were buying in the record stories," recalls Riepen.

Riepen is aware of the arrival of FM radio – a new, second broadcast band that allows music to air in stereo with no static, which makes it perfect initially for classical music stations.

Riepen also takes note that in New York City, San Francisco, and Pasadena, California, a few FM stations have begun broadcasting rock music on FM. He envisions a new kind of radio – a station where all kinds of music are played and the announcers speak in conversational tones rather than howling and shouting at their listeners. And instead of twenty minutes or more per hour of loud national commercials with their jingles pitching products from acne cream to drag races, the radio station would air only eight ads each hour, featuring local stores and community businesses.

Lacking a background in radio, Riepen decides to run his idea past broadcast professionals and visits the National Association of FM Broadcasters' 1967 convention, the week before the annual National Association of Broadcasters gathering:

> I thought I would go down there and tell them what I was thinking about doing and see what they say. So I told them what I thought — you know, limit the commercials to eight an hour and have a conversational tone and play album cuts. Well, they all asked me what my background was, and I told them I was a lawyer and I was doing graduate work at Harvard Law School. And they suggested that I concentrate on that and leave broadcasting to them because I was the dumbest person they have ever met. That there was nothing about my concept or approach to programming that was economically viable in America.

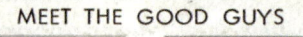

A WMEX weekly music survey featuring the WMEX Good Guys, September 3, 1965. *Source: LCMedia Productions.*

"He was what we needed," recalls Jim Parry, one of the early WBCN announcers. "He was an entrepreneur who had that kind of affinity for the culture—and at the same time, the personality of the entrepreneur, which is 'my way or the highway!'"

Riepen searches in Boston for a commercial radio station in financial trouble, one that may be willing to lease him some of its airtime. Going through Dun & Bradstreet business credit reports, he finds WBCN-FM, a struggling Boston classical music broadcaster that is on the verge of a second bankruptcy. Riepen contacts the owner, T. Mitchell Hastings, an electronics engineer and entrepreneur who developed and is marketing the Hastings FM Jr., which is billed as the world's first shirt-pocket FM radio. Hastings owns four classical music FM stations along the East Coast as part of the Concert Network, including WNCN, New York; WXCN, Providence; WHCN, Hartford; and WBCN, Boston, which is financially strained to the point where announcers are going on the air to ask for money.

"These stations were all essentially bankrupt because they were all classical music stations that couldn't sell any advertising and then, you know, begging on air for people to buy spots," recalls Steve Nelson.

"We had problems, you know," remembers Ron Della Chiesa, an announcer and program director at WBCN-FM, which was asking its listeners to send in donations to help keep the commercial classical music station on the air. "We had people coming in from the Associated Press. We had the newswire right on the studio, [and they were] disconnecting it and taking it out—because the bill hadn't been paid. And I went to him, and I said, 'Mr. Hastings, what are we going to do?' He said, 'Well, read from the newspaper.' That was it."

Riepen contacts Hastings and asks about using the radio station's airtime between 10:30 p.m. and 5:30 a.m.

"Ray was able to convince Hastings into just giving him the overnights because nobody listens to FM," recalls Tommy Hadges, an original WBCN announcer, noting that FM was a new innovation in radio at that time that had yet to fully catch on. "And nobody listens to WBCN, and nobody listens in the middle of the night."

Ray Riepen searches Boston for an FM station that is in financial trouble that would allow him to try out his new concept for radio in the overnight hours. *Source: David Bieber Archives.*

T. Mitchell Hastings owns the Concert Network, four FM radio stations along the East Coast, including WBCN (the *BCN* stands for "Boston Concert Network"). *Source: David Bieber Archives.*

The Hastings FM Jr. radio is billed as the world's first shirt-pocket FM radio. *Source: Hastings Products, Inc.*

T. Mitchell Hastings (left) and Ron Della Chiesa (right) at WBCN-FM. *Source: Ron Della Chiesa.*

```
        WBCN-FM—104.1 Megs.
 6:00—Back to the Bible
 6:30—Songtime
 7:30—Your Day With Father
 7:45—Fellowship Festival
 8:00—Good Morning
 9:00—Stereo Music Time
12:00—Luncheon Carousel
 2:00—Portraits In Melody
 5:00—Capsule Stock Market
 5:15—Music
 6:00—Candlelight and Silver
 8:00—Stereo Tape Festival
 9:00—Recent Releases
10:50—Dates and Places
11:00—Serenade
12:00—Potpourri for Connoisseurs
 1:00—Stereo Till Dawn
```

WBCN's broadcast schedule, 1967. *Source: LCMedia Productions.*

With airtime on WBCN secured, Riepen sets off in search of announcers for his new kind of radio. He drives around the Boston area while listening to college radio stations. When he hears an announcer he likes, he goes to the radio station while they are on the air, walks in, and introduces himself, telling them he is looking for announcers who would like to go on "real radio."

"I told them what I had in mind, and they probably thought I was crazy, too, because, you know, it didn't exist yet," recalls Riepen. "You know, if you worked at a college station maybe you had to try and be professional, and of course, professional means standard broadcasting, and I thought it was ugly radio."

For the students on the air at their college stations, Riepen's sudden and unannounced visit and offer of a job on the air are unexpected, to say the least.

"I was working at doing a show at the Tufts University station, and one evening, unannounced, Ray appeared there," recalls Joe Rogers. "I think it was easy enough for him to do because I am pretty sure we didn't lock the door."

Rogers says Riepen told him he was starting "a free-form radio station that would only be constrained by what you could imagine the listener would want to listen to." He said he was hiring entirely untrained people. "He didn't want professionally trained disc jockeys who had the proper voice to do this," recalls Rogers.

"Part of Ray Riepen's genius when he started WBCN is that he didn't hire professional radio people. He found kids, like me, who loved the music and had a bit of radio experience. The sound was very natural," recalls Richard Barna, a student at Brown University and on the air at the time at the Brown college station WBRU-FM who was hired by Riepen to be an announcer at WBCN. "It wasn't at all like Top 40, with which they were trying to compete."

"What he cared about was your passion for the music and what was called, at the time, the 'underground culture,'" says Andy Beaubien, an early WBCN announcer.

Joe Rogers, who would become the first person on the air on free-form WBCN-FM, recalls what happened then: "Soon after, there was a meeting in which all of us long-haired, untrained DJs mapped out a schedule. I got the Friday night time slot from 10 p.m. to 2 a.m. Then it turned out that the radio station was going to debut on a Friday night, and so they said, 'Rogers, it's you.' It wasn't because I was their ace designated leadoff hitter. My instructions were simply, 'Don't screw it up.'"

Soon after, on March 15, 1968, WBCN is born.

At 10:30 p.m., the station transitions from classical announcer Ron Della Chiesa and Aaron Copland's *Fanfare for the Common Man* to Tufts student Joe Rogers, who calls himself "Mississippi Harold Wilson" after the birthplace of the blues and the then-British prime minister. And while the station has no record library of suitable music to play, the announcers bring records from their own collections in milk crates or boxes when it's their turn on the air.

"And so, on March 15th, 1968, I carried my records up the stairs to the top floor of the Newbury Street building to the station. Ron Della Chiesa was there finishing his show with a perfectly nice piece of classical music, *Fanfare for the Common Man*. When his record ended, it was time for me to begin. I started by playing a song by the Mothers of Invention with some sort of farting, belching noise and then into Cream's 'I Feel Free.' It all began at that point. It went well enough to get through the next four hours," recalls Joe Rogers.

Ray Riepen searches for radio announcers at Boston-area college stations, including at WTBS-FM, the MIT station. *Source: Courtesy of the MIT Museum.*

But there is a hitch.

The daytime staff of the classical music station, which has its offices atop the brownstone on Boston's prestigious Newbury Street, tells Riepen they don't want the longhaired kids in their studios at night.

"I don't know if they thought we would steal the classical records or whether somebody would be smoking 'funny cigarettes' up there or what, but they didn't socially want the two groups to interact in any way," recalls Riepen.

"We were hippies," recalls Jim Parry. "We had long hair, we had rock and roll band shirts, and we did the usual substances."

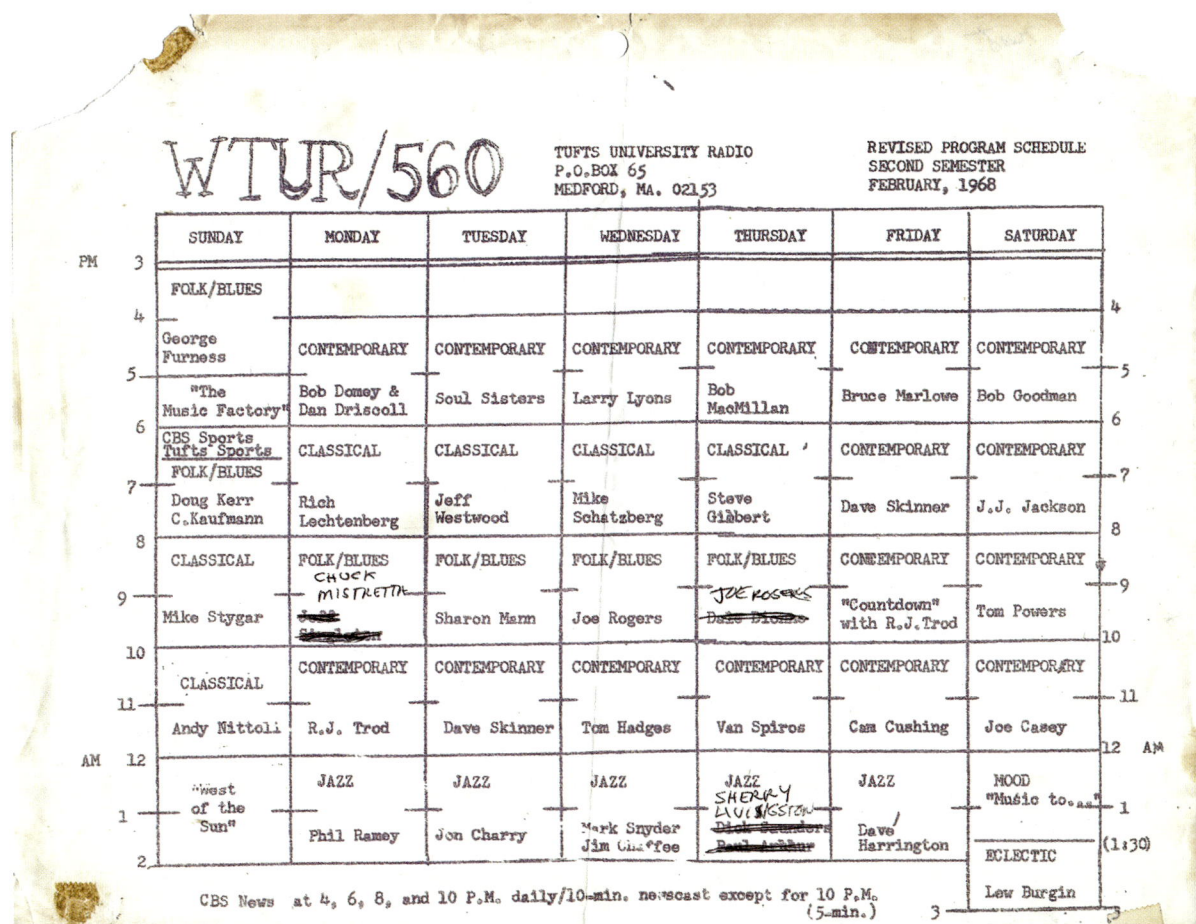

The schedule for WTUR, the Tufts University radio station, February 1968. Joe Rogers is a student with two weekly two-hour programs. Also on the air are future WBCN announcers Tommy Hadges and J. J. Jackson. *Source: Robert McMillan Jr.*

Joe Rogers, shown here in the WBCN air studio, is the first announcer on the air with the station's new format on March 15, 1968. He calls himself "Mississippi Harold Wilson." *Source: David Bieber Archives.*

Ray Riepen (second from the left, with glasses) recruits a staff for WBCN including young announcers, seen here in a promotional photo in 1969. *Source: Boston Phoenix Collection, Northeastern University Library.*

Chapter 3

Riepen solves the problem by purchasing two turntables, a microphone, and two small Sparta audio mixer boards — the kind a DJ might use at a bar mitzvah party — and he installs them in his rock club, the Boston Tea Party, in the cramped dressing room used by the bands. "The studio was literally on a side room backstage at the Boston Tea Party," recalls Tommy Hadges, "which was an amazing place to be sitting, because you'd see these bands going back and forth, and like, 'Oh look, there's Jefferson Airplane' or 'Oh look, there's The Who' — or whatever." However, for the emerging radio station, sharing a green room with rock bands did present a few problems, as WBCN announcer Jim Parry recalls:

> The record library was a closet about as wide as a door, with four shelves in it. It was also in the green room during shows at the Boston Tea Party. Ten Years After was performing one night, and they were admiring the record library, and Ray Riepen in an expansive mood says, "Hey, you guys want some records to take home?" Alvin Lee, who was the lead guitarist of the band said, "OK!" And he grabbed everything — all the records from B through D. He took them all and left. So we could not play anything from the Beatles to the Doors for about a month or so until they got replaced. It was kind of a loose operation.

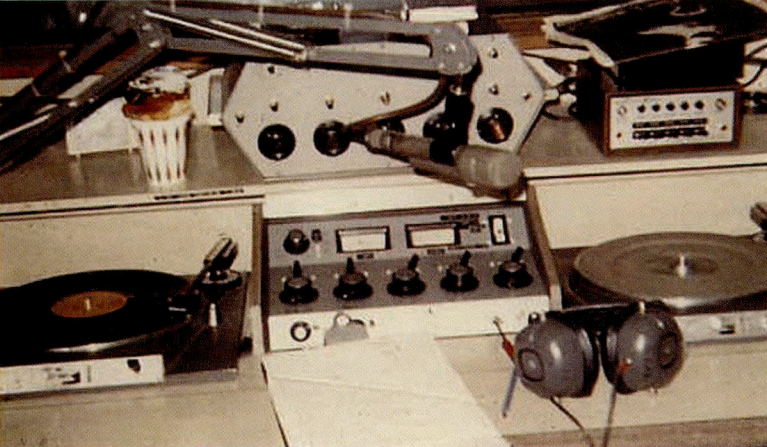

Jim Parry, one of the original WBCN announcers, at WBCN's offices. *Source: Boston Phoenix Collection, Northeastern University Library.*

WBCN broadcasts live from the dressing room at the Boston Tea Party using a makeshift studio comprising two turntables, a microphone, and a mixer. *Source: Don Sanford.*

Alvin Lee, guitarist for Ten Years After, accepts an offer while at the Boston Tea Party to take home albums from the WBCN record library, thus leaving the station without the Beatles or the Doors albums to play on the air. *Source: Jeff Albertson Photograph Collection, Special Collections and University Archives, UMass Amherst Libraries.*

"Ugly Radio Is Dead" posters, promoting the new WBCN-FM, appear throughout the Boston area timed to the format's launch on March 15, 1968. *Source: Tommy Hadges Collection, Special Collections and University Archives, UMass Amherst Libraries.*

Posters promoting the underground radio station immediately appear throughout the Boston area, proclaiming "Ugly Radio Is Dead."

An on-air request to listeners to send a postcard if they're listening to the station results in mail bags filled with responses that clog the stairwell leading up to the station's offices.

"By the middle of the next week, different announcers had done shows," says Joe Rogers, "and in the process, they had mentioned to the listeners that we would like to know where they were, what they were thinking, and if they had any requests, maybe they could send in a postcard. And they did. They sent in thousands and thousands of postcards to the station. We had not anticipated that and didn't dream of it. The mailman was bringing in duffle bags full of postcards from listeners."

Postcard from a store where "we play your music all day." *Source: Richard Barna.*

Postcard from a listener writing that "The Revolution is becoming ever more popular at Newton High, where I am a senior" and asking that "I am hoping that you will expand even further, for instance signing on at 6 [p.m.] instead of 10:30." *Source: Richard Barna.*

Charles Laquidara in the WBCN record library, circa 1970. *Source: Peter Simon Collection, Special Collections and University Archives, UMass Amherst Libraries.*

Chapter 3

WBCN's announcers frequently tell listeners to "Let us know what you like, and what you don't like," and the audience responds, recalls WBCN's creative services director, David Bieber, who, before working at the station, wrote a *Boston Magazine* article about it. During interviews for the book and film, David said:

> There was a real grassroots passion from listeners, people who were paying attention to what the station was doing and saying, and everyone had an opinion.
>
> And the joke often was in those days that every listener had an opinion. One would write to say, "I love when you play folk music but you play too much rock." And then somebody else would write, "I love when you play jazz but you play too much folk." But it was clear that people were giving what they heard on the air great consideration. One letter from a listener said, "I am very confused. Today, I was listening to your radio station and heard some very strange things going on. First, you played a speech by Dr. Martin Luther King preaching nonviolence. Immediately after that came the Jefferson Airplane telling me to tear down the walls and revolt. Then came a record preaching love, peace, and happiness." That shows you the spectrum of BCN sensibilities at the time.
>
> Another letter said, "Mostly I dig WBCN but I don't know what's happening to your heads recently. Every time I listen to it, it seems to be 90% hard-rocking, down and depressing blues. I am eight months pregnant and trying to recover from the flu. So I turned on WBCN and got a black mass followed by "Sympathy for the Devil." Couldn't you balance your programming a little more? My unborn baby has a pretty sensitive head, and damn strong feet, and every time he hears something he doesn't dig, he kicks me in the ribs. Besides he's a Pisces and they are super influenced by music before birth."
>
> That tells you how intertwined people's lives were with what WBCN was doing and playing and how influential the station was in their lives. And how personally they took everything that was being presented to them.

By the spring of 1968, you can hear WBCN throughout the Boston area, whether or not you have a radio with you, coming out of cars, dorms, apartments, and stores. *Source: Spencer Grant Collection, Boston Public Library.*

At Boston University, students can bring their headphones and listen to WBCN while studying. *Source: Boston University Photograph Collection of the Howard Gotlieb Archival Research Center, Boston University.*

"Pretty much everybody had the same records, but you couldn't hear it on the radio," says Norm Winer, who later became WBCN's program director. "Jefferson Airplane's debut album, Steve Miller Band, Quicksilver Messenger Service, Cream, Donovan, and the Beatles' more experimental stuff: we were playing album cuts from all these bands. WBCN was the response to the Top 40 radio stations playing a just a handful of songs on rotation again and again. WBCN was like a really cool friend that brought you into their living room and played stuff for you. We were taking people into our homes, and saying, 'Hey, you've got to hear this.'"

As early WBCN announcer Richard Barna says:

In the late 1960s, the music industry changed dramatically to that of singer-songwriters – people who had a message, who wanted to convey what they thought and felt, and who did it with a power, intensity, and an emotion that was unprecedented. People recognized it. So the music business changed. By 1968, 70 percent of the record sales were albums. But the Top 40 radio stations were still playing the pop singles.

At BCN, we played "sets" of music and created these musical collages live on air, real time, mixing the great music with sound effects, spoken word, comedy, jazz, and blues, even classical. And of course, we had no idea what was going to happen each time we started. They would follow themes based on the type of music or the lyrics blending together or a political or just funny topic, but we all prided ourselves on doing them as well as we possibly could. All the segues and the interrelationships between each piece kept the audience in a high state of attention. With this free-form format, we were constantly laying in new things, and listeners were kind of waiting, wondering, "What are they going to do next?"

As WBCN's Charles Laquidara recalls:

It is so vivid to me what it was like. You just walk into the radio station and all these albums – maybe six hundred or seven hundred albums on a wall. You could tell by the colors of the album covers what artists they were. I would choose four or five albums to get started with, and then throughout the course of the show, I would get inspired. I would think, "Ah, this song will go with that song," and then I would run up before the record ended and find that album and go to the other turntable and put on that record. Then I would queue it up as that song was ending. I would make the segue and hope that the two songs were in the same key. . . . That was was a magic moment when your two songs would go together. Listeners would say, "Oh man that was great! What Laquidara did there, it was fantastic!"

WBCN's new format is so successful that it expands within two months to twenty-four hours a day, and the sounds of the station can be heard throughout the Boston area. Charles Laquidara recalls the reach of the station: "You could hear it in the dormitory rooms, blasting out. In the stores. You could go from one end of Boston to the other end of Cambridge and not have a radio, and you could hear WBCN the whole way."

"By the time it went on the air in spring full time, you could walk down some of the streets in Boston, and people would have their windows open and their radio speakers literally on their window sill playing this to the world, and everybody is on the same station," recalls Steve Nelson.

"I have vivid memories of walking up Massachusetts Avenue in Cambridge," recalls photographer Barry Schneier. "Every store – whether it was the record store, a head shop, as we say, the Orson Welles Cinema – you heard it in every store. It really was the soundtrack of Boston at the time."

Peter Wolf is on the air overnights as the fast-talking "Woofa Goofa" spinning rock, soul, and R&B records until leaving the station to tour as lead singer of the J. Geils Band. *Source: Jeff Albertson Photograph Collection, Special Collections and University Archives, UMass Amherst Libraries.*

Musician James Montgomery remembers: "At the Boston University library, they had this really cool thing. You could just put headphones on and plug them in, and if you looked around the room, everybody in there was listening to WBCN."

"There was nothing else on the radio even close to what was happening [on WBCN]," says Charles "Master Blaster" Daniels.

By May 1968, WBCN's sound from the underground is heard during the days and evenings, while on the overnights Peter Wolf takes over. As Mitchell Kertzman says:

Peter Wolf was unlike any of us. We were college kids, and we were just who we were on the radio. Peter was a well-known musician in town, and he had a larger-than-life persona. Peter was doing 2 to 6 a.m. on the air, and you could just feel everything change when Peter walked in the room to do his shift. I would be on the air, and he would come in with his friend, Big Charles. He called him "Big Charles the Master Blaster." With Peter, it was literally a rock star coming for a few hours to the radio station. Peter's musical taste and talents were very much in the blues and R&B tradition. Peter's musical taste, energy, and shtick made him unlike anyone else.

"Here was a radio station that was an underground rock station, and Wolf was doing the overnight show. It was amazing," recalls Steven Segal.

WBCN announcers from the classical music era and later (left to right) tennis columnist Bud Collins, WBCN's Steven Segal, Peter Yarrow (of Peter, Paul and Mary), and WBCN's Joe Rogers, Sam Kopper, and Al Perry, circa 1969. *Source: Sam Kopper.*

Right
WBCN announcer Peter Wolf and his then-wife, actress Faye Dunaway. Ray Riepen calls Wolf's loud, fast talking in rhyme, which becomes infectious to listeners ("This is the Woofa Goofa, mama toofa!"), "a total violation of everything we stood for, but he was such a great guy and a great personality." *Source: Jeff Albertson Photograph Collection, Special Collections and University Archives, UMass Amherst Libraries.*

4

A New Kind of Radio

A New Kind of Radio

4

Ray Riepen's vision for WBCN is for listeners to hear all genres of music — including rock, folk, blues, jazz, and classical, among others (to hear a sitar, show tunes, or even comedy albums on the air was common) — but unlike the fast-talking DJs on the Top 40 stations of the day, WBCN's announcers speak in intelligent, conversational tones.

As a commercial station, WBCN's revenue comes from advertising, but from the beginning, the station's air staff insists that only ads for local businesses be accepted and refuse any spots from national advertisers or for any product that is not seen as being socially positive.

"In the early days of WBCN, the advertisers tended to be small shops, clothing stores, discount record shops. Those were the kinds of stores and businesses that we wanted to talk about," explains Tim Montgomery, who left his graduate business school studies to take a job at WBCN selling ads, which also meant writing and often producing them, before eventually rising to general sales manager. "We wanted advertisers that addressed the needs of our generation and weren't exploiting anyone. We didn't want automobile dealers, we didn't want national advertisers, we didn't want Coca-Cola, we didn't want anything that sounded like a jingle."

As WBCN announcer Tommy Hadges recalls:

Initially, the decision had been made that we didn't want to run any recorded commercials. The idea was that all of the ads would be live reads written by someone in the commercial department. Most of them were for local products or local shops.

Then the second decision was that there might be some limitation as to what sort of product we wouldn't want to have on the air. We didn't want to have the Clearasil ads.

Then the evolution was that we decided that we could record commercials, but we would want to do it internally. We wouldn't want to accept a national ad that was being used by a product in the rest of the country. We would do a special version of it that would be a little bit more BCN — a little funkier if you will.

The support of the community was strong enough that the station was actually making money relatively quickly. We didn't have to rely upon ad agency business. It was a refreshing thing to hear a station that didn't have the typical radio ads on it. Some of the live reads were the most entertaining things you could possibly ever hear.

We were so lucky to have been collectively handed the opportunity to do basically anything we wanted on the radio. That is the essence of complete freedom, isn't it?

There was a list [on the wall] titled "We don't want to advertise," which included everything we refused to advertise on the station. There was some joking on the list, but a lot of it was completely real.

WBCN sales office at 312 Stuart Street. WBCN announcer John Brodey, ad salesman Jack Kearney, Listener Line volunteer Arlene Brahm; (foreground) ad salesman Kenny Grenblatt (left to right). Advertising salespeople at WBCN are responsible for selling ads as well as writing the on-air copy, and they often record and produce spots for broadcast that are consistent with WBCN's air sound. *Source: Bill Curtis.*

WBCN's staff have a say regarding what sponsors and ads the station will accept for broadcast. *Source: David Bieber Archives.*

WBCN staff keep a running list of the kinds of ads they don't want to run, ranging from serious objections to the humorous. *Source: David Bieber Archives.*

In fact, a 1970 radio documentary by Pacifica station WBAI-FM in New York entitled *The Best Rock Station in the East: WBCN* describes the list that is posted on a bulletin board at WBCN, to which people have added their suggestions. It reads: "We don't want to advertise," followed by "cosmetics; hair oils; deodorants; underwear; anything about cars that has a usually sublimated appeal to inferiority, 'Drive a Mustang for virility, etc.'; WBCN news department; Doris Day; any product that purports to make a person better liked or more pleasing than his real self."

"For a sponsor to say, like, 'The real you's a drag, man,'" says WBCN's Charles Laquidara in the thirty-minute WBAI radio documentary, "but if you use our product, you can be better. Well, you know, we just don't like to do that. You know, it's just not real. It's not what's really happening. One of the reasons why they listen to us is to get away from that crap."

Ads are read live on the air by announcers, who have the freedom to riff on the advertising copy, enhancing the value to sponsors, while those that are produced as recorded spots by the station's announcers and ad sales staff are infused with a distinctly clever, countercultural tone.

For example, an ad for Jay's Motor Repair, a local motorcycle shop, features Jay, the owner, as he explains that he likes to fix motorcycles — except when he's stoned.

Weekly radio ads for New England Music City and the *Real Paper*, featuring the brilliant and hilarious comic Michael Fremer, serve up parodies of musical artists and current news events — with each week's ads becoming "must hear" radio discussed over water coolers.

As WBCN's popularity soars, so do its ad rates. "I was getting AM rates for a thirty-second spot," says Ray Riepen. "I had done that in fourteen months, so we revolutionized — and of course, a year later every station in the country tried to sound like BCN."

At the same time, the station airs public service announcements for social and radical causes, from offers of counseling for draft resisters to soliciting donations for the Black Panther Defense Fund. To its listeners, WBCN is a new kind of radio.

Michael Fremer's ads become "must hear" radio as a popular part of WBCN's programming. *Source: Michael Fremer.*

As a result of WBCN's popularity and credibility with its listeners, advertisers allow the station to write and produce ads that have a distinctly countercultural tone to them. WBCN's Andy Beaubien works on a spot in the station's production room. *Source: Boston Phoenix Collection, Northeastern University Library.*

A New Kind of Radio

WBCN, INC.

BOSTON, MASS.

104.1 MgHz FM Stereo

Wholly owned subsidiary of Concert Network, Inc.
Executive Offices — 312 Stuart Street, Boston, Mass. 02116
Phone — (617) 482-6410

President — R.R. Riepen
Vice President & General Manager — Leonard A. Cohen
Local Sales Manager — Alfred R. Perry
Program Coordinator — Charles Laquidara
Production Coordinator — Sam Kopper

FACILITIES:

Transmitter Atop John Hancock Building, Boston, Mass.
ERP —   50,000 Watts Horizontal
              50,000 Watts Vertical
Antenna Height: 570 ft. above sea level,
                500 ft. above average terrain

Reuters News Service
Associated Press

NATIONAL REPRESENTATIVE:

Greener, Hiken, Sears — 527 Madison Ave.
                        New York, N.Y. 10022
                        Phone: (212) 421-6260

WBCN, INC.

BOSTON, MASS.

104.1 MgHz FM Stereo

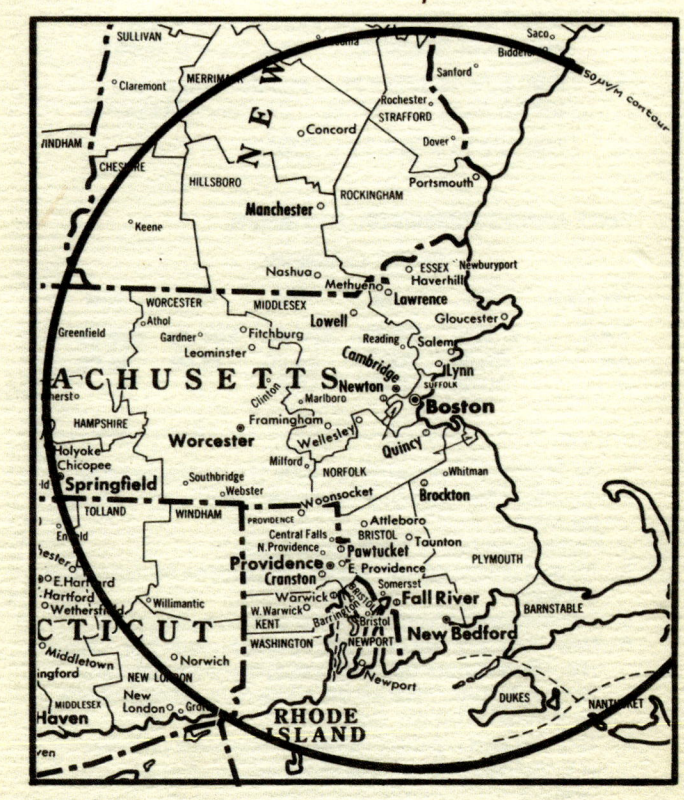

Wholly owned subsidiary of Concert Network, Inc.
Executive Offices — 312 Stuart Street, Boston, Mass. 02116
Phone — (617) 482-6410

A WBCN advertising rate card, May 1970.
Source: David Bieber Archives.

WBCN-FM 104.1 MgHz — BOSTON, MASS.

National & Local Rates Same
Rate Card No. 15 — Effective May 15, 1970

AAA 3:00 P.M. to Midnight — Monday thru Friday
     10:00 A.M. to Midnight — Saturday and Sunday

AA   6:00 A.M. to 3:00 P.M. — Monday thru Friday
     6:00 A.M. to 10:00 A.M. — Saturday and Sunday

A   Midnight to 6:00 A.M. — DAILY

SPOT ANNOUNCEMENTS: One Minute

Weekly Frequency

Per Week	1ti	6ti	12ti	18ti	24ti
AAA	$32.00	$28.00	$26.00	$24.00	$22.00
AA	26.00	22.00	20.00	18.00	16.00
A	16.00	12.00	10.00	—	—

1. 30 Second Announcements—80% of one minute rates
2. Maximum Saturation per advertised item — one minute per hour
3. Commercial Limit: 8 minutes per hour
4. All spot announcement categories combine for frequency discount.
5. Commercials delivered in stereo upon request.
6. Newscasts: one and one half times applicable one minute rate. Minimum six times per week; minimum schedule four weeks firm. Format: 10 sec. open — 60 sec. middle commercial — 10 sec. close.
7. This rate card is published for the covenient reference of advertisers and agencies and is not an offer of facilities.

WBCN PROPOSAL

CLIENT: _____

Announcements Weekly	Cost Each	Total
AAA _____	_____	_____
AA _____	_____	_____
A _____	_____	_____

Total
Weekly
Anncts _____ Total Weekly Cost _____

No. of Weeks: _____ Total Schedule Cost: _____

Starting _____ Concluding _____

Recommended Schedule:
Time

	S	M	T	W	T	F	S

Account Executive _____ Date: _____

5

1968: The Year That Everything Changed and That Changed Everything

1968: The Year That Everything Changed and That Changed Everything

5

For young people, 1968 begins as a year filled with hope and promise, driven by the mantra borrowed from the Beatles song that "All you need is love" — and possibly some LSD.

But overshadowing the dreams of a world living in peace are the realities of Lyndon B. Johnson's administration, including a military draft and an escalating undeclared war in Vietnam.

"By early '68, there was a sense of expectation and a political agenda that Lyndon Johnson's presidency was being threatened," recalls Sam Kopper, an early WBCN announcer. "This man, albeit, had a good domestic record on equal rights," says Kopper, referring to Johnson's progressive Great Society reforms and, perhaps most important, his signing of the federal Civil Rights Act of 1964. "But [Johnson] had a horrible foreign policy in that he was sending young men off to a war in Southeast Asia that we should not have been in."

"By late 1967 and early '68, there was a sense of expectation on the political agenda that Lyndon Johnson's presidency was being threatened by Eugene McCarthy," recalls David Bieber, WBCN's creative services director, referring to the Democratic senator from Minnesota who opposed Johnson's bid for a second term. "Young people were cutting their hair and shaving their beards to campaign for McCarthy, to 'Get Clean for Gene,'" recalls Bieber, referencing young people who got haircuts and put on business suits to knock on the doors of potential voters in support of the anti–Vietnam War "peace candidate," McCarthy. "There was a sense that we can change the dynasty of the tyranny of Johnson."

The pressure on Johnson by his critics has its desired effect. On March 31, 1968, Johnson goes on national TV with a message that nobody is expecting: "I shall not seek, and I will not accept, the nomination of my party for another term as your president," Johnson tells a stunned national television audience.

And in that unexpected moment, everything changes.

Four days later, on April 4, 1968, the great civil rights leader Martin Luther King Jr. is shot dead at age thirty-nine while standing on a balcony outside his second-floor room at the Lorraine Motel in Memphis, Tennessee.

Then, just eight weeks later, on June 5, 1968, Robert F. Kennedy, age forty-two, is shot and dies a day later, following an exhilarating victory speech in the California presidential primary. Bobby Kennedy had emerged as the beacon of hope for a generation of young people that witnessed the assassination of his brother, President John F. Kennedy, just four and a half years earlier.

By 1968, opposition to Lyndon Johnson's escalation of the U.S. involvement in the Vietnam conflict fuels growing protests against him that include the chant "Hey, hey, LBJ. How many kids did you kill today?" *Source: Peter Simon Collection, Special Collections and University Archives, UMass Amherst Libraries.*

Following pages
Anti–Vietnam War protest. *Source: Peter Simon Collection, Special Collections and University Archives, UMass Amherst Libraries.*

65

1968

The strong showing by U.S. Senator Eugene McCarthy of Minnesota in the Democratic presidential primary election in New Hampshire on March 12, 1968 (incumbent Lyndon B. Johnson receives 49 percent of the vote to McCarthy's 42 percent) leads Johnson to announce on March 31, 1968, that he will not seek reelection. *Source: Jeff Albertson Photograph Collection, Special Collections and University Archives, UMass Amherst Libraries.*

Eugene McCarthy addresses an overflow crowd estimated to be forty thousand supporters at Fenway Park in Boston on July 25, 1968. *Source: Courtesy of the MIT Museum.*

The impact is devastating. As Steven Segal, the early WBCN announcer known as "the Seagull," recalls:

> I was in Los Angeles when Bobby Kennedy won the primary, and as I was driving and listening to the results of the vote on the radio, and I was thrilled. "We won! We won!" And then suddenly, "Oh, my god, Robert Kennedy has been shot!"
>
> It was surreal. It felt like it was not really happening. I called a colleague and I said, "He is dead. They killed him." I can remember both of us crying on the phone, and there was a feeling of, "Oh, my god, they killed the movement." It is one of the clearest memories for me of that time. President Kennedy's brother. We could not believe it was happening again. It just took time to process. He was our last hope.
>
> Some of us got Clean for Gene. But without Martin Luther King and Bobby Kennedy, the movement had lost its power. There were still volumes and volumes of people who felt the same way, but there was no transformative leader at that point. It was a cold smack in the face. It was brutal, just brutal.

WBCN's Sam Kopper is getting ready to go on the air with his morning program on WBCN when he sees the wire copy reporting that Robert Kennedy has died moments earlier in Los Angeles at Good Samaritan Hospital:

> BCN had just gone full time in May [1968], and I was driving into the station to do the morning show. At that time, we had religious programming from about 5:30 in the morning until about 7:00 a.m., and I was listening to that. We were still on Newbury Street, and there was a teletype machine up on the fifth floor. When I showed up, there was paper copy that said Robert Kennedy [had died], and so I went on the air to say that, and it was one of these moments in life you feel like you were totally hit in the chest by the horror of it.

In August 1968, young people flood into the streets of Chicago, the site of the 1968 Democratic National Convention, to demand an end to the war in Vietnam and that the party nominate a presidential candidate who reflects their social and political concerns in the spirit of Bobby Kennedy. Chicago's mayor, Richard J. Daley, is having none of it and dispatches the police to maintain order in his city through any means necessary. What follows during the coming late-August days and nights is witnessed in horror by millions of Americans on TV screens in their living rooms as the television networks broadcast live coverage of young people and activists, along with journalists and bystanders, being confronted and then being brutally beaten in the streets by members of the Chicago Police Department as protesters hauntingly chant, "The whole world is watching."

A commission later investigates the events that occurred during the Democratic Convention and determines that the actions of law enforcement in response to the young people amounted to "what can only be called a police riot." Meanwhile, inside the convention hall, efforts to nominate a progressive candidate are beaten back by the Democratic party machine. Johnson's vice president, Hubert H. Humphrey, is nominated to run for president. Prior to becoming vice president, Humphrey had, during his fifteen years as a U.S. senator from Minnesota, championed progressive legislation. He was the lead author of the Civil Rights Act of 1964 and introduced a bill to create the Peace Corps in 1957, three years before it was first proposed by John F. Kennedy. He supported the creation of the food stamp program and of a National Peace Agency. However,

The Reverend Martin Luther King Jr. is assassinated on April 4, 1968, in Memphis, Tennessee. *Source: Peter Simon Collection, Special Collections and University Archives, UMass Amherst Libraries.*

Right
Robert F. Kennedy, seen here speaking to a civil rights demonstration in Washington, DC, on June 14, 1963, is shot and killed following the California presidential primary on June 5, 1968. *Source: Library of Congress.*

Chicago police stop protesters from marching from Grant Park to the International Amphitheatre, site of the Democratic National Convention. *Source: Ron Pownall.*

Following pages
Young people respond to the nomination of Hubert H. Humphrey as the Democratic candidate for president with chaos – huge marches and demonstrations. *Jeff Albertson Photograph Collection, Special Collections and University Archives, UMass Amherst Libraries.*

Chapter 5

Humphrey's liberal credentials had been severely tainted in the eyes of many critics, especially young people, for his failure to speak up during his time in the White House as vice president regarding the escalation of the Vietnam War.

"Bobby Kennedy was somebody who would be our champion," recalls Mitchell Kertzman. "[He was] somebody who could legitimately challenge for the Democratic nomination, somebody who we felt would end the Vietnam War. I don't think any of us really thought that Hubert Humphrey, who would become the Democratic candidate for president, was a great receptacle for our hopes and dreams."

In the fall of 1968, during the months leading up to the election, the chaos and generational divide of the nation continue to increase. "It was an autumn of chaos – huge marches, students demonstrating," recalls WBCN's David Bieber.

The situation is exacerbated by the third-party candidacy for president of George Wallace, who as governor of Alabama in June 1963 sought to fulfill his election promise of "segregation now, segregation tomorrow, segregation forever" by stopping the desegregation of schools – including by standing in the doorway of the auditorium at University of Alabama in Tuscaloosa to prevent two African American students from enrolling. In 1968, Wallace, running as a third-party candidate for president, wins five southern states while his campaign results in clashes between supporters and anti-Wallace demonstrators around the country.

In the end, riding a wave of support among Americans for his promise to bring law and order to the country and claiming he has a secret plan to end the war in Vietnam, which later is shown to have been a lie, Richard Nixon wins the White House by a little more than a half a percentage point, with Wallace getting nearly 14 percent of the popular vote.

George Wallace's third-party candidacy for president draws sharp opposition from young people and others nationwide due, in part, to his pro-segregation policies when he served as governor of Alabama.
Source: Jeff Albertson Photograph Collection, Special Collections and University Archives, UMass Amherst Libraries.

Right
"To the extent that we lost our innocence the night Robert Kennedy was assassinated, we lost our hope when Nixon was elected. . . . From then on, it was 'We are at war with Nixon,'" said Mitchell Kertzman.
Source: The Richard Nixon Presidential Library and Museum.

As WBCN's Sam Kopper says regarding the historical blur of events that was 1968:

Martin Luther King had just been shot a couple months before. You have the quick sequence of Johnson resigning, Martin Luther King's assassination, Robert Kennedy's assassination, and then Nixon winning the election. All the while, an ill-conceived, unjustified, idiotic war is going on. Nixon is telling us when he is running for president that he [has a secret plan to end the war and end it very rapidly]. It becomes obvious that is not what he is going to do. In fact, he heats it up. Tons of men are going to war, some of them not by choice because it was a draft, and they're getting killed. Over forty thousand Americans are killed, and Richard Nixon was there with his sweaty brow, his sweaty lip — you know, trying to justify all this stuff.

As Mitchell Kertzman recalls:

To the extent that we lost our innocence the night Robert Kennedy was assassinated, we lost our hope when Nixon was elected. Nixon was the death of hopes and dreams. His policies, his persona, became everything that young people were against, everything that the WBCN generation was against. There didn't seem to be any dialogue with Nixon. He was not paying attention or listening to young people. He had no empathy for what was going on in the streets. Nixon was trying to kill what was going on in the streets.

Nixon was and felt like the personification of American evil, of everything that was wrong in the country. From then on, it was, "We are at war with Nixon. We are at war with American political leadership." That changed the tone and the tenor of everything from political activity to what was going on the air on WBCN.

From that point on, opposition to the war in Vietnam and getting rid of Nixon become central raisons d'être of the radio station — a sentiment that would become shared by the majority of America's young people.

6

WBCN and the American Revolution

WBCN and the American Revolution

6

America's involvement in the Vietnam War peaks in 1968, as President Johnson approves the involvement of 550,000 U.S. troops for the undeclared war, at a cost of over $26 billion and 16,899 American casualties in that year.

Opposition to the draft has been simmering throughout the country, but it begins to boil over in Boston. A major flashpoint of the antidraft movement occurs on January 5, 1968, with the federal indictments and six months later the convictions of Dr. Benjamin Spock (at the time, America's most trusted pediatrician and the author of the ubiquitous *The Common Sense Book of Baby and Child Care*, which is read by millions of parents), Yale University chaplain William Sloane Coffin Jr., and three others—known collectively as "the Boston Five"—for conspiring to counsel draft registrants in Boston to turn in their draft cards in violation of the federal Selective Service Act.

Broadcasting with 50,000 watts in the thick of this growing generational conflict over the war, WBCN gives voice to the growing antiwar counterculture that permeates Boston and Cambridge, with its hundreds of thousands of college and high school students. As a clear signal of solidarity with opposition to the draft and the growing U.S. involvement in the war in Vietnam, as well as its general opposition to all things "establishment," WBCN begins to call itself on-air and elsewhere "the American Revolution."

"At that time the station was mostly about the music, but when the station leadership chose 'the American Revolution' as the theme, I think that's a recognition that there was more to it than just a lifestyle revolution, that it was also about a political revolution," recalls WBCN announcer Mitchell Kertzman.

"It's playing off 'Here's Boston. Boston was the hotbed of the American Revolution, the original one. This is a new one,'" says announcer Jim Parry.

Listener Steven Wayne recalls hearing the station in those early days: "My first memory of BCN was when—I don't know which disc jockey it was, but when they said, 'This is the American Revolution,' and you felt that they meant it."

WBCN's charter announcer, Joe Rogers, says calling the station "the American Revolution" stemmed not just from the generational rebelliousness that was in the air but from the importance that free speech and free expression had to everyone at the station during this period: "We felt with so many kids facing the draft and the war in Vietnam, that if we spoke up, maybe they would feel like they could speak up, as well."

Famed baby doctor and author Dr. Benjamin Spock of "the Boston Five" addresses an antidraft rally on Boston Common, next to codefendant the Reverend William Sloane Coffin Jr., July 10, 1968. *Source: Brearley Collection, Boston Public Library.*

A young man holding a burning draft card at the Arlington Street Church following a rally protesting the draft and a march to the church, October 16, 1967. *Source: Peter Simon Collection, Special Collections and University Archives, UMass Amherst Libraries.*

Originally a slogan printed on posters featuring Joan Baez and her two sisters, Pauline and Mimi, "Girls say yes to boys who say no" is an attempt to undermine America's connection between manhood and military action. Here the words are worn by a young woman during an antiwar protest at MIT. *Source: Courtesy of the MIT Museum.*

Chapter 6

WBCN calls itself "the American Revolution" as a way of associating itself with the growing and increasingly visible resistance and opposition to the draft, including this march of five thousand protesters on Boston's Freedom Trail on April 3, 1968. *Source: WBCN and The American Revolution Documentary Collection. Special Collections and University Archives, UMass Amherst Libraries.*

Protesters outside the federal courthouse in Boston during the sentencing of Dr. Benjamin Spock and "the Boston Five," July 10, 1968. *Source: Brearley Collection, Boston Public Library.*

WBCN's first bumper sticker featuring the peace sign, circa 1968. *Source: Joe Rogers.*

However, unlike the free-wheeling underground newspapers and magazines of the day, like *Avatar* in Boston – which merrily push the edges of public decency by printing the "f-word" or nudity, only to face an occasional fine or confiscation of their publications by prudish police or politicians – WBCN is a federally licensed 50,000 watt commercial radio station heard in Massachusetts and neighboring Northeast states, which means conforming to government regulations regarding what the station can – and cannot – say and play on the air.

And the young announcers immediately run up against the Federal Communication Commission's rules regarding the lyrics of songs the station plays – or wants to play – including such album cuts as "We Can Be Together" by Jefferson Airplane ("Up against the wall, motherfucker"), "Working Class Hero" by John Lennon ("They hurt you at home and they hit you at school / They hate you if you're clever and they despise a fool / 'Til you're so fucking crazy you can't follow their rules"), and Country Joe and the Fish's antiwar "Fish Cheer" as performed live at Woodstock (instead of spelling out "F-I-S-H," they sang, "Give me an 'F.' Give me a 'U.' Give me a 'C.' . . .")

"These were the times when the Rolling Stones came to play the Ed Sullivan TV show," recalls WBCN announcer Joe Rogers, "and they could not play their song 'Let's Spend the Night Together.' That was their hit song. But were not allowed to say the word *night*. Mick Jagger had to say 'Let's spend some *time* together' because the concept of spending the night together was too risqué."

Rogers notes that WBCN's announcers, like young people generally, watched as the Smothers Brothers, two comedians who had a popular CBS-TV variety program, were publicly forced off the air in April 1969 for their humorous and persistent criticism of the White House and the Vietnam War.

"They were struggling with what they were allowed to do and what they couldn't do. And clearly, we at WBCN – we ignored most all of those rules, and that was something the audience could hear. And hopefully that made it easier for them to be themselves," says Rogers.

"We didn't really care what the rules were. We tried to – well, we did, we made our own rules. We formed a radio consciousness that was further and further and further more political and more dangerous, and we worked hard to be dangerous," recalls Steven Segal. "It was, 'Okay, can we say *shit* on the air? Can we say *fuck* on the air?' So it became a game: can we sneak the word on the air?"

J. J. Jackson, one of the original WBCN announcers, told an interviewer in 2012:

One of the things we were supposed to do was to push the edge of the envelope. And it wasn't so much that you were concerned about offending someone, because obviously the audience you are playing to is not going to be offended, but because of the FCC, and all you need to do is to get a letter and you've got this incredible fine you've got to deal with and all of that.

"Each announcer had his or her own FCC license and you could lose your job there or any place else by losing your licence," adds Joe Rogers.

Ray Riepen recalls,

Somebody would write a letter to the FCC and then next thing you know I would get a letter. And then I would have to go down there and they would have a – I don't know what they call them – but they would have a conference and there would be some administrative person in the Federal Communications Commission in Washington wanting to know what kind of a deal I was running up there.

In fact, often such language was not gratuitous or used simply for the shock value but was a thoughtful expression of musical artists who could find no other word or phrase to express their outrage at the war in Vietnam and other social injustices.

According to Al Perry, WBCN announcer turned general manager, "Using an obscenity like that—it was part of the song. You really didn't have a right to cut that out. And there were times when songs like that needed to be played. Period."

"More and more artists were putting political messages in their songs and I think that appealed to a lot of people because they wanted something a little bit more than just 'Baby, I love you,'" recalled WBCN announcer Eric Jackson. "People wanted 'Baby, I love you—but we got something we've got to do.'"

"I had done some work in some civil rights organizations in and around my hometown in New Jersey," continues Jackson,

> and so I was used to music being a powerful force for motivation and inspiration. So, what we were seeing in the sixties and seventies is that commercial music was now becoming this sort of inspirational force. Jazz was also starting to deal [with current events], especially the titles, maybe even if they weren't lyrics—the titles were starting to speak in that same kind of direction.

Additionally, following criticism from Nixon's White House of popular music that in its view promoted or glorified the use of illicit drugs, the station's playing of these songs—like the Beatles' "Lucy in the Sky with Diamonds" (the title of which contained the letters of the popular psychedelic drug LSD); "Eight Miles High" by the Byrds ("Eight miles high and when you touch down / You'll find that it's stranger than known"), or "White Rabbit" by Jefferson Airplane ("One pill makes you larger/ And one pill makes you small . . . / Remember what the Dormouse said: / 'Feed your head'")—become defiant and rebellious acts.

"We didn't really care what the rules were.... We formed a radio consciousness that was further and further and further more political and more dangerous, and we worked hard to be dangerous," says WBCN announcer Steven "the Seagull" Segal. *Source: David Bieber Archives.*

In the fall of 1969 — in another audacious stance for free expression and opposition to the establishment, even when the establishment is the music industry itself (which foreshadows the "take-down" copyright battles of the digital internet era) — WBCN receives an unauthorized copy of a recording containing the then-unreleased and rough Beatles songs-in-progress taped during the recording sessions for the band's upcoming album, *Let It Be*, with the working album title of *Get Back*. Lore has it that the rough-mix acetate has been assembled by Glyn Johns, the engineer working on the album, in order for the band to listen to the music tracks while they are working on the album in order to give feedback to Johns but not to be distributed outside of the group.

"Steven got a hold of the Beatles album before anyone else did, and the instructions were 'Make sure you don't play it on the air,'" announcer Joe Rogers gleefully recalls. "And so, of course, he did. I endorsed the idea. The tape was there, and it's meant to be played, and so it would have to be played. Not much thought went into the idea: there was the tape, and there was the tape recorder. Let it be!"

Steven "the Seagull" Segal at WBCN's studios. The use and celebration of mind-altering drugs, including marijuana and LSD, become a central part of the counterculture as young people and others seek ways to explore their own thinking, expand their consciousness, and find alternative ways of viewing and living their lives. *Source: Peter Simon Collection, Special Collections and University Archives, UMass Amherst Libraries.*

WBCN announcer Maxanne Sartori. *Source: Bill Spurlin.*

WBCN airs the rough, not fully formed versions of such Beatles classics as "Let It Be," "Get Back," and others, allowing listeners to hear the songs for the first time, albeit in rough forms, as announcer Steven Segal tells listeners: "We will be, in some way, stopped from playing this album in the next couple of days [because] people take it extremely seriously, because it's the Beatles."

Three decades before the Digital Millennium Copyright Act of 1998 made YouTube "take downs" of copyrighted material common, Segal only half-jokingly tells the station's listeners: "If you're taping this off the radio, someone's going to come to your house, and say 'Listen, I'm sorry: you can't play that album in your house.' In fact, if you've taped that, you may be the first on your block to get a telegram from Apple [the Beatles' label] saying, 'Don't play that record in your house. You can't even have it. Flush that album down your toilet.'"

"It was typical for Steven to take on anybody," says Tommy Hadges, WBCN announcer. "So the fact that he is attacking the biggest band in history, at least at that time, you'd have to say, 'Well, that's what he does.' ... And what a great controversy Steven created because who wouldn't have wanted to record that and have it and wait for the Capitol [Records] guy to show up at their door or get a telegram from the Beatles saying, 'Stop playing my album.' It would be fabulous to actually have that ever happen to anyone."

Looking back fifty years later, Steven Segal has no regrets or second thoughts about it, saying, "There was no burning question that we would play it [the Beatles record]. We got it. We are going to play it. Who is going to tell us not to play it? They can tell us not to play it, and we are going to play it anyway because we are WBCN, and it is the Beatles. . . . So it is a very natural thing. We weren't scared. What are they going to do to us? Send us a telegram?"

The spirit of rebelliousness and chaos reflected on WBCN is summed up by bass player David Hull, who performed with Joe Cocker and Buddy Miles and later toured with Aerosmith:

> **Rock music has always been about creating chaos and raising hell. That's what it supposed to do if you are doing your job right. It always had a sense of anarchy and belligerence to it. It's in peoples' nature at that age to be belligerent. It is a biological fact it is hormonally driven, it is cerebrally driven, it's just there.**
>
> **A lot of us became musicians because of our age and the events in our country. We were extremely angry and felt bitterly betrayed by our country. Fusing that attitude with the inherent anarchy and chaos of rock and roll was an extremely potent thing. BCN became the mouthpiece for that. It became the delivery system for that music to the audience, to all of us. There was an unbelievable sense of community at that station. It inspired and turned a great loyalty on the part of the music community.**

By 1969, WBCN has outgrown its original home in the cramped, fifth-floor walk-up Newbury Street studios of the failing classical music station, and it is about to lose its annexed space in the dressing room of the Boston Tea Party, which moves to a larger location on Lansdowne Street across from Fenway Park in July 1969. The radio station moves to small, austere offices at 312 Stuart Street, in downtown Boston, across from the Greyhound bus station, where guests attempting to enter WBCN at night or on the weekends are told to use a pay phone in the bus station to call the studios to be let in.

Top
WBCN announcers and staff pose with Ray Riepen (back row, far right) for a promotional photo, 1969. *Source: Boston Phoenix Collection, Northeastern University Library.*

WBCN air staff in the studio at 312 Stuart Street, circa 1970. Left to right: Michael Ward (engineer), Steven Segal, J. J. Jackson, Al Perry, Sam Kopper, Jim Parry, and Joe Rogers (aka Mississippi Harold Wilson). *Source: David Bieber Archives.*

Joe Rogers and J. J. Jackson in a promotional photo, 1969. *Source: Boston Phoenix Collection, Northeastern University Library.*

Charles Laquidara on the air at WBCN's 312 Stuart Street studios, circa 1970. *Source: Jeff Albertson Photograph Collection, Special Collections and University Archives, UMass Amherst Libraries.*

Announcer Tommy Hadges on the air, 1968. *Source: WBCN promotional photo, WBCN and The American Revolution Documentary Collection. Special Collections and University Archives, UMass Amherst Libraries.*

Below
"Sound waves . . . wave back!" A WBCN promotional poster, circa 1970. *Source: WBCN and The American Revolution Documentary Collection. Special Collections and University Archives, UMass Amherst Libraries.*

WBCN and the American Revolution

"We were in a small studio over a luncheonette, run by a guy name Flash," recalls Danny Schechter, WBCN's "News Dissector." "We were up on the third floor, so you could smell – you know, if the burgers got burned, the smell somehow came up. We had a relatively small space and a lot of people because the station had become a twenty-four-hour station."

"I remember when bands would come, and they'd look around, and there would be all kinds of crap on the walls and piles of junk on the floor," says WBCN announcer Tommy Hadges. "They'd get instantly comfortable. It was so different than if they were going to the professional radio stations elsewhere in town. They immediately relaxed and sat down. Maybe there wasn't a chair, maybe they had to sit on the table. That was possible. The studio functioned very well, and all of the equipment itself was impeccably bought and maintained. So technically it was great, but everything else about the place was a mess."

WBCN's studios at 312 Stuart Street in Boston, above Flash's Snack and Soda Shop. *Source: Bill Lichtenstein.*

The front office of WBCN's studios at 312 Stuart Street, Boston.
Source: Tommy Hadges Collection, Special Collections and University Archives, UMass Amherst Libraries.

A window covered with stickers looking into WBCN's main air studio from the front office. *Source: Boston Phoenix Collection, Northeastern University Library.*

WBCN and the American Revolution

B.B. King (right) being interviewed by WBCN's Kenny Greenblatt in the station's production room, 1970. *Source: Charlie Sawyer.*

Photographer Peter Simon, seen here with sister Carly Simon, is a frequent visitor to WBCN, circa 1970. *Source: Peter Simon Collection, Special Collections and University Archives, UMass Amherst Libraries.*

Chapter 6

One frequent visitor to the station is Peter Simon, brother of singer Carly Simon. He is one of several photographers studying as an undergraduate at Boston University who go on to chronicle the era on film.

> I was such a fan at first that I sort of got to know the WBCN staff and volunteers, and then they began feeling comfortable with me as a photographer. And I would show up and photograph them here, there, and everywhere. Then at one point, we all gathered into their little record library, which was tiny. One of the DJs, John Brodey, decided it would be cool to take off his clothes, and that's the 'X-rated' version of that picture. It was like one family — one big happy family.

WBCN's Maxanne Sartori and Charles "Master Blaster" Daniels at the WBCN studios, circa 1971. *Source: Peter Simon Collection, Special Collections and University Archives, UMass Amherst Libraries.*

Members of the WBCN air staff in the record library at the 312 Stuart Street studios. Back row (left to right): Tommy Hadges, Charles Laquidara, Jim Parry; middle row: Norm Winer, Danny Schechter ("the News Dissector"), John Brodey, Maxanne. Front row (seated): Dinah Vaprin, January 1972. *Source: Peter Simon Collection, Special Collections and University Archives, UMass Amherst Libraries.*

7

Campus Unrest

Campus Unrest

7

In 1969, Richard M. Nixon takes office as president and soon after promises to transfer the responsibility of fighting the war in Vietnam to the South Vietnamese through a process he calls "Vietnamization," stating in December 1969 that the war is coming to a "conclusion as a result of the plan."

However, by 1970 it becomes clear that the undeclared war in Vietnam is continuing to escalate.

"The Vietnam War hung over everything," recalls WBCN ad salesman Tim Montgomery. "If you graduated from high school or college in that time, probably your first concern as a male was, 'Am I going to be drafted?'"

Bob Slavin, a WBCN announcer, recalls the draft lottery that was set up to randomly select which young men would be sent to Vietnam:

> Two-hundred sixty-three. That was my lottery number: 263. Back then, you would be drafted if you had a low number. If you had number one, you were gone. You got your number by the date that you were born. My birthday is September 9th, which was number 263 out of 365, so I didn't get drafted. I was really, really, really happy. My college roommate didn't get a good number and was very much at risk of being drafted, so he joined the Peace Corps and went to Jamaica for a couple of years. So it was very real.

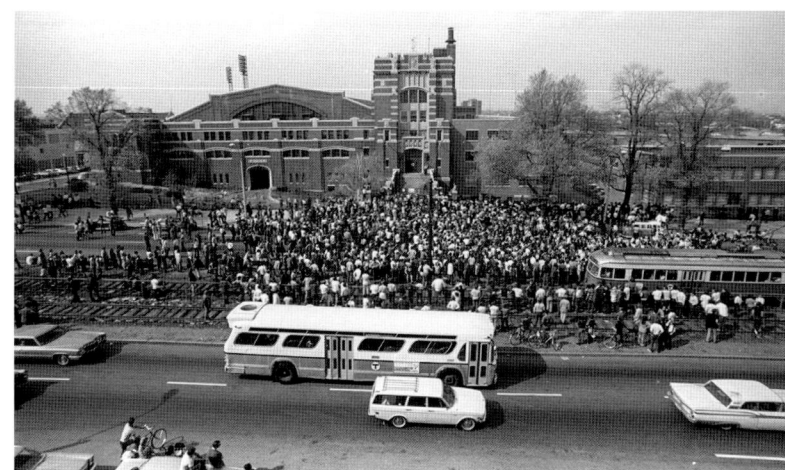

Students protest the war in Vietnam at the Commonwealth Armory in Boston, 1970. *Source: Spencer Grant Collection, Boston Public Library.*

Students protesting the draft and the war in Vietnam at Boston University, 1970. *Source: Peter Simon Collection, Special Collections and University Archives, UMass Amherst Libraries.*

A protest against the war in Vietnam on Boston Common, circa 1969. *Source: Jeff Albertson Photograph Collection, Special Collections and University Archives, UMass Amherst Libraries.*

Harvard's Center for International Affairs, including Professor Henry Kissinger (front row, third from left), 1959. Kissinger continued to teach at the Center for International Affairs until December 1968, when he left for Washington to become national security advisor in the Nixon administration. *Source: Harvard Center for International Affairs.*

As Norm Winer, who would become program director at WBCN, recalls:

> I will always remember that I was number 359, and that's out of 365 days on the calendar. So you might think with a child on the way and new at my job at WBCN that I would be somewhat secure, but I didn't know that these would be the same rules in three months, so I certainly didn't feel secure. I tried my best the morning at the [draft board] physical to try to get out of it. I was trying to be totally unstable and erratic, but, ironically, they remembered my name from the radio, and I couldn't get away with it. They said, "No, you are not crazy. We listen to you all the time on the radio. You're fine. Move along."

Students oppose the draft as well as the government's on-campus Reserve Officers' Training Corps (ROTC), which provides a free college education to those in the military training program. At the same time, Boston becomes the center of increasing discussions and awareness, particularly on college campuses, about the previously hidden deep connections between the triad of the government, the major corporations that are profiteering from the war (including those that are designing and building weapons), and the university-based researchers and academic centers that are working under contract to develop everything from the latest antipersonnel weapons to policies and strategies for fighting the war.

As Danny Schechter recalls:

> Boston was a battleground of ideas. It wasn't just a community. This was the place that Henry Kissinger taught at Harvard. And so were activists opposing the war, and there was a back and forth. There were protests at MIT. There were protests all across the Boston area in all these universities — because we saw the universities as part of the war machine, the war system, and the universities were providing intellectual capital as contractors for the Pentagon. They were providing studies and research and training, and we opposed that. We want to expose it.

An increasing number of students and on-campus antiwar organizations like Students for a Democratic Society (SDS) demand that their schools end involvement with the ROTC program, stop war-related research and related activities, and distance themselves from the U.S. Vietnam War effort.

At Harvard University, where Michael Ansara was an undergraduate, he recalls the urgency for students to find a way to stop the war. "Boston was seething," recalls Ansara. "There were hundreds of thousands of college students here, most of whom by then had turned against the war. So we began to look at every way that we can impede and oppose the war."

On April 9, 1969, a day after posting a list of demands on the door of the Harvard president's residence, approximately seventy students force their way into Harvard's University Hall and escort eight deans out of the building before locking themselves in.

"The Harvard strike got a lot of attention because Harvard gets a lot of attention," says Danny Schechter, who was writing at the time for the Cambridge-based radical underground newspaper the *Old Mole*. "This is the elite, the crème de la crème of American students," says Schechter, who says he arrived at the Harvard dean's office to find it packed with students in blue jean jackets and t-shirts defiantly and openly smoking marijuana.

A strike poster with what becomes the iconic red fist is created by Harvard student Harvey J. Hacker at the Harvard Graduate School of Design. *Source: Harvey J. Hacker.*

A Harvard strike poster with student demands: "Strike for the eight demands strike because you hate cops strike because your roommate was clubbed strike to stop expansion strike to seize control of your life strike to become more human strike to return Paine Hall scholarships strike because there's no poetry in your lectures strike because classes are a bore strike for power strike to smash the corporation strike to make yourself free strike to abolish ROTC strike because they are trying to squeeze the life out of you strike." *Source: Harvey J. Hacker.*

STRIKE FOR THE EIGHT DEMANDS STRIKE BECAUSE YOU HATE COPS STRIKE BECAUSE YOUR ROOMMATE WAS CLUBBED STRIKE TO STOP EXPANSION STRIKE TO SEIZE CONTROL OF YOUR LIFE STRIKE TO BECOME MORE HUMAN STRIKE TO RETURN PAINE HALL SCHOLARSHIPS STRIKE BECAUSE THERE'S NO POETRY IN YOUR LECTURES STRIKE BECAUSE CLASSES ARE A BORE STRIKE FOR POWER STRIKE TO SMASH THE CORPORATION STRIKE TO MAKE YOURSELF FREE STRIKE TO ABOLISH ROTC STRIKE BECAUSE THEY ARE TRYING TO SQUEEZE THE LIFE OUT OF YOU STRIKE

Students at Harvard occupying University Hall, April 9, 1969.
Source: Timothy Carlson.

Campus Unrest

Chapter 7

"It was occupied," says Danny Schechter. "This is before the Occupy Movement. [The office was] occupied by all of these activists smoking dope in the dean's office. And I talked to some of the people from SDS, Harvard SDS. I said, 'You've got to stop this immediately because this will become the story that you're defacing the university. Get these people out of here right now.' And so they did. They got all the students out of there. I said, 'Are all the doors locked?' They said, 'Yes.' I said, 'Good, let's go into the filing cabinets.'"

SDS's Michael Ansara recalls what happened next:

We seal off the offices, and the offices are filled with files. The files were locked, but in those days those metal cabinets had a very simple locking system. I took a standard metal bookend, put it in, and pop – the file cabinet opens. And so they're looking through them. And what they are looking for is any files that say "CIA, Central Intelligence Agency," any file that say "ROTC, Reserve Officers' Training Corps," any files that say "Dow Chemical" or other major corporations. And we were finding them.

"We began to find all kinds of secret documents," says Danny Schechter. "We found letters from the Pentagon to Harvard, from the CIA to Harvard. 'Henry Kissinger will be in Saigon next week.' He was a professor at Harvard. All these materials were there, and we said, 'We've got to publish this somehow. How are we going to get these materials out of here?'"

Schechter recalls that the Massachusetts State Police surrounded Harvard Yard, were limiting students who wanted to come and go through the gates, and were checking those who were leaving:

We had these green book bags, and we filled one with these documents. I took one of the students, and we came to the entrance with the State Police on one side of the fence and the activists on the other side. I pretend to pick a fight with him. I screamed, "Let me out of here! I hate this revolution! Look what you are doing to Harvard! You are destroying the whole place! I can't stand it!" A cop comes over and said, "Let this guy leave," and the cop escorts me out, not knowing that in my bag are all these documents. I then brought them down to the *Old Mole* offices in Central Square.

In order to get the documents out of Harvard Yard, which is surrounded by police, Danny Schechter has to create a spontaneous diversion. *Source: Peter Simon Collection, Special Collections and University Archives, UMass Amherst Libraries.*

SPECIAL BUST SUPPLEMENT • FOR REGULAR CONTENTS, SEE INSIDE

OLD MOLE

15¢   NUMBER 11   A RADICAL BI-WEEKLY   BOSTON, MASSACHUSETTS   APRIL 11 – APRIL 24

HARVARD CIA FILES

Exhibit A

> President and Fellows of Harvard College
> Holyoke Center 458
> Cambridge, Massachusetts 02138
>
> **LIBERATED**
>
> PROPOSAL
> to the
> Central Intelligence Agency
> for
> GRAPHICAL DISPLAY AND EXTENSIBLE LANGUAGES
> IN TEXT MANIPULATION SYSTEMS
>
> A. G. Oettinger
> Principal Investigator
> June 10, 1968
> Desired Starting Date: July 1, 1968

HARVARD=CIA=STATE DEPARTMENT=MURDERERS=FORD FOUNDATION=PENTAGON

The next day, the *Old Mole* has a special edition filled with the documents from inside the halls of Harvard, with a front-page headline citing the "liberated" Harvard CIA files. "It showed how compromised the administration was," says Schechter, "and how supportive it was of the CIA and various government contracts in support of the war in Vietnam. It was an important moment in the Harvard strike."

At dawn the next day, Harvard President Nathan M. Pusey gives the word, and local police officers and state troopers enter Harvard Yard in riot gear and nightsticks in hand. For twenty-five minutes, TV news cameras and photographers capture the bloodshed as law enforcement officers club and then forcibly evict and arrest almost two hundred of the occupying protesters, mostly Harvard students. This leads to wider protests, including two mass meetings at Harvard Stadium, and a vote by the Harvard community—both students and faculty—to go out on what would be an eight-day strike.

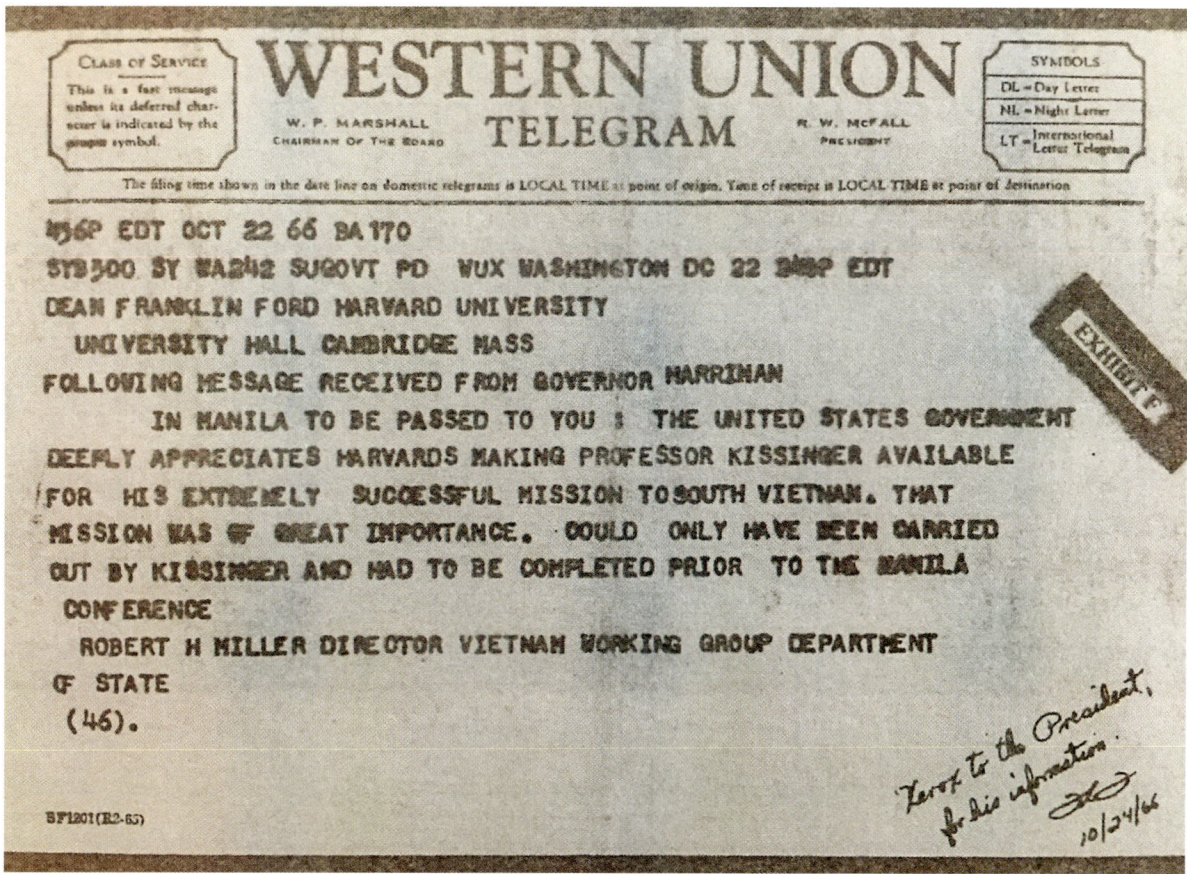

Harvard documents printed in the April 11, 1969, issue of the *Old Mole* reveal a tangled web of connections between the university, federal government, and war-related corporations. *Source: WBCN and The American Revolution Documentary Collection. Special Collections and University Archives, UMass Amherst Libraries.*

The U.S. State Department's telegram to Harvard Dean of the Faculty Franklin L. Ford offering appreciation for "Harvards [sic] making Professor Kissinger available for his extremely successful mission to South Vietnam," dated October 22, 1966. *Source: WBCN and The American Revolution Documentary Collection. Special Collections and University Archives, UMass Amherst Libraries.*

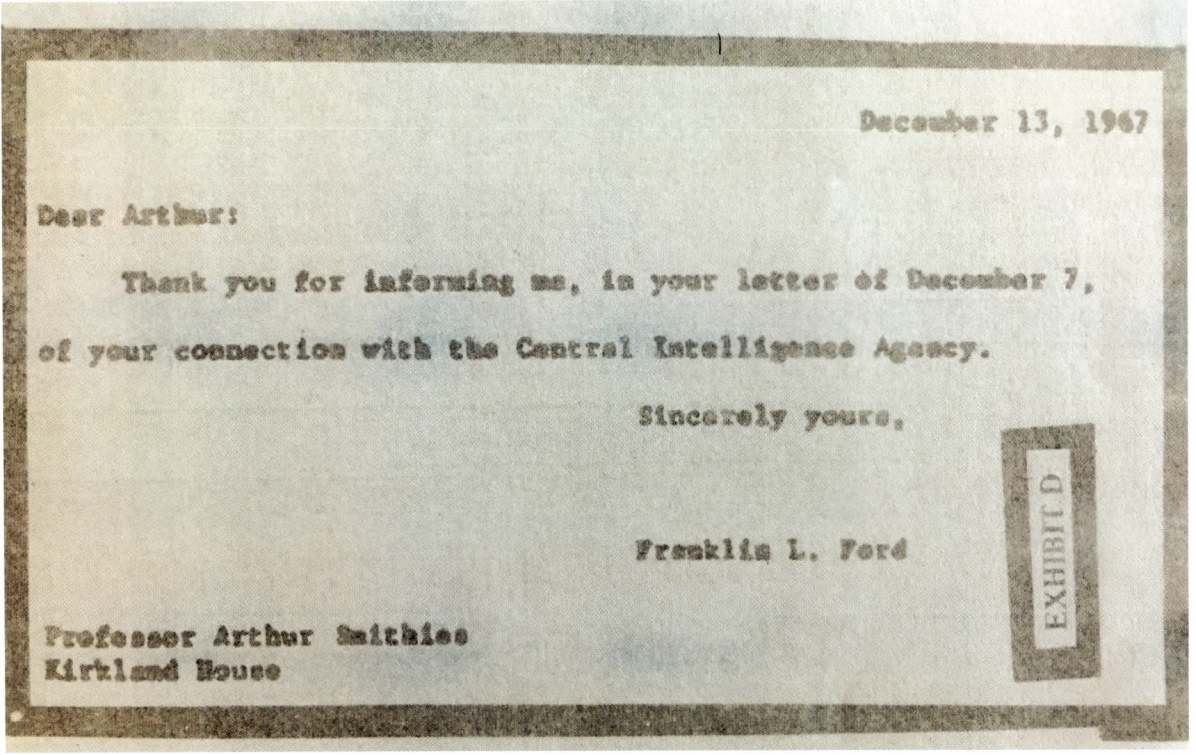

Note from Harvard Dean of the Faculty Franklin L. Ford to Harvard professor Arthur Smithies, master of Kirkland House, concerning what was revealed to be Smithies's ten-year "connection" with the CIA. *Source: WBCN and The American Revolution Documentary Collection. Special Collections and University Archives, UMass Amherst Libraries.*

Copies of the *Old Mole*, with the confidential Harvard documents, are sold on the streets of Boston and Cambridge. *Source: Nick DeWolf Photo Archive.*

Chapter 7

"More than 400 policemen charged University Hall early this morning and forcibly – and sometimes violently – removed several hundred students who were occupying the building." *Harvard Crimson*, April 10, 1969. Source: Harvard Crimson.

Massachusetts State Police enter University Hall to evict and arrest occupying students, April 9, 1969. Source: Dan Brody.

Campus Unrest

Boston University professor Howard Zinn addresses an antiwar demonstration outside Harvard Stadium. *Source: Jeff Albertson Photograph Collection, Special Collections and University Archives, UMass Amherst Libraries.*

Right
MIT professor Noam Chomsky speaks to an antiwar rally. *Source: Peter Simon Collection, Special Collections and University Archives, UMass Amherst Libraries.*

"They effectively brought the war right back into Harvard Yard and galvanized the Harvard community to go on strike," observes Ansara.

At a press conference, Pusey says that his decision to call police onto the campus resulted from reports that students were going through confidential files in University Hall.

Meanwhile, one mile east on Massachusetts Avenue, students at the Massachusetts Institute of Technology are organizing to stop the development of military weapons systems at an on-campus laboratory.

Bill Zimmerman—who makes front-page news in 1973 as the pilot indicted for airlifting food and medical supplies to Native Americans under federal siege at Wounded Knee, South Dakota—was living in Cambridge in 1969 and recalls the growing opposition to the war on Boston-area campuses, including Harvard, MIT, and elsewhere:

> Protests were being staged across the country starting in 1969. Many of those demonstrations got very militant because it was clear that the government was paying no attention to protests. Protests were widespread but seemed to have no impact on policy, so they began to evolve into greater resistance. Resistance meant burning draft cards, trying to close down induction centers, blocking troop trains, and marching on Washington. People tried to close down university research facilities on their campus or in their city because those research facilities were contributing to the war effort by developing new weapons to be used against the Vietnamese. And since these weapons were actually killing people whose lives the antiwar movement was trying to save, some of those demonstrations got very hostile, very militant, and frequently led to physical confrontations between demonstrators and police. That's what happened at MIT in November of 1969, with a month of protests called the "November Actions."

Marsha Steinberg, who would join WBCN's news department, was a member of the radical Weathermen faction of Students for a Democratic Society and recalls the increasingly militant demonstrations at MIT:

> One of the amazing things about Boston is that it is filled with high-end universities with huge research departments. In the sixties, a lot of corporations wormed their way into these universities and provided a lot of money to set up their own research in the context of the university to do research related to the war. There was some direct action of people in the streets trying to protest that nexus between the war and the university. For example, the train tracks in Cambridge became a target where people would sit down and block trains that brought supplies to war-related corporations. At MIT, they actually tore up the tracks, which obviously prevented those trains from being there. It was all a direct attack on the war and corporations that were in it. It showed a level of militancy in the antiwar movement at that time. People had now gone from protesting in the parks to tearing up the train tracks that were servicing these corporations. It was amazing to see it, and only WBCN in town would report on it in any detail.

A target of the "November Actions" at MIT is the Instrumentation Laboratory (I-Lab), the on-campus research facility where principal work on the MIRV multiple-warhead missile system is being conducted. *Source: Courtesy of the MIT Museum.*

Following pages
Protesters seeking to block the entrance to the MIT Instrumentation Laboratory (I-Lab) clash with Cambridge police, November 5, 1969. *Source: Peter Simon Collection, Special Collections and University Archives, UMass Amherst Libraries.*

Campus Unrest

8 | Peace Is in the Air

Peace Is in the Air

8

As the public opposition to the war in Vietnam grows, WBCN gives an ongoing voice to those who are against the conflict. This includes many from university campuses, such as outspoken faculty critics of the war like MIT's Noam Chomsky and Boston University's Howard Zinn.

Meanwhile, the station provides a powerful soundtrack of "music with a message" that fuels the growing opposition to the war. Songs like "Volunteers" by the Jefferson Airplane, "Gimme Shelter" by the Rolling Stones, and "I Ain't Marching Anymore" by Phil Ochs, among many others, became iconic antiwar anthems and calls to action. Plus, the comedy of political satirists like David Frye and Rich Little, who impersonate and ridicule Richard Nixon, are interspersed on the air with the music, along with the more surreal and esoteric comedy groups like the Firesign Theatre and the Conception Corporation and the edgy humor of Lenny Bruce, which help frame up the social, political, and cultural issues of concern to the station's largely youth listeners.

Perhaps the most significant moment for the station and the effort to end the Vietnam War comes on October 15, 1969.

The blue "Work for Peace" buttons with a white dove help spread the word about the Moratorium to End the War in Vietnam on October 15, 1969. *Source: WBCN and The American Revolution Documentary Collection. Special Collections and University Archives, UMass Amherst Libraries.*

In the spring of 1969, a businessman and peace activist from Newton, Massachusetts, Jerome Grossman, who helped spearhead the peace candidacy of Eugene McCarthy for president in 1968, envisions a national strike that would demonstrate to the White House the resolve of the American people who are against the war and would provide a jolt to President Nixon to end it. When Grossman fails to receive support for such a radical, national action, the idea of a one-day "moratorium" replaces it.

"We had seen that Nixon and his administration had no plan to end the war," says activist Michael Ansara. "And so at this point, there was as close to a general strike as we could possibly figure out, and it was called the Moratorium: stop what you are doing, and take time out to register your opposition to the war."

For weeks, WBCN broadcasts to its listeners news of the upcoming moratorium against the Vietnam War — the first nationwide mass demonstration against the conflict — which in Boston is to be held on the Boston Common on October 15, 1969, as well as in cities throughout the country. Given its success, it would be followed by a national Moratorium march in Washington, DC, a month later, on November 15, 1969, and then another protest in Boston on April 15, 1970.

WBCN's first news director, Norm Winer, a recent graduate from Brandeis University, recalls the efforts made by the radio station in support of the massive protest. "We were pretty tireless in making people aware of it," recalls Winer. "It would have been very difficult to have been in Boston at that time and been part of that community and not been aware of exactly what, why, and when and where that event was taking place." This includes broadcasting the schedule of events, phone numbers where people could call to volunteer their time to help organize the protest, and the time and place that schools throughout the Boston area (including colleges, high schools, and junior high schools) would be gathering locally in order to march together to the demonstration down the major Boston thoroughfares, including Beacon Street, Commonwealth Avenue, and Massachusetts Avenue, which all feed into downtown Boston and Boston Common.

Supporters of the Vietnam Moratorium in Boston, 1969.
Source: Ted Polumbaum/Newseum collection.

Marchers from junior high and high schools in Newton walk the seven miles to Boston Common, joining up with students from other schools and colleges along the way, including Boston University, Northeastern, MIT, and Harvard. *Source: LCMedia Productions.*

The Harvard University Band plays the theme from the movie *Exodus* at a predemonstration rally on Cambridge Common that draws fifteen thousand people to hear speakers including Harvard biology professor George Wald (who tells the crowd: "I'll tell you how to get out of Vietnam. In ships"), before marching to Boston Common for the Moratorium, October 15, 1969. *Source: Dan Beach.*

Boston-area Vietnam veterans march to Boston Common to join the call for peace at the Moratorium, October 15, 1969. *Source: Dan Beach.*

"You had the law schools marching to the Common, you had high schools marching to the Common, you had suburban housewives leading delegations of suburban housewives," recalls activist Michael Ansara. *Source: Dan Beach.*

Peace Is in the Air

Marchers crossing the Charles River with MIT behind them on their way to Boston Common for the Vietnam Moratorium, October 15, 1969. *Source: Courtesy of the MIT Museum.*

"The Boston Common was the perfect place for the Moratorium," notes Robert Cox, the head of Special Collections and University Archives at the University of Massachusetts at Amherst. "The Boston Common served as a geographic location of social and cultural exchange since the seventeenth century, a place where citizens and noncitizens alike could come together in a true common place."

"In Boston, every single college and university basically shut down," recalls Michael Ansara. "You had the law schools marching to the Common, you had high schools marching to the Common, you had suburban housewives leading delegations of suburban housewives."

Such "feeder" marches mean, for example, that in Newton, a few hundred seventh-, eighth-, and ninth-grade students from Weeks Junior High School march the eight miles to Boston Common walking down Commonwealth Avenue, where along the way they are joined by students from the area's other junior high schools and high schools and then by students and faculty from Boston College and Boston University, before the marchers, having swelled to tens of thousands in number, arrive at Boston Common. At the same time, high school students from Lexington and other high schools west of Boston walk up Massachusetts Avenue, with students and faculty from Harvard, MIT, and other schools joining them along the way. To those who participate, the experience is inspiring and exhilarating.

"I was a student at Emerson College at the time," recalls photographer Barry Schneier. "The march began, and I remember marching down Commonwealth Avenue with thousands of people. People were calling out to onlookers, saying, 'Join us! Join us!' People are joining as we went down Commonwealth Avenue and further into Boston. Some of the smaller colleges started to empty out, and by the time we got to the Common, there was a massive crowd and a sense that we are not going to tolerate this war anymore. We have had enough. We felt incredibly powerful. We realized that we had shut down colleges that day. We had turned the attention away from studying to be an accountant or whatever it was to address this incredible atrocity that was going on."

"There was this momentum building of hurt," says Schneier. "We were so hurt that our country would do this, that our country would continue to proceed and sacrifice lives for a conflict that everybody knew really wasn't justified. It just wasn't right. It didn't make sense, and we just knew it had to stop. We just had to see it stop."

On October 15, 1969, there are Moratorium events against the war in Vietnam in more than two hundred cities and towns across the country that are attended by over two million people. *Life* magazine writes that it is "a display without historical parallel, the largest expression of public dissent ever seen in this country," and observes that "the antiwar movement for the first time reached the level of a full-fledged mass movement." But the sea of protesters who flood and overflow Boston Common is the most impressive event of the day. CBS News needs a helicopter to film the more than 100,000 people on Boston Common, calling it "an immense crowd, the largest Vietnam peace demonstration ever seen."

Among the list of speakers in Boston at the Moratorium and a second one held on April 15, 1970, were future presidential candidate Senator George McGovern, who tells the crowd: "Let's stop saving face and begin saving lives." McGovern urges the immediate withdrawal of U.S. troops from Vietnam and says "To those who say [the withdrawal of American troops] will cause a bloodbath in Vietnam, I say there is a bloodbath now."

"People were calling out, saying, 'Join us! Join us!' People are joining as we went down Commonwealth Avenue and further into Boston," recalls photographer **Barry Schneier.** *Source: Dan Beach.*

Marchers arrive at Boston Common from around the city to find 100,000 people — the largest Vietnam war protest to date — and a significant police presence. *Sources: WBCN and The American Revolution Documentary Collection, Special Collections and University Archives, UMass Amherst Libraries (students with signs); Eric Engstrom (poster); Dan Beach (helmeted police).*

Abbie Hoffman delivers a memorable speech comparing the John Hancock Building to a hypodermic needle and imploring the crowd to start a revolution, April 15, 1970. *Source: Paul Johnson.*

The John Hancock Building alongside Boston Common. *Source: Spencer Grant Collection, Boston Public Library.*

Perhaps the most memorable speaker for those in attendance at the April Moratorium is activist and founder of the Youth International Party, or Yippies, Abbie Hoffman, who grew up in Worcester, Massachusetts. Abbie's appearance at the Moratorium comes just after his trial with the other members of the "Chicago 8" for conspiracy to incite riots in Chicago during the 1968 Democratic Convention. "Abbie Hoffman gave his usual great speech with his funny lines," recalls Steven Wayne, an activist and WBCN listener who heard Hoffman on Boston Common. "But one of the immortal lines was when he pointed over to the John Hancock Building and compared it to a hypodermic needle." Abbie Hoffman observed (as the crowd looked and cheered) what would be obvious to anyone seeing the old John Hancock Building, twenty-six stories high, which was just blocks from Boston Common downtown – that the top looked like a giant syringe needle:

> **John Hancock Building. Hypodermic needle. Look at it. John Hancock Building. Fucking John Hancock: John Hancock was a revolutionary. He was no goddamn life insurance salesman.**
>
> **I'll tell you what's wrong with this society. What's wrong with this society is that people are no goddamn good unless they've got ten goddamn life insurance [policies]. Fuck that kind of society. We're going to destroy that kind of society. And we're going to do it. We're going to do it like those freaks two hundred years ago did it, like John Hancock.**
>
> **I'll tell you, April 18, 1775 [referencing the lines of "Paul Revere's Ride" by Henry Wadsworth Longfellow]: Everybody who is here who is now alive remembers that famous date and year.**
>
> **Paul Revere. Paul Revere, standing on the bank of the Charles River. Look up at the church, see the fucking strobe lights, mount up his motorcycle ride. Right on, Paul Revere! He rode out through MIT, out through Harvard Yard and Arlington, and Lexington and Concord, screaming and yelling, "The pigs are coming! The pigs are coming! The pigs are coming!" He said, "Get your shit together. We gotta have a revolution."**

"We all laughed," recalls Wayne. "But you know, he said, 'It's time to up the ante here.'"

Meanwhile, the FBI is keeping a close watch on all, with the extent of the surveillance not fully known until years later. Documents obtained under the Freedom of Information Act for this book and documentary film indicate the FBI was keeping close tabs not only on college students who were involved with the antiwar movement in the Boston area but on high school and junior high school students, as well. These documents, provided to FBI director J. Edgar Hoover, ended up in the FBI's files detailing those working to end the war in Vietnam.

For many like Steven Wayne, an unforgettable highlight of the Moratorium was a peace sign that appeared in the sky over the city. "A skywriter put a peace sign up in the sky, and everybody cheered when it was announced that BCN had paid for it. It was clear that BCN was with us," says Wayne.

"Here it was large in the sky by the radio station I was working for," says WBCN's Debbie Ullman. "That was a thrilling thing."

The peace symbol was the brainchild of the late WBCN salesman Kenny Greenblatt, who worked with general manager Al Perry to make it happen.

"The peace symbol came from a fellow named Wayne. He worked out of an airport in Hampton, New Hampshire. He had contacted Kenny Greenblatt, and initially we used him to do some BCN skywriting," recalls Al Perry.

"I seem to think I might have wrote a check for that myself because we didn't have a lot of money. And there were times when I just wasn't going to go into someone's office who was over me at the time and fight with them," recalls Perry.

May 28, 1970

REC-6

Mrs. ▬▬▬

Dear ▬▬▬

ALL INFORMATION CONTAINED
HEREIN IS UNCLASSIFIED
DATE 5/24/79 BY nek

        I received your communication on May 25th. The interest which prompted you to bring this matter to my attention is indeed appreciated.

                        Sincerely yours,

                        J. Edgar Hoover

b6
b7C

NOTE: Our files contain no record of Mrs. ▬▬▬. The "National Strike Information Center" has been previously brought to our attention and is the subject of a pending inquiry. It is self-characterized as a central house for all information regarding strike activities at high schools, colleges and universities across the country. It sets forth data regarding proposed activities at various educational institutions. Upon approval of this letter, it is recommended it and its enclosure be furnished to the Domestic Intelligence Division for information and any additional action felt appropriate.

FMG:jls (3)

MAILED 10
MAY 28 1970
COMM-FBI

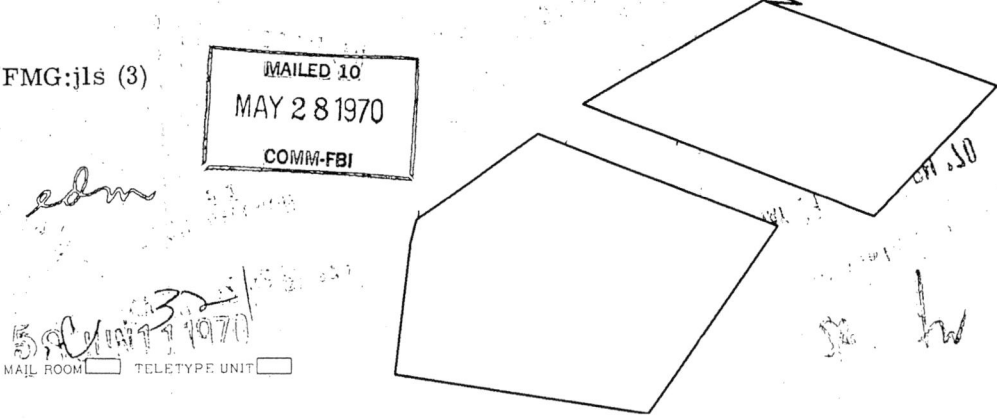

A letter from FBI director J. Edgar Hoover.
Source: Federal Bureau of Investigation.

Region 3 -- Boston-Cambridge

The MIT Moratorium Committe Reports that the canvassing of Boston are research companies has received a boost from two quarters. The ITER Corporation has sent a notice to each of its employees informing them of the visit of canvassers from Harvard and MIT while Polaroid Corporation issued telegram forms to its 9000 employees and agreed to pay for any message they wish to send their congressmen. Cardinal Cushing College has joined MIT in canvassing.

Emerson College is the regional office for the economic boycott. Call 617-235-0320, ext. 270 or 496. Harvard has added the Panther demand to the Coke leaflet and is asking Coke to give up some of its air time.

Harvard is also giving draft resistance information. Call 616-876-4074 or 617-491-1559, ext. 4820

MIT and Tufts want names and addresses of people leaving Boston for the summer who are willing to work. Address lists will be compiled and mailed to all people in one are along with lists of local organizations and suggestions for action.

The Strike Coordinating Committee of the Harvard Grad School of Education demands that the Board of Overseers take the following specific actions believed to be in the spirit of the strike and the three national demands:

1. That they withdraw all Harvard stock holdings in Southern racist utility companies.
2. That they withdraw any endowment or other funds from banks which support the economy of the Republic of South Africa.
3. That they immediately and totally abolish ROTC at Harvard.
4. That they immediately issue a statement condeming the war in Southeast Asia and demand an immediate withdrawal of U.S. troops.
5. That they remove any and all financial aid which Harvard directly or indirectly contributes to the war in Southeast Asia.

Lesley College in Cambridge has established a child-care center for mothers who would like to participate in strike efforts. The hours are 8AM-5PM daily. For further information call 617-547-2296.

The following extensions should be used when calling the number 864-6900 at MIT:

City telegram, ext 1627, 1628
MIT telegram, ext 2331
Route 128 leafleting, est 1602
Cambodia teachout canvassing, est 2051, 2052, 2053, 2130
New Congress Peace Candidate Electioneering, ext 2331
Tax resistance, ext 1627, 1628
Lobby, ext 1602
Church canvassing, ext 2983
High school canvassing, ext 1740
Local business canvassing, ext 1602

The press Center at MIT will include your information in regular releases. Contact Press Center in Bush, room 10-105, ext. 7014

The following is the most complete list of high and junior high schools reporting on strike or as engaging in strike activity.

Massachusetts:
Newton South and North, Brookline, Cambridge High and Latin, Lincoln-sudbury, Lexington, Milton Academy, Palfrey Street School (Watertown), Framingham North, Randolph, Lynn, Medford, Haverhill, Swampscott, Walpole, Waltham, Wellesley, Roxbury Latin, Watertown, Brown and Nichols, Acton, Arlington, Bedford, and Salem, all in the greater Boston area. In and about Worcester are: St. Johns, North, South, Dougherty, and Bumcoat. In the rest of Massachusetts: Natick, Phillips Andover, Weston, Winchester, Needham, Sharon, and Quincy.

Emerson College in Boston has established their FM radio station, WERS, 88.9, as the official high school strike information station. They will be co-ordinating and announcing high school information for the Boston area.

In addition, two junior high schools, Weeks in Newton and Warren JHS, report strike activity.

New York:
Brandeis, Seward Park, Julia Richmind, Washington Irving, Wingate, Stuyvesant, Raflyn, Plainedge, Eastmeadow, Macarthur, Abbeyville, Farmingdale, Tilden, Far Rockaway, Horace Mann, Great Neck North,

Detailed activities of college, high school, and junior high school students involved in lawful anti–Vietnam War political and educational activities, from the files of the FBI. *Source: Federal Bureau of Investigation.*

The peace sign that WBCN pays to have written in the sky for the Vietnam Moratorium can be seen throughout Boston. *Source: Donald Steele.*

Chapter 8

On the day of the Moratorium, the peace sign can be seen throughout Boston, along with the call letters "WBCN." The peace sign and the demonstration become iconic when an image of them by photographer Yale Joel appears as a two-page spread in the middle pages of the following week's *Life* magazine, which has the story of the Moratorium on its cover.

"On my coffee table at home, someone put out a book about peace," recalls Al Perry, "and if you flip through it, that peace symbol is in it."

Reflecting on the day's events and the significance to the tens of thousands of young people involved, Norm Winer says:

> You know, we're each powerless. None of us—and being so young, too, we feel totally, as individuals, we feel powerless in the larger scheme of things. You know, it is hard to get your parents' attention or your boss's attention or your teacher's attention through most of your life at that point. You have very limited experiences, and the causes that we held precious and the issues that we felt were priorities were things that we might never have had the chance to express adequately. Through this collaborative experience, we were able to get the world's attention and make our feelings known. It elevated our aspirations to doing that and validated us, validated the battle.

Chapter 8

Moratorium attendees watch the peace sign being written in the sky above Boston. *Source: Nick DeWolf Nick DeWolf Photo Archive.*

The image of the peace sign over Boston becomes iconic when it is used as a two-page photo spread in *Life* magazine. *Source: Yale Joel Collection of the Howard Gotlieb Archival Research Center, Boston University.*

The Moratorium in October 1969 on Boston Common "elevated our aspirations . . . and validated us, validated the battle," says Norm Winer. *Source: Dan Beach.*

Peace Is in the Air

9

WBCN: The Hub of the Community and Soundtrack of the City

WBCN: The Hub of the Community and Soundtrack of the City

9

Long before cell phones and GPS, before Google and Facebook, and before Twitter and Tik-Tok—in fact, back when the internet is just a sketch in a Defense Department notebook—WBCN serves as the social media of its time. This is in large part the result of two concurrent events.

First, Ray Riepen's breakthrough vision for the radio station is that he will hire college students, rather than radio professionals, to serve as announcers and that they will speak with their audience in conversational tones.

Second, as WBCN announcer Tommy Hadges points out, "We were treating radio not as a performance but as a relationship with our listeners." In fact, this novel approach to radio broadcasting stands in stark contrast to the history of radio until that point, which largely involved announcers, presenters, and actors who delivered music, news, or entertainment programs to their listeners. And while WBCN's arrival happens a full three years before National Public Radio's first broadcasts in 1971, it foreshadows the kind of "we're all just sitting around the living room talking" approach to radio that you can commonly hear today on NPR and community radio stations. But it was unheard of on the radio in 1968.

A newspaper ad for WBCN focuses on the station's role in keeping the community informed of important news and events, circa 1971. *Source: LCMedia Productions.*

As an example, in May 1969, the Who are backstage at the Boston Tea Party, where they are performing the rock opera *Tommy* for one of the first times in America. The band members—including Pete Townshend, Roger Daltrey, John Entwistle, and Keith Moon—are invited over to the open radio mike by Steven Segal, who is then on the air live on WBCN from the club's backroom. He asks about the Who's *Tommy* album, which is being released in the United States that weekend. In fact, the band sees the artwork for the U.S. release album cover for the first time. And then Pete Townshend, who wrote most of the rock opera, explains in detail the meaning of the story of *Tommy* and its connection to the life story of Indian spiritual master Meher Baba, of whom Townshend was a follower.

"There's the Who, explaining the meaning of their lyrics and why they wrote the rock opera," notes Norm Winer, WBCN program director. "It's not something particularly unusual today, where we hear that sort of thing all the time, especially on public radio, where musicians or writers or artists stop by a radio station to discuss their work. But honestly, in those days, for a musician or a band to come by a major commercial radio station and play some music and talk about it in that kind of detail; that was really the beginning of it."

Through moments like this and an open approach to communications with its listeners, WBCN offers its audience interactions that are similar in nature to what social media offers today.

"BCN did a very good job—as the youth movement got more political—of not being the leader," notes WBCN announcer and later software entrepreneur Mitchell Kertzman. "In other words, people didn't go to the streets because BCN told them to go to the streets. It was the internet of its day, when you could communicate with the station. The station would communicate. It was the community resource of how you knew what was going on."

"Our audience, they had to be informed, you know, about what was happening to their country, what was happening locally," says general manager Al Perry.

Announcers on the air at WBCN see radio "not as a performance but as a relationship with the station's listeners," says Tommy Hadges. Pictured is the control board in the WBCN air studio, January 1972.
Source: Peter Simon Collection, Special Collections and University Archives, UMass Amherst Libraries.

Perry talks about the responsibility of the station to its listeners and community in terms of the Federal Communication Commission's vision of how federally licensed radio stations were intended to serve the public: "In many ways, you could argue that the relationship WBCN had with its listeners was closest to what Congress had in mind when it passed the Communications Act of 1934, which created the FCC and licensed radio stations and later television – that is, broadcasters should 'serve the public interest, convenience, and necessity.'"

In its time, WBCN becomes a hub and source of critical information for young people seeking to stay in touch with each other in order to navigate their rapidly changing world with its deep generational divide.

Who to call for advice if you just got your draft notice? Who to ask for help if your roommate has taken some bad LSD? What about if you need a ride to the music festival happening next weekend in another part of the country? Or if you must hear the new Jimi Hendrix album, which hasn't arrived yet in stores? The phones at WBCN ring, with little break, sometimes two and three calls at once and often during nights and weekends, when the only person at the station to answer the phones and help callers is the announcer on the air.

The situation comes to a head one night in mid-1970, when Charles Laquidara, while doing his 10 p.m. to 2 a.m. radio show, answers the phone and finds himself drawn into a call from a listener who needs urgent help. Laquidara lets an album play through on the air while he takes the call. As is typical for WBCN, he comes on the air to explain to his listeners what has just happened.

"I just want to share something with you, okay?" says Laquidara, opening the microphone. "All right, since I have been on the air at ten o'clock, I had a really hard time – like getting a show together the way I would really like to. I guess, we would really like some volunteer help down here. Like, you know, we are not in a position to pay bread for it, but we really need help answering phones and connecting people up with the right numbers and things."

Soon after, in the fall of 1970, the radio station launches "the Listener Line," a telephone number answered from early morning until late night by volunteers, some as young as fourteen, as the station's listeners are encouraged to call with any question or issue they might have – or for help with any problem they might have – and they do.

"All stations had request lines, but deep down inside you knew they weren't really listening to what you said, even if they answered the phone," says WBCN announcer Bob Slavin. "If you called BCN's Listener Line, you would instantly realize, 'Oh, geez, these people really do care about what I have to say.'"

"I remember they had a complete reference library. People would call in to ask where they can get a good pizza. They'd want to know things that nowadays, you'd ask Siri on your iPhone," recalls Tommy Hadges.

One of the functions of the Listener Line was a service called "Traveler's Friend." "Traveler's Friend was a way to connect people who had a car with those who did not," recalls Tim Montgomery, ad salesman at the station. "So if you needed to go to New York, we'd put that out there on the air, and someone would say, 'Yeah, I'm driving to New York Saturday morning at 10 a.m., and I will pick you up in Harvard Square.' It's pretty amazing when I think about it."

"It was a very mobile society, but we lacked the resources to hop on planes and go wherever we wanted, and although we did a lot of hitchhiking back in those days, it wasn't really recommended,"

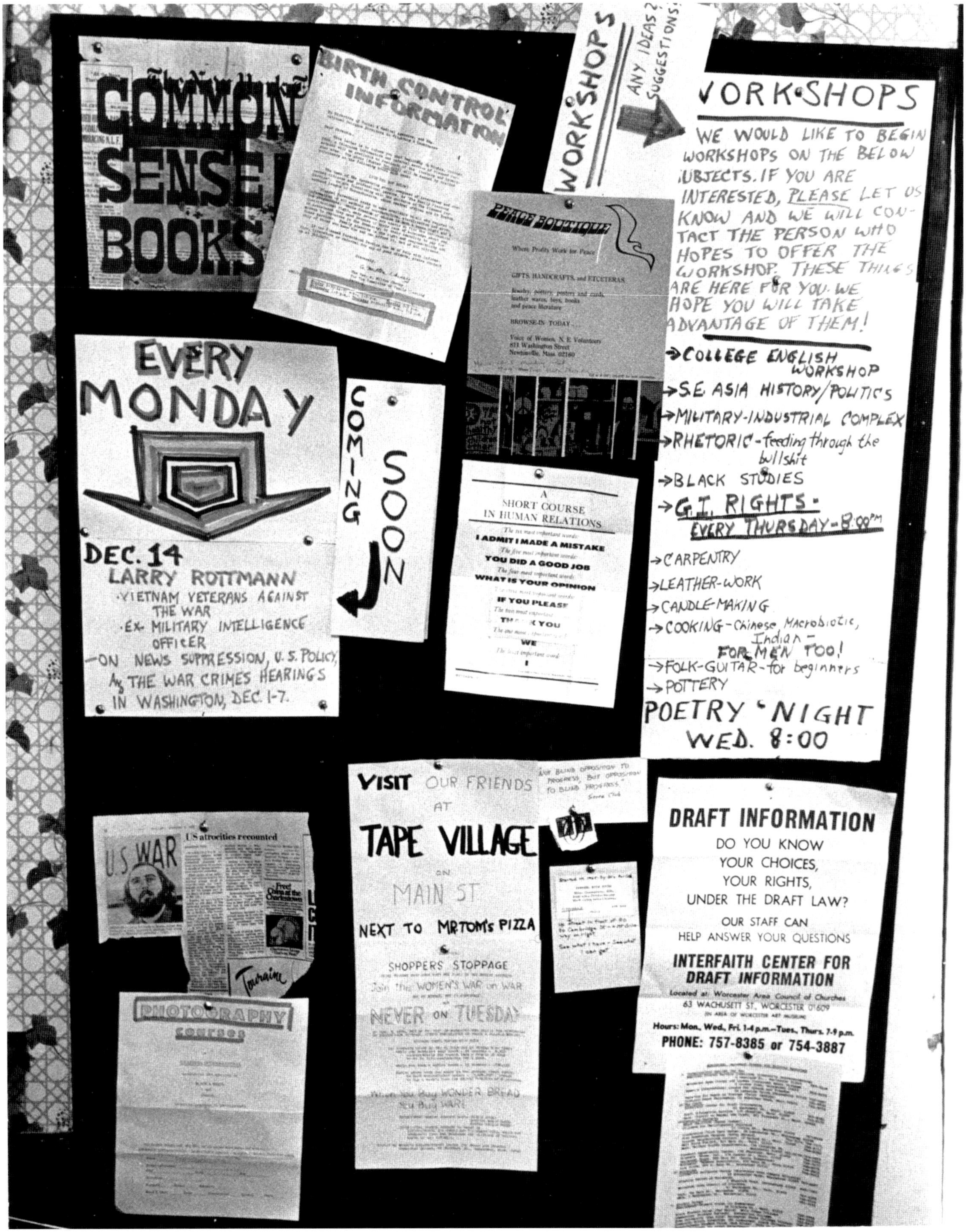

COMMON SENSE BOOKS
BIRTH CONTROL INFORMATION
WORKSHOPS
ANY IDEAS? SUGGESTIONS?
WORK•SHOPS
WE WOULD LIKE TO BEGIN WORKSHOPS ON THE BELOW SUBJECTS. IF YOU ARE INTERESTED, PLEASE LET US KNOW AND WE WILL CONTACT THE PERSON WHO HOPES TO OFFER THE WORKSHOP. THESE THINGS ARE HERE FOR YOU. WE HOPE YOU WILL TAKE ADVANTAGE OF THEM!
→COLLEGE ENGLISH WORKSHOP
→S.E. ASIA HISTORY/POLITICS
→MILITARY-INDUSTRIAL COMPLEX
→RHETORIC - feeding through the bullshit
→BLACK STUDIES
→G.I. RIGHTS - EVERY THURSDAY - 8:00PM
→CARPENTRY
→LEATHER-WORK
→CANDLE-MAKING
→COOKING - Chinese, Macrobiotic, Indian - FOR MEN TOO!
→FOLK-GUITAR - for beginners
→POTTERY
POETRY NIGHT WED. 8:00
PEACE BOUTIQUE
Where Profits Work for Peace
GIFTS, HANDICRAFTS, and ETCETERAS
Jewelry, pottery, posters and cards, leather wares, toys, books and peace literature
BROWSE-IN TODAY
Voice of Women, N. E. Volunteers
811 Washington Street
Newtonville, Mass 02160
EVERY MONDAY
DEC. 14
LARRY ROTTMANN
·VIETNAM VETERANS AGAINST THE WAR
·EX-MILITARY INTELLIGENCE OFFICER
-ON NEWS SUPPRESSION, U.S. POLICY, & THE WAR CRIMES HEARINGS IN WASHINGTON, DEC. 1-7.
COMING SOON
A SHORT COURSE IN HUMAN RELATIONS
I ADMIT I MADE A MISTAKE
YOU DID A GOOD JOB
WHAT IS YOUR OPINION
IF YOU PLEASE
WE
I
US WAR
US atrocities recounted
VISIT OUR FRIENDS AT TAPE VILLAGE ON MAIN ST NEXT TO MR TOM'S PIZZA
SHOPPERS' STOPPAGE
Join the WOMEN'S WAR on WAR
NEVER ON TUESDAY
When You Buy WONDER BREAD You Buy WAR
PHOTOGRAPHY COURSES
DRAFT INFORMATION
DO YOU KNOW YOUR CHOICES, YOUR RIGHTS, UNDER THE DRAFT LAW?
OUR STAFF CAN HELP ANSWER YOUR QUESTIONS
INTERFAITH CENTER FOR DRAFT INFORMATION
Located at: Worcester Area Council of Churches
63 WACHUSETT ST., WORCESTER 01609
Hours: Mon., Wed., Fri. 1-4 p.m.–Tues., Thurs. 7-9 p.m.
PHONE: 757-8385 or 754-3887

Left

Before the internet and social media, bulletin boards are one way people communicate with the community about events and services being offered. WBCN becomes an electronic bulletin board for its listeners both through its broadcasts and its Listener Line. *Source: David Bieber Archives.*

Volunteers like Linda Shapiro (on phone at left) answer WBCN's Listener Line. Behind her are the reference books used to help answer the wide variety of questions received. *Source: Tommy Hadges Collection, Special Collections and University Archives, UMass Amherst Libraries.*

The WBCN Listener Line volunteers are an important part of the station and the WBCN family. Shown here are (left to right) John Ragucci, Tina Armstrong, Pam Mitchell, Lori Goldman, and Andi Johnson, at WBCN studios, circa 1974. *Source: LCMedia Productions.*

The Hub of the Community and Soundtrack of the City

says Norm Winer. "So the goal of Traveler's Friend was to find someone who was part of the community – someone who you could relate to, someone with whom you shared interests – with whom you could share a ride if one of you were driving there – to Florida or to New York, Hartford, Birmingham, maybe Yellowstone, or some rock festival in some unknown city unless they banned it before you got there."

"Traveler's Friend was something that could only happen back in those times. It was a product of a particular moment," says Joe Rogers. "We made these arrangements and never heard terrible feedback from it. As a full-grown adult in this time in my life, I shudder to think that sort of risk was taken. But there was never a case of something bad happening from that that we ever heard about. We only heard good things."

Another unique service of the Listener Line was the "Cat and Dog Report," where people could call in with lost pets or animals to give away, and they would get read on the air.

"You would say 'Hey, I lost my cat,'" recalls announcer Charles Laquidara. "'What color was the cat? Okay, what color eyes did it have?' Or 'Listen, I am giving away – this dog had puppies.' So it was called the 'Cat and Dog Report.' And it was popular."

"People would want to call the Listener Line when they had a problem, and it would be the first call that they would make," recalls Joe Rogers.

"I can remember people who were suicidal, that our Listener Line people would stay on the phone with them for hours. And acid casualties," recalls Steven Segal.

For the station's youth audience, the Listener Line is Google before there is a Google. Additionally, the Listener Line allows WBCN's audience to serve as the eyes and ears of the station and the city, to call in with information – about free concerts, rallies and demonstrations, protesters being arrested, teach-ins and musical and political events – that the station can share with its listeners. Those who phone the station are aware that they are always just a thrown switch away from finding themselves live on the air, where an entire city can respond to whatever their issue or matter of concern is.

"It was a tremendous service for the community," says Tommy Hadges. "Kate Curran was a volunteer herself who organized the entire group. It was a completely voluntary service, and it was a very important part of the station."

This kind of interactive communication made WBCN vital to the lives of its audience and relevant throughout the city. As Danny Schechter, WBCN's "News Dissector," explains:

> The reason WBCN could do these sorts of things and even do them in a sort of profitable way was that management got out of the way. The original general manager, Al Perry, he was *part* of the station. That the engineers *were part* of the station. You didn't have big corporate overlords like you have in most media companies who are managing everything, all while controlling everything.
>
> I worked in television, where the control room is the metaphor for all of television. And after a signal leaves the control room, it goes to master control, so *control* of the airwaves is the big word. At BCN, *control* wasn't the big word. *Creativity* was the big word, and *community* was the big word.
>
> *Consciousness* was another word that really defined the station, and this appealed to young people who were revolting against the system and saw and heard in the station a reflection of themselves and their own values, their own culture, their own music, and they were attracted

For WBCN's young audience, the Listener Line's Traveler's Friend — which matches up people who are driving to points around the country with those who are looking for rides and can split the driving and cost of gas — is an alternative to hitchhiking for those who cannot afford the cost of a bus or plane ticket. These hitchhikers are lined up at the entrance of the Massachusetts Turnpike near Copley Square in Boston seeking rides to such destinations as Albany, New York, and Hartford, Connecticut, November 1970. *Source: Nick DeWolf Photo Archive.*

WBCN staff photo in front office at 312 Stuart Street, January 1972.
Back row (from left): T. Mitchell Hastings, Michael Joyce, Tim Montgomery, Phil Belanger, Kathleen Curran, Bill Lichtenstein, Amanda Sullivan, Bill Spurlin, Cindy Collamore, John Brodey, Danny Schechter, Charles Laquidara, Tommy Hadges, Jack Kearney. Second row (on floor and desk, from left): Kenny Greenblatt, Al Perry, Jim Parry, Carla Epple. Front row (from left): Maxanne and Norm Winer. *Source: Peter Simon Collection, Special Collections and University Archives, UMass Amherst Libraries.*

to it. And it had an impact that goes beyond just entertainment and music. It was a vital force in the community, and that's unique in broadcasting, you know. I worked in many other broadcasting companies where everything is overmanaged, overcontrolled, overregulated.

Since BCN allowed creativity — it gave it a chance — and its openness to free expression and support for anti-establishment and even radical activities, the station drew the attention of the leading political and social activists and critics of the time [many of whom would call into the station or drop by WBCN's studios].

WBCN attracted support from some of the top rock and rollers in the world, who came to the station and who loved being there and who wanted to come back. BCN was really part of the whole rock and roll culture. I mean, we heard names like John Lennon, but when I interviewed John Lennon, he knew all about BCN. He loved BCN.

In fact, Danny Schechter interviews ex-Beatle John Lennon and Yoko Ono in Boston when Yoko attends and addresses the first International Feminist Planning Conference at Lesley College from June 1 to 4, 1973, sponsored by the National Organization for Women and featuring representatives from twenty-seven countries. Among other things, Danny's interview uncovers the fact that John helps out at home with cooking and cleaning — not news by today's standards, but in the context of 1973, this revelation that ex-Beatle John Lennon is a feminist becomes newsworthy. Included in their broadcast discussion:

Danny Schechter: Lo and behold, John and Yoko surfaced in Cambridge — not at all deported from the United States. What are you doing here? I guess we should do that for starters. Yoko?

Yoko Ono: Well, I'm here because I'm a woman, and it's just very interesting to meet other sisters. And meeting is a very important thing . . .

Danny: What did you get out of it? What have the sessions been like?

Yoko: I found that women are very powerful. And they have sort of immense power that's hidden in them. They have to hide it in the society because it's a male society. And they were taught to hide their power. They were taught to look helpless and all that, you know. And now they're sort of bringing it up. And one thing I want to say to the brothers is that — don't be scared of them, don't be threatened by the power that we're bringing out, because it's like we were icebergs, you know. The whole bottom is hidden in the water. And that hidden power, when it's offered to the society, is going to be a great force. We're offering something to society, to you. And they can use it in strength, you know.

Danny: How have you felt about this conference here and about — your involvement, John, in the women's movement as it were, the kind of feminist ideas?

John Lennon: Well, my involvement started when I met Yoko. At that time, there was no word for it — *feminism*, you know. There was two artists living together, and she happened to be the female, and she wanted equal time and equal space. And that started a sort of dialogue between us, which went on and on, and then a sort of women's movement came out around the — about a year or two after we've met. And I was sort of naturally related to it . . . . But they're all here, you know. And the point about this thing is, it's the first international feminism conference. And in that way, it's historic and important. The fact that they're all trying, you know, and they're all dialoguing and all, you know. The sort of radicals are saying, "Well, what about this?" and liberals are saying, "Well, in our country we have to do this." . . .

Danny: Without getting too personal, what changes has John gone through? I mean, how has John's consciousness been transformed?

Yoko: I know that you might think it's very trivial. But if he makes biscuits and boils rice, for instance, and it was sort of like – I mean, you know, in our household nobody has to do it. You know, luckily we don't have to do it. But the fact that he's learning what it is to cook, you know: cooking is like art. I mean, it's a very interesting experience. So in a way, men, because of the social set-up and convention, that they were deprived from the pleasure of learning how to cook, learning how to knit or whatever. Those things, they're deprived from it too. And now he's starting to open up that side, which is beautiful.

Danny: Are you a good cook?

John: [In a high-pitched voice] *A man's work is never done, my dear*. No, I just wanted to do it, you know, so I've only actually cooked one meal.

John Lennon and Yoko Ono at Lesley College in Cambridge, where Yoko Ono performs at the first International Feminist Planning Conference, June 1973. *Source: Lesley University.*

WBCN's Danny Schechter "the News Dissector" interviewing John Lennon and Yoko Ono while they are in Cambridge for the first International Feminist Planning Conference at Lesley College, June 1973. Schechter later recounts that in the photo, Lennon is showing him, as the interview is beginning, that his microphone is not plugged in. *Source: Stephen Goldstein.*

The Hub of the Community and Soundtrack of the City

Danny: And I cook every week.

John: Well, I know there is a lot of guys can cook you know. It's just something I never – but most guys can't.

Danny: I really can't cook, but I cook anyway.

John: Well, that's how you learn. I just started trying to do it because it's like, you know, all the females are brought up not knowing, say, for instance, how to work tape recorders or fix their bike or whatever it is. And men are brought up not knowing how to cook or look after themselves, you know, and if you have a sort of split from your partner or leave home, it's like hardly knowing half of what's going on. You know, if nobody was around, I'd probably starve to death.

Danny: The Beatles wash their own dishes?

John: I don't know anything about the Beatles.

Danny: Aside from that level of sharing work and stuff, I mean, do you feel that you've been going through changes about your own role, your own relationship to Yoko, your relationship to other women, to other men?

John: Man, it's completely changed. It's been a process of four or five years. And I just – it was like having one eye shut. Once you start acknowledging, yes, that women are oppressed slaves, and then you start seeing it in those terms, it's just an eye opener, and you can never go back even though you still intellectually you can grasp it. But when it starts sort of happening in all over your body, that's when the changes really come. Although we're not a completely liberated couple, and we still go through a lot of struggle, and it's usually for space you know.

Yoko: But it's a good struggle because – I don't even know if it's a good struggle, I'm just saying that it's a struggle, but as John said, we can't go back, so we're doing it, you know.

Another frequent guest at WBCN's studios or on the phone in the station's early years is activist Abbie Hoffman, who, like WBCN's Norm Winer, attended Brandeis University. As Winer recalls:

> It was very easy to suppress the voice of dissent in those days, but Abbie raised the argument to a whole other level. He created a whole new stage on which he could appear and get the public's attention. He was taken on by late-night talk shows, and of course, he was embraced by WBCN. . . .
>
> Abbie was a Bostonian and he never worked for the radio station but we took him in. He was consistent with our mentality and with our with our sensibility, I mean the revolutionary ethic that we wanted to espouse . . . . He was one of the smartest people. He was so good at presenting himself and be able to identify all of his concerns of the public and things that we weren't even aware of yet. It was a pleasure to deal with him. He was an intense and engaging public speaker – really, really funny. Truly a fascinating man.
>
> Abbie's gift is that he brought attention to issues, people, and news that otherwise would have gone unnoticed just because it was lost in the monotone of American politics. He was a performance artist as much as he was a political figure and countercultural icon. He was presenting to the public to get their attention, and even though he was very much a part of our world, his profile was that dramatic and conspicuous that he got the attention of mass media.

Michael Ansara knew Hoffman as an organizer:

> Abbie had a brilliant sense of the media. He knew how to crystallize the counterculture and produce a moment. He was as much a cultural figure as a political figure. I was more serious about organizing and politics, and so he and I sort of diverged. I wanted to build an organization.

Abbie Hoffman (center), who frequently appears on WBCN's airwaves, in the studio with WBCN announcers Debbie Ullman and Charles Laquidara, July 1971. *Source: Jeff Albertson Photograph Collection, Special Collections and University Archives, UMass Amherst Libraries.*

WBCN through the eyes of famed cartoonist Gahan Wilson, whose monster-influenced characters were seen in the *New Yorker* for fifty years. Here, a WBCN announcer as a Wilson-envisioned monster broadcasts on Friday the 13th, and lets listeners know about an upcoming witch coven and monster rally in Cambridge. *Source: LCMedia Productions, Inc.*

Chapter 9

He wanted to get media and was terrific at it. In the great march on the Pentagon, he and Allen Ginsberg and others wanted to levitate the Pentagon, and I was saying, "What are you talking about? I'm way too serious for this. Levitate the Pentagon? Come on, just focus on our politics." He was an intensely popular, charismatic figure. You knew that every time you talked to Abbie, there would be some provocative quote that would come out, guaranteed.

Others who pass through the doors and onto the airwaves of WBCN during this period are Bernadette Devlin, the Irish socialist activist and member of the British Parliament; poet Allen Ginsberg, who stops by the station one afternoon to help read the news interspersed with poems about corporate pollution of the environment; and actress and activist Jane Fonda.

Charles Laquidara recalls one night in November 1970, when "the Listener Line person came in and said, 'There's a musician downstairs. He just played at the Arc, and the other musician—I guess they both played at different places. Uh, Jerry Garcia . . .' And I said 'From the Grateful Dead?' 'Yeah.' 'Who's the other one?' 'Duane Allman from the Allman Brothers.' 'Yes, send them up. We will play. Yeah, cool.'"

Bernadette Devlin, the Northern Irish civil rights activist and member of the British Parliament, visits WBCN's studios, seen here with Danny Schechter (left), February 18, 1971. *Source: Jeff Albertson Photograph Collection, Special Collections and University Archives, UMass Amherst Libraries.*

Jane Fonda speaks with WBCN while in Boston, June 1972. *Source: Jeff Albertson Photograph Collection, Special Collections and University Archives, UMass Amherst Libraries.*

The Hub of the Community and Soundtrack of the City

So they come up, and we're, "So what do you got now for us?" And we're doing this on air. We were smoking dope. These guys—there is Jerry Garcia and Duane Allman. I mean stuff like that couldn't happen today with musicians, unless they were paid big bucks by, you know, a record company or somebody to go and do that. But here are these two guys coming up. They each played their respective gigs. They came up, and they played for two hours.

Another unexpected musical moment happens when WBCN announcer Jim Parry, while walking to work, recognizes blues and gospel singer Rev. Gary Davis, whose finger-picking guitar style had influenced folk artists from Bob Dylan to John Sebastian to Dave Van Ronk. Davis is sitting across the street from the radio station at the Greyhound bus terminal waiting for a bus that is several hours away. Parry introduces himself and asks Davis, who has his guitar with him, if he would like to come by the station to talk and play on the air, which turns into an unexpected live musical performance.

As WBCN's influence grows in Massachusetts and the other New England states where the station's 50,000-watt signal can be heard, announcers from the station travel to attend the first Alternative Media Conference held at Goddard College in Vermont in June 1970. The conference is a chance for WBCN's staff to meet two thousand others, including underground radio station programmers and alternative journalists from around the country. Attendees include Freak Brothers cartoonist Gilbert Shelton, Baba Ram Dass, *Rolling Stone* photographer Robert Altman, and Marvel Comics' Stan Lee, with musical performers including Dr. John, Cactus, and the J. Geils Band.

Those who attend say the conference is life-changing and perhaps the most important event of the era because it allows them to see that they are part of a much bigger, national effort to use media to help create social, political, and cultural changes in cities and towns throughout America. The conference leaves the WBCN announcers and staff with a new sense of mission and empowerment about using their radio station to create positive social and political changes.

This spirit of using the radio station to promote positive social change was described in an interview with WBAI-FM, New York, for its 1970 radio documentary on WBCN. In it, WBCN announcers Charles Laquidara and Joe Rogers speak of their efforts to ask listeners over the air to send telegrams to Massachusetts governor Frank Sargent, a Republican, to express their opinions about the recent conviction and imprisonment of birth control advocate Bill Baird, who is serving a sentence for dispensing birth control to college students, a felony at the time in Massachusetts. Soon after, the governor frees Baird pending an appeal, and according to Laquidara and Rogers, the governor specifically cites the number of telegrams he received as the reason, which they cite as evidence of a newfound power of radio to mobilize listeners.

This new spirit of collaboration between underground journalists and broadcasters and their audiences around the country is not lost on the FBI, which is keeping close tabs on the growing counterculture and anti–Vietnam War movement. In a July 13, 1970, FBI memo, obtained for this book and the documentary film, the Bureau details the events at the Alternative Media Conference, noting that "Individuals at stations are realizing they have a responsibility to the community . . . and issues that are overlooked on radio." Among those whose name and number show up in the FBI file is WBCN's Charles Laquidara.

Jerry Garcia of the Grateful Dead stops by WBCN's studios unannounced with the Dead's Bob Weir and Duane Allman of the Allman Brothers Band to perform following a Grateful Dead concert at Boston University and an Allman Brothers gig at the Boston Tea Party, November 21, 1970. *Source: Jeff Albertson Photograph Collection, Special Collections and University Archives, UMass Amherst Libraries.*

Left
Duane Allman of the Allman Brothers Band performs live on the air on WBCN following the band's gig at the Boston Tea Party, November 21, 1970. *Source: Jeff Albertson Photograph Collection, Special Collections and University Archives, UMass Amherst Libraries.*

Right
Other musicians who are fans of WBCN include Ringo Starr, with (left to right) Epic Record's Lenny Collins and WBCN announcers Tommy Hadges and John Brodey, 1978. *Source: Tommy Hadges Collection, Special Collections and University Archives, UMass Amherst Libraries.*

Middle right
George Harrison with (from left) WBCN's Maxanne Sartori, WRKO's Carol Singer, Don Dumont of Warner Brothers Records, and WBCN's Al Perry, 1976. *Source: Al Perry.*

Bottom right
Muddy Waters (center) celebrating his birthday following a live broadcast on WBCN seen with (from left) Peter Wolf, J. Geils Band; Al Perry, WBCN; Magic Dick (Richard Salwitz), J. Geils Band; and Dick Wingate, Chess/Janus Records, April 22, 1975. *Source: Dick Wingate.*

Livingston Taylor is a frequent guest on WBCN, including on commercials and station IDs, circa 1970. *Source: Peter Simon Collection, Special Collections and University Archives, UMass Amherst Libraries.*

Top right
WBCN staff attend the Alternative Media Conference at Goddard College in June 1970, later calling the chance to network with others working in the underground media around the country one of the most important experiences of the era because it helps them see their work in a national context. *Source: Stephen Goldstein.*

Bottom right
Baba Ram Dass, the spiritual leader whose work inspires everyone from Steve Jobs to George Harrison, speaks to the attendees at the Alternative Media Conference, June 1970. *Source: Peter Simon Collection, Special Collections and University Archives, UMass Amherst Libraries.*

145

UNITED STATES DEPARTMENT OF JUSTICE
FEDERAL BUREAU OF INVESTIGATION
Boston, Massachusetts
July 13, 1970

In Reply, Please Refer to
File No.

NATIONAL STUDENT STRIKE (NSS)

The National Strike Information Center (NSIC) at Brandeis University, Waltham, Massachusetts, started as the central clearing house for receipt and dissemination of information on a nationwide basis concerning the student strike and now that striking students are turning their energies to local organizing, it is the NSIC's function to aid them in any way possible. The foregoing is set forth in each copy of the NSIC Newsletter, which is the official propaganda organ of the NSIC.

People from college and commercial rock stations, underground papers and those interested in television and film attended, but the definition of alternative media was intentional not spelled out by the organizers of the conference who hoped that a self-selective process would occur. Record promoters and other "hip capitalists" were there to discuss business and to capitalize on the youth market. It was felt that the use of this media was no alternative inasmuch as the various stations still have to sell products to survive which puts "radical" programmers in compromising positions with sponsors or management. Commercial radio presents real problems for creative people and college and non-commercial stations often have insufficient funds or manpower.

The broadcast media are often stifled by "control" and fear of the Federal Communications Commission which prevents the station from fulfilling its obligations by presenting program of community interest. "Individuals at stations are realizing they have a responsibility to the community and many expressed interest in programs about community projects and issues that are overlooked on radio. Local organizers can rap with these people on the air, send them stories or tapes and provide them with local news. Many stations are anxious to help and some of the people to talk to at radio stations around the country are:

BERNE FROMM, WBFO *Radio Station*
3435 Main Street
Buffalo, New York

CHARLES LAQUIDARA (WBCN (FM)) *Radio Station*
312 Stuart Street
Boston, Massachusetts
Program Coordinator

FBI files obtained through the Freedom of Information Act reveal the FBI's awareness of WBCN's role in using radio to help create social change. *Source: Federal Bureau of Investigation.*

Perhaps most emblematic of WBCN's efforts to give a voice to those who previously didn't have one is a program created by announcer Jim Parry called *Feedback*. As Parry recalls:

> I created and liked doing *Feedback*. It was the opportunity for listeners to make and send in tapes of whatever they wanted—rants, music, you name it—and we would take ten minutes every day and play whatever listeners sent us. With the possible exception, at that point, that we couldn't air four-letter words, essentially everything else was fair game. We got tapes from a lot of really awful bands and some very good bands. There were a few people who got involved in really nutty rants who had some personal vendetta against something that made absolutely no sense except in their particular worldview. But we got a lot of good stuff. People had something to say, and they sent it in. We did that for five years. It was democracy in action. You got a chance to say what you wanted to say in a medium that was widely listened to. That is almost impossible today because big corporations control the stations.

10

WBCN News and Public Affairs

WBCN News and Public Affairs

10

From WBCN's beginning in March 1968 as an underground free-form radio station, newscasts and public affairs reports are not part of the regular scheduled programming.

"In the very beginning, we did not have news," says WBCN announcer Sam Kopper. "Our attitude was, all these other radio stations generally have five minutes of news at the top of every hour, and some of them have a half hour of news at six o'clock, so news is perfectly well covered."

"We didn't have news, you know. We didn't know what to do," recalls station founder Ray Riepen. "We were getting heat on that from the FCC. You had a certain obligation as far as the FCC was concerned to provide news and public affairs."

In fact, news reports on radio stations in the mid-1960s generally involved what is called "rip and read," a process by which the announcer on the air would grab a hand full of news reports from an Associated Press or a United Press International teletype machine, which continuously prints out news stories on long rolls of paper. The announcers, in turn, rip the stories they want to read on the air from the rolls of printed paper — hence, "rip and read."

The stories in radio newscasts of the era often include as little information as a newspaper headline ("North Vietnamese troops and Viet Cong guerrillas launch surprise attacks throughout South Vietnam on the Lunar New Year. The Pentagon says rockets, grenades, and fires reduce portions of Saigon to rubble") and frequently not much more, often passing along the official government line on a story, without significant detail or context.

Beginning with WBCN's coverage of the 1969 student strikes, increasing in the wake of growing protests against the Vietnam War, and fueled by the experiences of the station's staff at the Alternative Media Conference in June 1970, it becomes clear to Ray Riepen and others at the station that WBCN needs to provide its listeners with an ongoing, independent source of news and information about events both in the Greater Boston area as well as national and international affairs that are relevant to their lives but are being overlooked elsewhere.

Norm Winer, then a recent Brandeis University graduate and part-time WBCN announcer, convinces the station to let him become the station's first news director. Winer sees his task as to cover the news that is relevant to the young people who make up most of the station's audience, in a manner that will reach and resonate with them. As Winer recalls:

They had a news room, and they had a news machine, but they didn't have anyone doing the news. So I convinced them that, "Hey, you need someone to do news. I read the *New York Times* every day. Let me be your news director, and you can pay me a criminally small amount of money to do that, but I'll gladly do it. And I'll do fill-in DJ work whenever I can." So I became the station's first full-time news director.

News for BCN was like music on BCN. The initial conception was that it would be the stuff you wouldn't hear anywhere else. The same issues that were relevant to us were also relevant to the audience. So we knew which political issues were the most compelling, which were the most important, and which ones were the most immediate when it came to our listeners' concerns.

Tape cassettes are a new technology, as are portable cassette recorders that journalists can easily carry around to record sound. Devices such as Sony's first portable cassette recorder, the handheld TC-100, with its piano key operations, are ubiquitous and allow reporters to wander around, in and out of crowds and protests, capturing audio along the way. As Winer recalls:

There was a matter of me going out to a demonstration and being swept along with the other protesters, being arrested or held or whatever, and subsequently, I would reveal my press credentials, and they would let me go. I would come back to the radio station and do a delayed newscast and reveal to everybody what was going on. That was the nature of how we did it.

Our coverage of protests was different than what you might hear on the local TV evening news or read in the *Boston Globe*. We could clearly state and articulate the cause that was involved, and perhaps most important, we could depict for our listeners why all these people were there. You know, we gave them the scenario – whether it was a bombing, whether it was a takeover, whether it was a demonstration. We covered all of these stories because they were something that affected all of us. And it was nice to know that Boston was not isolated – that this was something that was going on in Madison and on the West Coast and New York and Columbia University, and all of these events were connected, and it was our jobs to connect those dots for the people in Boston.

Norm Winer (right), recently graduated from Brandeis, becomes WBCN's first news director. Shown with WGBH's David Silver, host of *What's Happening Mr. Silver?*
Source: Peter Simon Collection, Special Collections and University Archives, UMass Amherst Libraries.

The coverage of news brings a new seriousness of tone that is noticeable on the air, in contrast to the station's first year, when it predominantly played music. It reflects a growing resolve among young people — and increasingly among older Americans who are growing weary of the war in Vietnam — that everything that could be done needs to be done to remove Nixon from office.

This interplay between music and entertainment and news and information is noted by Winer in a 1970 interview with WBAI-FM in New York as part of its radio documentary about WBCN: "People say we're a music station, and people tell us, 'Be happier on the air,' they tell the individual announcers. But I can't separate playing records from what's going on with those [wire service] machines in there, in the newsroom. Our lives reflect what's going on in the world more and more. And to try to look askance or play pretty music while Nixon is ordering troops into Cambodia cannot be done."

By July 1970, efforts to identify a permanent full-time news director result in the hiring of Robert "Bo" Burlingham, a Princeton graduate, local activist, and SDS member. Burlingham replaces Winer, who returns to announcing at the station. However, what no one at the station knows at the time is that Burlingham has bona fide radical credentials as a member of the revolutionary group the Weathermen.

Burlingham is introduced to the station by Harvard SDS leader Michael Ansara. "Charles [Laquidara] wanted me to do the news for BCN," recalls Ansara. "He kept saying, 'Come do the news. Don't just come on and say here's a demonstration. You should do the news.' But I didn't want to do it. It's not me. I'm an organizer. I'm not the news."

Ansara recalls that

> by chance, a dear friend of mine, Bo Burlingham — one of the sweetest people in the world — shows up on my doorstep. And much to my great sadness, he was caught up in Weathermen — and now, much to my great delight, he and his soon-to-be-wife, Lisa, show up on our doorstep and say, "We're out of Weathermen." They looked as if they'd never seen the sun, as if they'd been in some underground prison. They were pale and had no clothes other than the clothes they were wearing. My wife and I took them in, and they lived with us for a while, and then they got on their feet.

According to Bo Burlingham:

> I joined the Weathermen in September of 1969. I joined because I was as desperate as everybody else since it looked like the war was going on interminably and we had no faith in Nixon to end it. There was a lot of talk about how we needed to have a real revolutionary response to this, but most of it was just talk. It was mostly people in universities who were keeping their students deferments by sitting around coffee tables talking about how we need a revolution. The Weathermen actually seemed like they were serious about doing something, so I decided that I would go with them.

Burlingham says his time with the increasingly radical organization — which had taken its name from a line in the Bob Dylan song "Subterranean Homesick Blues" ("You don't need a weatherman / To know which way the wind blows") — initially involved an assignment for him and his fiancé, Lisa, in a group of four members of the Weathermen that traveled around the Midwest. However, everything changed one day in March 1970. As he recalls:

An explosion on March 6, 1970, in a Greenwich Village townhouse in Manhattan that is being used as a bomb factory by the Weather Underground kills three and sends two others fleeing into hiding. *Source: David Bieber Archives.*

Chapter 10

I remember going to work at the University of Dayton and seeing a newspaper that had an article about how there had been an explosion at the townhouse in Greenwich Village. It was clear from the people involved that this was a Weathermen townhouse and that people were, in fact, making bombs.

The bomb blast occurs on March 6, 1970, and it levels a brownstone at 18 West 11th Street in New York City's Greenwich Village. Three members of the Weathermen—Ted Gold, Diana Oughton, and Terry Robbins—are killed by the blast, and two other members—Kathy Boudin and Cathy Wilkerson—survive and flee. Burlingham continues:

This was the level of seriousness that we never had before. I was shocked by this. It was shortly after that that we decided we had to go someplace else. We wound up coming to Boston. I was not in touch with any of the powers that be in what was becoming the Weather Underground, as an increasing number of members of the Weathermen went underground and into hiding.

I was in the situation where I needed to get a job. I needed to have some way to support myself. So I asked Michael [Ansara] if he knew of any place where I might go to work, and he said that he heard WBCN was looking for a news director.

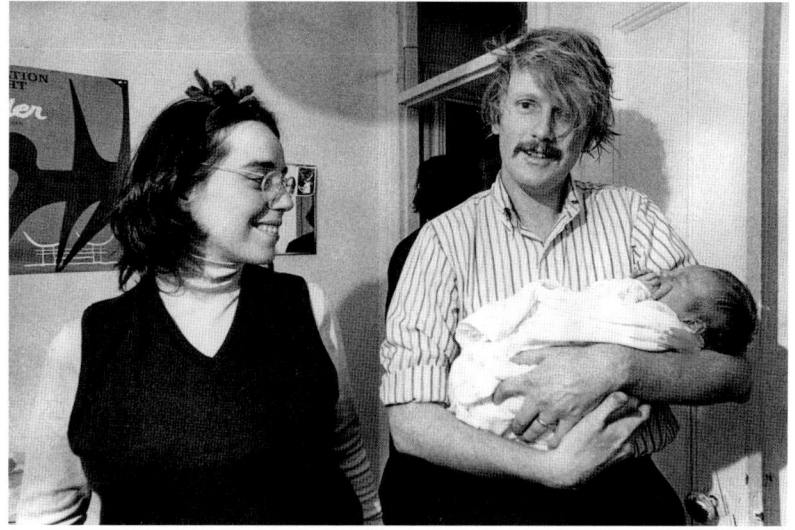 

With help from friend Michael Ansara, Bo Burlingham, seen here with his wife, Lisa, is hired to be news director at WBCN. *Source: David Bieber Archives.*

Working with a team of volunteers, including Danny Schechter (seen here), news director Bo Burlingham begins producing daily newscasts on WBCN. *Source: Jeff Albertson Photograph Collection, Special Collections and University Archives, UMass Amherst Libraries.*

154

Michael Ansara remembers: "Both Bo and Lisa were looking for jobs. I asked Bo, 'Well, what have you done?' Bo says, 'When I went to Princeton, I had a really popular radio program.' So I brought Bo to BCN and introduced him to Charles [Laquidara] and Ray [Riepen], and they hired him on the spot to do the news."

Once at WBCN, Bo recalls, "We came up with a plan that we were going to get together a team of people, including Danny Schechter, who were going to gather the news during the day, and then Charles Laquidara was going to read it, with rock and roll and all sorts of other things going on."

The team's plan to produce the news worked perfectly for two days, and then, on July 23, 1970, Burlingham recalls:

> I was at the station, and we had a meeting over lunch and after everyone left. I was still eating my sandwich when I heard the AP ticker machine go off. So I got up to look and see what the news story was. It said, "Flash. Flash. Flash. Detroit, Michigan, Attorney General John Mitchell announced today that 13 leaders of the Weathermen organization were indicted for conspiracy to [bomb] federal buildings.

NBC News reports that "A federal grand jury in Detroit charged the thirteen top leaders of the Weathermen with plotting to bomb public buildings in Chicago, Detroit, New York, and Berkeley, California. According to Attorney General John Mitchell, the indictments grew out of an investigation begun after three other Weathermen blew themselves up in a fashionable townhouse in New York's Greenwich Village in March."

Bo Burlingham looks at the list of those indicted, and says it "started off with a bunch of names of people who I knew were underground." Among them were Weathermen Mark Rudd, Bill Ayers, and Bernardine Dohrn, who had disappeared after the New York City townhouse explosion. "And then it got to some names of people who I knew weren't underground. And I said, 'Oh, too bad for them.' And then I got to the last name on the list, and it said Robert Burlingham, and I couldn't believe it. I was totally stunned. I had really not been involved at all in the underground."

Bo takes the story to show announcer Charles Laquidara.

"Bo comes in with this thing he ripped," recalls Charles Laquidara, "and he says, 'Charles, we have a problem. Read this.' And I looked at it, and it says, 'Attorney General John Mitchell has just announced that indictments are being issued in Detroit for 13 Weathermen.'" And I said, 'So what's wrong with this?" and he says, "Seventh name." I looked down, seventh name, Bo Burlingham: my news director."

The bulletin with news of the Weathermen indictments comes over the station's Associated Press teletype machine. *Source: Tommy Hadges Collection, Special Collections and University Archives, UMass Amherst Libraries.*

13 WEATHERMEN INDICTED IN PLOTS

U.S. Grand Jury in Detroit Charges Bombing Plans

By JERRY M. FLINT
Special to The New York Times

DETROIT, July 23—A Federal grand jury today indicted 13 persons, including the leaders of the Weatherman, on charges of conspiring to bomb and kill. Ten of the 13 are already being sought on fugitive warrants in other Federal or local cases.

The Weatherman originally was a faction of the Students for a Democratic Society. The faction openly advocates violence to bring about a revolution or revolutionary changes in the American system.

The indictment attempted to link Weatherman meetings in Flint, Mich., last December and in Cleveland in February with bomb making in New York and an arms cache found in Chicago and meetings among the 13.

The indictment charged:

"It was part of the conspiracy that the defendants and the unindicted co-conspirators, together with others not known to the grand jury, would organize a 'central committee' to direct underground bombing operations of the defendants and co-conspirators; that this group would be assigned to Berkeley, Calif.; Chicago, Ill.; New York, N. Y., and Detroit, Mich.; that clandestine and underground 'focals,' consisting of three or four persons, would be established; that the 'focals' would be commanded by the 'central committee' in the bombing of police and other civic, business, and educational buildings throughout the country."

The indictment charged that members of the so-called focals would travel around the country using false identities and communicating through coded messages, obtain firearms and explosives, and use them to bomb police and other buildings and to kill and injure those inside.

The 13 indicted persons were:

Mark Rudd, 23 years old; Bernadine Dohrn, 27; William Ayers, 25; Kathy Boudin, 27; Linda Evans, 23; Cathy Wilkerson, 25.

Also Dianne Donghi, 21; Russell Neufeld, 22; Jane Spielman, 23; Ronald Fliegelman, 26; Larry Grathwohl, 22; Naomi Jaffe, 27, and Robert Burlingham, 24.

Of these, the first five were also indicted in Chicago in April—part of the Chicago 12—on charges stemming from the Weatherman violence there in October, 1969.

Miss Evans was arrested in New York earlier this year and released on bail. The Federal Bureau of Investigation announced tonight that Miss Donghi was arrested in New York this afternoon and would be arraigned Wednesday in the Federal Court in Brooklyn. Mr. Neufeld was picked up by the F.B.I. at a hospital in Chicago where he worked. The remaining 10 are being sought on fugitive warrants from other cases.

Named in the indictment as co-conspirators but *not* defendants were 15 other persons, including two, Ted Gold and Diana Oughten, who were killed in a March 6 explosion at what has been called a Weatherman bomb factory in Greenwich Village, New York, and a third, Terry Robbins, who was believed killed in the explosion.

The indictment named 21 "overt acts" leading to the conspiracy charge.

Left
News of the Weatherman indictments in the *New York Times*, July 24, 1970. *Source: New York Times.*

An FBI Wanted Poster seeking those indicted along with Bo Burlingham. *Source: U.S. Department of Justice.*

Ray Riepen tells Bo Burlingham that since WBCN is federally licensed, it makes him "nervous to have a guy that's indicted for dynamiting federal buildings on the payroll," but he offers Burlingham a job with the newspaper Riepen co-owns, the *Cambridge Phoenix*. *Phoenix* newspaper staff shown here (left to right): Joe Pilati, Marsha Clayton Daniel, Stephen Diamond, Jeffrey Tarter, April Smith, Robert Ventola, Elliot Blinder, Jean Bergantini Grillo, Peter Simon, Stephen Davis, 1969.
Source: Jeff Albertson Photograph Collection, Special Collections and University Archives, UMass Amherst Libraries.

Bo calls Michael Ansara, who picks him up at the radio station, and the two go to a bar in Kendall Square, Cambridge, to talk.

"I remember sitting there, and the news coming on the television, and they began the first story, which was about this indictment in Detroit," says Burlingham. "They began putting pictures up, and so I am worried that they might put my picture up, and so I was hiding my face as much as I could. Thankfully, they didn't. It was mainly the most famous members."

While waiting to speak with attorneys, Michael says he and Bo "go to speak with Ray Riepen to tell him what's happened but also to let him know that Bo needs the job."

Ray recalls the visit from Bo and Michael:

Bo came to my office with Mike, and he tells me, "I've been indicted, and I thought you ought to know." He explained that he had been a part of the Weathermen. And I said, "Well, geez, this is a federally licensed business. It makes me nervous to have a guy that's indicted for dynamiting federal buildings on the payroll. I've got to let you go, but I'll give you a job at my newspaper [referring to the year-old alternative weekly *Cambridge Phoenix*, which Ray Riepen has just purchased]. Which he [Bo] thought was pretty nice in light of everything.

"Ray said, 'I am a part owner of a newspaper called the *Cambridge Phoenix*, and if you wanted to go work there, you could do that.' I thought that was very generous of him," recalls Burlingham.

"So that's what we did, and he wrote for the newspaper for a year or two, and then I think he went to *Mother Jones* out on the West Coast," says Riepen.

Despite the seriousness of the situation, there was humor that was not lost.

"Meanwhile, we are getting lawyers to work on the case," recalls Michael Ansara. "I mean, Bo is doing the news on WBCN, and the FBI had no idea that he's in Boston."

"All charges were dropped," recalls Norm Winer. "There were all sorts of illegalities and irregularities. And so we needed a new news director, and that's when Danny Schechter came into the picture."

The News Dissector

11

The News Dissector

11

In the wake of Bo Burlingham's sudden departure from the WBCN news department, stepping into the job as news director in July 1970 is twenty-eight-year-old alternative journalist Danny Schechter. During his time at WBCN, Schechter not only creates a news department that is commensurate with the radical, underground sound of the station but helps reframe the very nature of news and news reporting, challenging the beliefs that news can or should be purely objective and that it's wrong for journalists to have and express a point of view in their stories.

Additionally, Danny is credited with being among the first to examine news itself with the kind of incisive media analysis that now, fifty years later, is common as media critics routinely tear apart news stories for their sources, their language, and the ways they reflect the values of whoever owns the news outlet publishing the story.

From his initial days at the station, Danny's focus is on stories that WBCN's young listeners care about but that are rarely covered by the mainstream "straight" press. These include the Vietnam War and the growing opposition to it; emerging social movements for racial, women's, and gay and lesbian equality; environmental awareness; and struggles for liberation around the world, from South Africa to Central and South America.

In the wake of Bo Burlingham's departure, Danny Schechter takes over the news at WBCN as the station's "News Dissector."
Source: Jeff Albertson Photograph Collection, Special Collections and University Archives, UMass Amherst Libraries.

Danny Schechter in his office, the WBCN newsroom, where he records interviews and other audio material and writes two newscasts a day. *Source: Tommy Hadges Collection, Special Collections and University Archives, UMass Amherst Libraries.*

Danny Schechter delivers his newscasts from the WBCN production studio twice daily – a thirty-minute newscast around 6 p.m. and a fifteen-minute newscast at 10 p.m. – although on a day with major news events, the news can run much longer. *Source: Jeff Albertson Photograph Collection, Special Collections and University Archives, UMass Amherst Libraries.*

"I first met Danny Schechter because he was active in a lot of the local rallies and demonstrations from the organizational standpoint, and that's how I knew of his skills as an orator and a mover and shaker," recalls WBCN's first news director and later program director Norm Winer.

Schechter describes how, during one of his first newscasts, he acquires the nickname "the News Dissector," which would stay with him for the next four decades at WBCN and later through his work at CNN and ABC News:

> I wrote a script, and I brought it to the DJ [Jim Parry] to read for the newscast. He takes a look at what I typed out, and he said, "I can't read this. I can't even understand what it's saying. It's a sloppy mess! You read it!"
>
> So I said, "You want me to read it? Are you sure?" I was very self-conscious about having a Bronx accent that wouldn't play well in Boston given the traditional rivalries of the Red Sox and the Yankees. Also, I wasn't expecting to be on air. And so he says, "You do it. I have to go to the bathroom." He then introduces me: "And now Danny Schechter, the News Inspector, the News Ingester, the News Dissector." And I love that idea of the news dissector, and so it sort of stuck. And that's how I got on the air doing the news — because Jim had to go to the bathroom. It's a typical BCN story.

"The title stuck because that was Danny's whole approach to the news," recalls Jim Parry. "He was not going to sit there and read straight wire copy. He was going to tell you how it came to be that way. He was going to tell you what the implications of that were — what the story behind it was. He was, in fact, 'the news dissector.' So it turned out to be very apropos."

Danny creates two daily newscasts for WBCN — at 6 p.m. and 10 p.m. — that he hosts along with guest commentators, many who have a radical perspective, who put the stories into context, particularly the coverage of the most important stories of the day: the war in Vietnam, the draft, and the growing youth-fueled opposition to both.

"This was an era in which the Vietnam War hung over everything, and it was the issue that galvanized the opposition. It was the issue that galvanized the Republican righteousness and patriotism and led to all kinds of oppression and massive demonstrations and even a bomb attack on the Pentagon. While I was at BCN, I tried to cover the Vietnam War in a different way than it was being covered by other media outlets in the U.S. That meant getting information from other sources, like Agence France-Presse or the British news agency Reuters."

Danny Schechter's newscasts are interspersed "with snatches of music" and other audio clips, and he would "synthesize it all in a kind of performance art," recalls Sid Blumenthal, a former writer for the *Boston Phoenix* and political adviser.
Source: Jeff Albertson Photograph Collection, Special Collections and University Archives, UMass Amherst Libraries.

The News Dissector

"What made Danny's work special [was that] Danny was willing to speak plain English with simple common sense, enriched by knowledge and penetrating insight," says former MIT professor and political commentator Noam Chomsky.

In fact, Chomsky's own contributions to WBCN's news coverage include his insights about language, as WBCN's news stands in contrast to the nightly TV newscasts and other news media that use the syntax of the Nixon administration, which calls the North Vietnamese "the enemy" in the undeclared conflict and reports the war's daily body counts as if reporting on a sports event.

WBCN breaks ranks with the Associated Press and other news media by refusing to refer to the North Vietnamese as "the enemy" in newscasts, recalls WBCN announcer Bob Slavin.
Source: United Electrical, Radio, and Machine Workers of America (UE) Records.

As an example, WBCN announcer Bob Slavin recalls changes Danny would make to news reports from the Associated Press wire:

> **The Associated Press copy would come over, and it would talk about the Vietnam War. It would make a reference to "forty of the enemy that were killed," and Danny would scratch out the word "enemy." It seems so obvious, but at the time you didn't mess with AP, you don't mess with the news. But, of course, you mess with AP. At the time, all you were hearing was, "the enemy this" and "the enemy that." But they weren't our enemy. They weren't my enemy. We were killing people who were presented as our enemies, and they weren't.**

"Here in Boston, the intellectual tone is set by universities," says Schechter. "And at these schools, you had some leading critics of the Vietnam War like Noam Chomsky [of MIT] and Howard Zinn of Boston University, who I brought on the air at BCN, and they became commentators. We showed that independent and dissenting ideas could find a large audience if they were presented in a style with a sense of humor and with some real content to it."

As David Bieber, who later became the station's creative services director and ad hoc archivist, recalls:

> **Danny Schechter and even before him Norm Winer, who was the first news director at WBCN—they were connected to the outsider politics. Danny was connected to everyone from Jane Fonda to Abbie Hoffman to John Lennon and Yoko Ono. I'm sure that he had a personal phone directory that included all their home numbers, and he could reach them and get them to comment, and they in turn, when they had a vital message to deliver, knew who would air it. And their words would go through unfiltered, you know, because we were so like-minded, and that was really hard and rare to find.**

Soon after, the news department expands. First, Danny, who is producing two newscasts a day without a staff, asks a fourteen-year-old Listener Line volunteer, Bill Lichtenstein, to run up the street with a tape recorder to speak with people attending a demonstration at what was then the Boston Police Headquarters, on Berkeley Street, just a few blocks from WBCN's Stuart Street studios, protesting the shooting and killing of Black Panther leader Fred Hampton in Chicago. As Bill recalls: "He gave me a Sony cassette recorder, and told me to ask people at the protest, 'Why are you here?' which, of course, is the perfect question for a fourteen-year-old covering their first news story, a demonstration."

Bill later reports live on the air from various demonstrations and news events around Boston, including from inside Harvard's Center for International Affairs in Cambridge, the former office of Henry Kissinger, as protesters break into the building on April 18, 1972. While inside, protesters ransack the offices and "liberate" files, some of which end up in print in *The CIA and the Cult of Intelligence*, written in 1974 by Victor Marchetti, a former special assistant to the deputy director of the Central Intelligence Agency, and John D. Marks, a former officer of the U.S. Department of State. It is the first book that the U.S. government ever goes to court to censor before its publication.

Meanwhile, Andy Kopkind, a brilliant alternative journalist who has been fired from *Time* magazine following an arrest for being gay, and his life partner, John Scagliotti, who goes on to create the public television series *In the Life* and the Emmy-winning documentary *Before Stonewall*, join the station, followed by Marsha Steinberg, a former Weathermen member, who has served time for her role in the "Days of Rage" protest in Chicago shortly after the beginning of the Chicago 8 conspiracy trial.

MIT professor Noam Chomsky (left, seen sitting in his office circa November 1970) and Boston University professor Howard Zinn (right, seen here at B.U. in January 1970) are regular commentators on Danny Schechter's newscasts, helping to put the day's news into a social, political, and historical context.
Source: Jeff Albertson Photograph Collection, Special Collections and University Archives, UMass Amherst Libraries.

The News Dissector

Antiwar protesters break into the Harvard Center for International Affairs to target research and other work being done by the university in support of the war in Vietnam, April 18, 1972. *Source: Spencer Grant Collection, Boston Public Library.*

During a break-in at Harvard's Center for International Affairs, WBCN's Bill Lichtenstein reports live on the air via telephone, describing the scene before police arrive. *Source: Spencer Grant Collection, Boston Public Library.*

Right
The aftermath of the break-in at the Center for International Affairs results in riot police being dispatched and a curfew that night for Harvard Square. *Source: Cambridge Historical Society.*

Says Michael Ansara:

Danny Schechter's WBCN news department was the most radical news department in the country. It was groundbreaking. The WBCN news team didn't have a model for how to do the news. There wasn't a model that said, "You have on three talking heads. You ask these questions. You turn to these experts." They were creating what it would mean for a rebellious rock and roll, free-form FM station to start incorporating news. They were free to try and fail. They were free to succeed. They tried everything. It was by far the most creative news department in the country and probably of journalism at its time.

In order to make the news relevant and engaging to the station's youthful audience, Danny and staff, particularly Bill Lichtenstein, begin to experiment with adding music and comedy to their reports by taking news clips and "actualities" — for example, a speech from Richard Nixon or an interview with a prominent administration official — and turning them into powerful audio montages by adding music and comedy to offer perspective to the day's events and to put stories into a broader social and political context. This montage format for news was innovated by "Scoop" Nisker of KSAN-FM radio in San Francisco, but WBCN adopts it whole-heartedly, and it is infused into the ongoing delivery of news on the station.

Says Ansara:

They were combining music with hard news, along with parodies and comedies about the news, culture, materialism, and corporate life. It undermined the political, cultural, and commercial order. And it did so brilliantly, in a way that later on, many radio programs would attempt to follow. I think it paved the way for the cable, comedy news programs that we have today. If you go back and you listen to BCN at the time, they're starting to do those things that will end up with Jon Stewart and Stephen Colbert. I think it all goes back to Charles, Danny Schechter, and the whole amazing group of people at BCN in those years.

This approach is part of what helps make Schechter's newscasts at the time, according to Noam Chomsky, "the most credible news source in Boston" and the ancestral forerunner of today's programs whose credibility stems from their fusing together of news, commentary, and comedy, like Jon Stewart's *The Daily Show*, Bill Maher, and Stephen Colbert. And Schechter's impact on the news media is even more broadly profound and lasting, particularly his approach to media criticism, which includes examining the source of news reports; the interests of the owners of the news organization reporting the story; the sources and experts in the story; and even the very language used, an analysis that becomes an early forerunner of media criticism that is so common today.

Schechter's newscasts combine reports, commentary, music, and comedy in order to put the day's events into context, pioneering a style of newscasts that becomes even more credible to the audience than just straight reporting. The twice-daily live news broadcasts, seen here with Schechter (left) and Charles Laquidara (right) were compared to "performance art." *Source: Boston Phoenix Collection, Northeastern University Library.*

"Danny [Schechter] was a real scholar," recalls Noam Chomsky. Schechter is shown here with his CIA file. *Source: Clif Garboden Collection, Special Collections and University Archives, UMass Amherst Libraries.*

Chapter 11

Chomsky recalls:

> Danny was a real scholar. One of his main topics of inquiry and research was South Africa. He, in fact, came from a background of student radicals who were interested in supporting South African liberation, and that was not a small issue at the time. But in the sixties, to try to bring out some of what was happening under the apartheid regime was pretty unusual. That was a major part of his own research and inquiry that had spread far larger to investigating the nature of the power system and the structure of the imperial world order. It was serious institutional and political analysis, which was a real breath of fresh air in the conformist environment at the time.

Chomsky adds that when it came to news reporting at the time, Danny provided a stark exception to the rest of the media: "And that's why people who had a different picture of the world, including many young people, tuned in to hear Danny Schechter the News Dissector at six o'clock. Then you got a picture of what was actually happening from a very different point of view."

Danny's visionary and incisive approach to news and reporting is recalled by WBCN's Charles Laquidara in a *Boston Globe* article written by Bill Lichtenstein following Danny's death from cancer in 2015: "We all would see the hypocrisy in the Vietnam War and what was going on in Chile and South Africa and how we were being manipulated by the establishment. But Danny saw it before anybody . . . [WBCN] is where all the young people in Boston got their news. People tuned in to Danny as today people tune into Jon Stewart, [Stephen] Colbert, and Bill Maher — to find out what's really going on."

Sid Blumenthal, a former *Boston Phoenix* writer, author, and senior adviser to both President Bill Clinton and Secretary of State Hillary Clinton, recalls Schechter's unique style in preparing and delivering the news:

> The Boston of [the early 1970s] . . . was a crucible for redefining journalism. . . . Danny's six o'clock reports were essential listening. He had a thrilling way of combining fact and analysis, in a stream of information about the most important events that could be heard no place else.
>
> Danny brought me in to participate in some of the editing of his reports and documentaries and even put me in for a week to fill in on news broadcasts. Observing Danny at work was like being a hurricane chaser; but in the whirlwind of this hurricane, order miraculously emerged.
>
> Danny would race into the studio . . . clutching handfuls of crumpled papers with notebooks bulging out of his pockets. He had scrawled his reports in bits and pieces across dozens of pages. He alone could decipher what he had written. Rushing on the air, he interspersed his broadcasts with snatches of music that he seemed to have located out of the ether. He managed to synthesize it all in a kind of performance art. It was breathless, compelling, and frequently hilarious.

Another who recalls Danny's performance art–like news presentations is David Bieber: "I can still picture Danny . . . surrounded by papers with his scrawl all over the sheets of paper. It was all spontaneous and brilliant. It was the kind of thing that you thought, 'Wow, he must have been spending a month getting this news prepared.' And in fact, he did it multiple times a day. It was phenomenal. It was a whirlwind."

Danny's critical approach to news has an influence on other journalists and the ways they approach their work.

Journalist Jonathan Alter, who was a senior editor and media critic for *Newsweek* for two decades starting in 1983, says listening to Danny's newscasts as an undergraduate at Harvard in the 1970s led him to adopt Danny's "spirit of skepticism and the rejection of tired assumptions and conventional wisdom . . . [while Alter worked] inside the belly of the beast," as Alter refers to his decades working as *Newsweek*'s media critic.

Alter cites examples of "Danny Schechter–style media criticism" that appeared in his media column in *Newsweek*, including "Why the *New York Times* won't cover the AIDS epidemic and why they don't include the names of partners in obituaries when people die of AIDS? . . . And, why had the media gone soft on Ronald Reagan?"

Regarding Danny's activist and advocacy reporting style, Alter is emphatic that it didn't compromise his role as a journalist: "Danny put truth and the interest of the listeners above all else. That's what made him a great journalist."

There is perhaps no better example of Danny Schechter's role as a journalist while walking the line as activist than the morning when the FBI showed up at his home to arrest one of his roommates, who was responsible for a humanitarian act of civil disobedience.

"This was a story that came directly to me. It woke me up one morning, and I covered it, and then we played the whole tape on BCN. It was great radio," recalls Schechter. "I lived in a house with a number of other people who were activists. One of them, Bill Zimmerman, was a pilot, and he had delivered food to the Indians in Wounded Knee."

Bill Zimmerman was an activist who started Medical Aid for Indochina to help purchase medical supplies and equipment to rebuild hospitals damaged in North Vietnam, Laos, Cambodia, and parts of South Vietnam by the United States. In February 1973, acting as a protest against the conditions of reservation life in America, approximately two hundred members and followers of the American Indian Movement take over and hold the town of Wounded Knee, South Dakota, on the Pine Ridge Indian Reservation. The federal government responds by surrounding the protesters and refusing to allow anything through, including food and medical supplies.

"We realized one could drop food into the village via parachute and there would be very little the federal forces could do," says Zimmerman. "And so we made a drop of food and supplies on April 17, 1973."

"Eventually, the FBI found out about who was behind these planes and this whole action and came to my house, where Bill also had a room, to arrest him," recalls Danny Schechter.

"They came in. All of them had their guns drawn, and they were making a lot of noise, so the other people who lived in the house woke up," recalls Zimmerman. "Danny immediately produced a portable tape recorder and went up to one of the FBI agents and introduced himself as Danny Schechter, the News Dissector, and said, 'I am here covering the bust.'"

Danny Schechter: And who are you, sir?

FBI agent: My name is Bob Smith, I am with the FBI.

Danny Schechter: Bob Smith?

FBI agent: That's right. You got the tape recorder going?

Danny Schechter: Yes, sir, I certainly do.

FBI agent: All right, what's your name?

Chapter 11

Bill Zimmerman conducts an air drop of food and medical supplies to the Native American protesters who seized the Pine Ridge Reservation in Wounded Knee, South Dakota, resulting in a federal indictment of Zimmerman and an FBI raid to arrest him at his home in Somerville, Massachusetts, where Danny Schechter also lives (see next page). Schechter covers the early morning raid and reports it on the radio. *Sources: Bill Zimmerman; Bill Lichtenstein (house exterior).*

Warrant for Arrest of Defendant (Rev. 7-52) Cr. Form No. 12

United States District Court
FOR THE

District of South Dakota, Western Division

UNITED STATES OF AMERICA

v.

William B. Zimmerman

No. CR73-5087

To¹ any United States Marshal, Special Agent of the F.B.I. or any other authorized officer:

You are hereby commanded to arrest William B. Zimmerman and bring him forthwith before the United States District Court for the District of South Dakota in the city of Rapid City to answer to an Indictment charging him with

impeding Federal Officers during civil disorder as charged in Count I; conspiracy to commit offenses against the United States as charged in Count II; travel in interstate commerce with intent to incite a riot as charged in Count III

in violation of Title 18, Sections 231(a)(3), 371 & 2101 U.S.C.

Danny Schechter, "the News Dissector," with daughter Sarah, circa 1977. *Source: Clif Garboden Collection, Special Collections and University Archives, UMass Amherst Libraries.*

Danny Schechter: Dan Schechter, WBCN in Boston. I am covering this here.

FBI agent: Are you a resident of this dwelling?

Danny Schechter: No, I am covering this arrest. What's happening here?

FBI agent: We have a warrant for other people. Are you a resident of this dwelling?

Danny Schechter: Can you tell me who you have a warrant for?

FBI agent: I don't have to tell you anything.

Danny Schechter: You don't have to tell me anything?

FBI agent: Now, if you interrupt, you are interfering with justice. We have told you we have a warrant for this man and other men. Now, do not interfere with justice. I am telling you now.

"They weren't expecting that there would be somebody, a journalist, in the house actually covering it," recalls Schechter. "And so they threatened me with arrest myself saying that I was interrupting justice. And Zimmerman was arrested. He was indicted in Boston. But the charges were later dropped, which is often the case—that the FBI would violate its own rules and legal protocols."

"His sense of theatrics was amazing," says WBCN announcer and later program director Tommy Hadges. "In other words, the whole idea of challenging these guys, 'I am a reporter, and I am covering this story right now,' the fact that, 'This is my house, and I am just coming downstairs at six o'clock in the morning.' He is probably wearing his bathrobe or something. I am sure that they never get this sort of reaction, so that is so great, so typical of the guy."

The WBCN news department also benefits from Ray Riepen's third venture, following the Boston Tea Party and WBCN. In October 1969, Riepen purchases the year-old *Cambridge Phoenix* to publish it as "Boston's answer to the *Village Voice*," and he staffs the paper with a host of bright and talented young writers, many of whom would go on to have stellar careers in journalism, including David Ansen, Stephen Davis, Joe Klein, Jon Landau, Dave Marsh, Janet Maslin, Paul Solman, Craig Unger, and Ed Zuckerman and photographers including Peter Simon and Jeff Albertson.

"The boundaries between the *Phoenix* . . . and WBCN were fluid," writes Sid Blumenthal. As a result of this overlap, the work of the *Phoenix* staff often mixes with that of WBCN. Perhaps most visible to WBCN's radio audience and the *Phoenix*'s readers are regular, highly attended WBCN-*Phoenix* softball games in parks around the city starting in 1971.

Cambridge Phoenix writer C. Wendell Smith covers home plate as WBCN's Charles Laquidara rounds third base in the first WBCN/*Phoenix* softball game, June 1971. *Source: Jeff Albertson Photograph Collection, Special Collections and University Archives, UMass Amherst Libraries.*

Cambridge Phoenix writer Stephen Davis (right) with Ric Aliberte (left) at the first WBCN/*Phoenix* softball game, June 1971. *Source: Jeff Albertson Photograph Collection, Special Collections and University Archives, UMass Amherst Libraries.*

Cambridge Phoenix editor Harper Barnes at the first WBCN/*Phoenix* softball game, June 1971. *Source: Jeff Albertson Photograph Collection, Special Collections and University Archives, UMass Amherst Libraries.*

WBCN's Al Perry at the first WBCN/*Phoenix* softball game, June 1971. *Source: Jeff Albertson Photograph Collection, Special Collections and University Archives, UMass Amherst Libraries.*

WBCN's 1971 softball team, including (back row, left to right) Bill Lichtenstein, Tim Montgomery, Donna Montgomery, Bill Spurlin, John Brodey, Cindy Collamore; (third row, left to right) Steven Capen, Merril Shabot Leferman; (second row, left to right) Sam Kopper, Debbie Ullman, Valerie [last name unknown], Lee Buckley; (first row, left to right) Paul [last name unknown], Danny Schechter, Norm and Meredith Winer, Charles Laquidara, Steve "Mono" Crowley; (front row) Jack Kearney. *Source: Peter Simon Collection, Special Collections and University Archives, UMass Amherst Libraries.*

The News Dissector

12

The Second Wa

The Second Wave

12

By the mid-1960s, second-wave feminism begins to wash over virtually every institution and aspect of American society. By doing so, it transforms the traditional roles and identity of women — as it quickly spreads beyond the United States and throughout the Western world.

In contrast to first-wave feminism of the 1800s and early 1900s, which focused largely on the rights of women to vote and own property, second-wave feminism focuses on basic life issues that remain at the core of feminism today, including the role of women in the family, equality in the workplace (including equal pay and the "glass ceiling" that limits the rise of women occupationally), reproductive rights, and domestic violence, among others.

From WBCN's launch in 1968 through mid-1970, the station attracts and builds an enthusiastic and loyal following of listeners, both male and female, with its reputation for being on the cutting edge — if not the radical fringe — of culture, politics, and social change. But the station is also a product of its time and place, and as such, it reflects the kinds of lagging social attitudes and behaviors about gender equality that permeate the era with regard to the roles of men and women at the station and on the air. This is true even though WBCN is generally far more socially conscious, youth-oriented, and just plain hip than any other station on the radio.

By February 1970, the station has been on the air for two years. The owner is male as is the full-time airstaff, which is described by announcer Charles Laquidara in a 1970 radio documentary about WBCN made by WBAI-FM, New York, as a group of innovative "guys."

Despite WBCN's countercultural roots, the music and advertising it broadcasts often reflect the values and realities of the male-dominated world of the time, from Rolling Stones songs like "Under My Thumb" ("Under my thumb / She's the sweetest pet in the world / It's down to me / The way she talks when she's spoken to / Down to me, the change has come / She's under my thumb") and "Stupid Girl" ("I'm not talking about the kind of clothes she wears / Look at that stupid girl / I'm not talking about the way she combs her hair / Look at that stupid girl / The way she powders her nose / Her vanity shows and it shows / She's the worst thing in this world / Well, look at that stupid girl") to Jimi Hendrix's version of "Hey Joe" ("Hey Joe / I said where you goin' with that gun in your hand? / I'm goin' down to shoot my old lady / You know I've caught her messin' 'round with another man") and even the Beatles' "Run for Your Life" ("Well, I'd rather see you dead, little girl / Than to be with another man / You better keep your head, little girl / Or I won't know where I am") and "Getting Better" from the *Sgt. Pepper's* album ("I used to be cruel to my woman / I beat her and kept her apart from the things that she loved / Man, I was mean but I'm changing my scene / And I'm doing the best that I can").

Charles Laquidara's well-meaning public service announcement – recorded to help Project Place, a local community service program – becomes the target of a feminist protest for asking for help from "chicks who can type." *Source: Tommy Hadges Collection, Special Collections and University Archives, UMass Amherst Libraries.*

Below
Project Place, Boston, 1970. *Source: Jeff Albertson Photograph Collection, Special Collections and University Archives, UMass Amherst Libraries.*

Chapter 12

The vast majority of music heard on the air at WBCN is from male artists, with few exceptions that largely include female folk artists (Joan Baez, Melanie, Joni Mitchell, Laura Nyro), rhythm and blues singers (Aretha Franklin, Mavis Staples), and female lead singers with male bands (Janis Joplin with Big Brother and the Holding Company, Grace Slick with the Jefferson Airplane). But even among female artists, few songs address the social inequities or difficulties faced by women in ways that are empowering to women or relevant to the patriarchy of the time.

The station's advertising is also focused largely on male listeners who, more often than not, control the disposable income, so that even a clothing store that sells custom-crafted women's clothing pitches itself to guys, as in this radio ad for the Middle Earth Boutique in Rockport, Massachusetts, which concludes: "What a good feeling a man can give a woman by taking her to Middle Earth Boutique, to have something made for her body – and his eyes."

Much of this was taken in stride or accepted as part of the status quo by station listeners, including many women, until early in 1970, when Rochelle Ruthchild, a college history professor and loyal fan of the radio station, is listening in her car. "I loved BCN," she recalls. "I listened to it all the time. My car radio was just – that was where it was set, on BCN."

Ruthchild recalls listening and being stunned to hear a taped public service announcement on the air seeking "therapists" to volunteer at Project Place, a local drug rehabilitation program and crash pad for runaway kids: "I was in my Saab, and I turned on the radio. I hear Charles Laquidara – and I love Charles Laquidara. He makes this announcement saying that Project Place needs volunteers – and, 'If you're a chick and can type, call us.' And I thought: I cannot believe this."

The public service announcement Ruthchild hears was written and produced by Charles Laquidara, who recalls his thinking in that moment: "At BCN, we used to do public service announcements for Project Place, where people in need could go to sleep, eat, and receive medical care. They needed some volunteers. They needed doctors and interns. So I made a PSA saying, 'Hey, Project Place needs some help, so if you are a doctor – or if you're a chick who can type and would like to help out to volunteer your time – that would be cool.'"

One member of the WBCN staff saw the potential issue with the ad. "Even our own enlightened male announcers may not have been quite so enlightened because, again, they are coming from an old world and moving into this new one," says Tim Montgomery. "Calling women 'chicks': I think some people thought was a hip thing to do, but I think women were reading Betty Friedan, you know, at the time," he says, referring to the author and activist whose 1963 book *The Feminine Mystique* is credited with helping spark second-wave feminism.

Rochelle Ruthchild raises the matter at a meeting of Bread and Roses, the recently formed women's liberation group. It is one of several overlapping efforts in the Boston area by and for women to come together and through consciousness-raising discussions and direct action to address and find creative solutions to the sexism and misogyny faced by women.

"I had been going to Bread and Roses meetings," she recalls, "and I thought we have to do something about this. I love this radio station. They can't be doing this. I thought we were supposed to be equal and not to be described as little animals. It just infuriated me. So I went to Bread and Roses, and someone there said 'We need to get some chicks.'"

Another member of the group is able to obtain a box of live baby chicks – and what happens in the middle of the next day couldn't have been more of a surprise to all involved. Ruthchild and a

By the early 1970s, WBCN's lack of a full-time woman on the air stands in contrast to the growing national feminist movement and demands for equality including in the workplace. In this photo, members of the feminist collective Bread and Roses march in Boston to demonstrate for equal rights and to celebrate International Women's Day, March 8, 1970. *Source: Don Preston.*

Women march in Boston to celebrate International Women's Day, March 8, 1970. *Source: Liane Brandon.*

Chapter 12

group of more than thirty women from Bread and Roses visit WBCN's office at 312 Stuart Street in Boston — unannounced. Crowding into the tiny elevator, it requires several trips for the women to reach the station on the third floor.

"Our poor manager, Len Cohen, was sitting there in his office when the secretary came in and said, 'Mr. Cohen, somebody is here to see you,'" recalls Laquidara. "And then she looks behind her, and they come charging in. A group of thirty women with a cardboard box — and they opened it up and dump eight baby chicks on to his desk. And they say, 'These are chicks. We are women!'"

"We walked into the office, and they had no idea," recalls Rochelle Ruthchild. "They were like, 'What is going on here?' We walked in, and we scattered the chicks. And we said, 'These are chicks. We're not chicks.' It was a time of very creative protests of all kinds, and the notion at the time was that feminists didn't have a sense of humor, which is obviously not true."

In fact, the cleverness of their protest is reported in the *Boston Globe* ("Women liberationists dump chickens, saying WBCN ad was for the birds" read the headline), and Bread and Roses hammers out an agreement with WBCN shortly thereafter to address their two demands.

"One of the demands was that we wanted a woman DJ, and we wanted an hour of airtime to present our feminist perspective since they clearly didn't have one," says Ruthchild.

According to Charles Laquidara, he and the station got the message. "Within two weeks we had our first women's show on the station," he says. "And needless to say, that ad went right out the window."

"What happened was it showed we were open to criticism, and we took it and we did something about it, which I think was — you know, most times things like that, they just kind of think it will quiet down in two weeks, and it will be gone," reflects General Manager Al Perry.

In the wake of the protest, WBCN commits to hiring a full-time female announcer and offers Bread and Roses an hour of air time so its members can produce and broadcast what will be the first feminist women's program heard on a major commercial radio station. It airs on March 8, 1970, for International Women's Day.

"We planned it all out. We read news articles and poetry. We played some songs. We talked about violence against women, reproductive rights. We talked about the major issues of the day, and we put it all together in an hour, and it was aired on BCN," says Rochelle Ruthchild.

The groundbreaking program is composed of a free-wheeling and, for many, eye-opening discussion about fundamental issues regarding the social roles of men and women, including, according to the *Harvard Crimson*, "examples of prejudice against women — in advertising, music, and publications." Several women involved later describe the program as like sitting in on an early consciousness-raising session among women, discussing their frustrations and concerns regarding gender inequalities and talking about solutions.

The other demand made by Bread and Roses was for WBCN to agree to hire a full-time female announcer.

"There were no women on the air at BCN," says announcer Tommy Hadges. "So the decision to hire a woman was a very important step for the station to take." Ultimately, a total of three women are hired as announcers, including Maxanne Sartori, Debbie Ullman, and Dinah Vaprin.

"Both Maxanne and Debbie Ullman were hired in rapid succession," recalls program director Norm Winer. "Maxanne had established herself in Seattle. She was on a radio station in Seattle before she came to Boston. And one of the great things about Maxanne: her ears were impeccable.

WBCN's general manager Leonard Cohen becomes the target of the Bread and Roses protest when a box of live baby chicks is dumped on his desk to cries of "Those are chicks. We are women!," February 13, 1970. *Source: David Bieber Archives.*

A *Boston Globe* article detailing Bread and Rose's protest at WBCN, February 13, 1970. *Source: Boston Globe.*

Women liberationists dump chickens, saying WBCN ad was for the birds

By Parker Donham
Globe Staff

About 35 young women, protesting "male supremist policies" at the hip rock music station, WBCN-FM, swarmed into the station's Stuart street studios yesterday afternoon and threw eight live baby chicks on the station manager's desk.

The women objected to an advertisement the station ran for the Drug Dependency Treatment Center seeking volunteer doctors and therapists. The ad included the notation, "If you're a chick and can type, they need typists."

The women also complained that the station's selection of music, its hiring policies and the language its disc jockeys used was male supremist.

A statement released by the women asked, "Could a radio station get away with an ad that ran, 'And if you're black, we need janitors?'

"The male supremist assumption was that 'chicks,' by their very nature, type," the statement continued. "We do 15 words a minute at birth and work our way up."

The women, most of whom were of college age, represented Bread and Roses, a radical female liberation group which takes its name from a song about women strikers in Lawrence at the turn of the century.

They demanded that the station give them an hour of prime time on Mar. 8, which they said was International Women's Day, to discuss their views.

Station manager Leonard Cohen granted their request but production director San Kopper said later that the time period would be shortened unless the presentation included music.

The station appeared to be an unlikely target for a demonstration. Its announcers are young, long-haired, and casually dressed, and its programming appeals to youthful advocates of radical lifestyles.

The demonstration touched off some soul-searching among the station's staff members, most of whom agreed the advertisement was offensive.

SHE BACKS WOMEN PROTESTERS—
Debby Ullman, an account executive at WBCN, tells station manager Leonard Cohen her views on women's liberation protesters. (Ellis Herwig Photo)

Kopper described his encounter with the protesters:

"I came into the room and said hello to the first chick—and I called them chicks—and she laid into me with these chickens. She wanted to make the biologic difference clear."

She said, "These are chicks — I'm a woman." Kopper said the women's tactics made him "really disgruntled," but he added that the commercial was a "self-admitted slip."

Charles Laquidera, the announcer who wrote and recorded the advertisement, said it had been produced as a public service for the organization, which aids drug addicts.

"Women's liberation has got to come," Laquidera said. "It's an important issue, but it's not as important as the issue that ad was directing itself to." He said the commercial was recorded hurriedly because the Center had an acute need for help. It has subsequently been withdrawn.

One member of the WBCN staff, account executive Debbie Ullman, agreed with the demonstrators' general criticism of the station.

"WBCN isn't taking a leadership role in the women's liberation movement that it is in other aspects of the movement," Miss Ullman said.

She said male employees of the station had been upset because "it's the first revolutionary issue in which they've been confronted as the enemy. They've been able to approve when similar tactics have been used against others."

The Bread and Roses members had met earlier with Miss Ullman and two other female employees of the station, who perform secretarial duties, to explain that the demonstration was not an attack on them.

The fourth female employee of the station is Business Manager Sandra Newsam. Station officials said they have been seeking qualified women for on-the-air work.

SEN. COHEN
...changes mind

Cohen calls house cut partisan issue

One legislator who has changed his mind on the House cut issue is Sen. Beryl W. Cohen (D-Brookline), who will vote against the reduction when it comes to a vote Feb. 25.

"It's a partisan issue—Republican versus Democrat," said Cohen in explaining why he will vote against the reduction he

Ducks saved from Wellesley oil

WELLESLEY—The search for oil covered ducks will continue today along Cole Spring Brook where 30 wild and domestic ducks and geese were rescued from an oil slick yesterday.

A spillage of a few gallons of oil at the F. Diehl Co. oil yards entered a storm drain and was carried about a quarter of a mile into the pond behind the town hall. From there it spilled into the brook on Washington st.

Domestic ducks and geese in the pond became caught in the oil and were taken to Angell Memorial Hospital where they were washed. Wild ducks in the stream also were caught in the oil.

Department of Public Works Supt. Everett R. Kennedy said he had been notified shortly after the oil was spilled and chemicals were introduced immediately into the water to disolve the oil. He said the slick was now well below the danger level.

Authorities at Angell Memorial believe at least another 100 wild ducks may be affected and they have a rescue team working today.

The birds are taken first to the Boston hospital and washed. They are then sent to Nevins Farm in Methuen where they are cared for until they molt and grow new feathers. About eight months are required before the birds can be sent to a wildlife preserve and finally released.

Maxanne heard bands that none of us heard, and I'm talking about Aerosmith. Some of us minimized their importance, thinking that they were too derivative of the Rolling Stones. That was an obvious comparison in the beginning. You know, Maxanne heard the quality of what they did — the musicianship, song writing, and so on — and very quickly she was proven right."

Although today it's a legendary part of the story of Aerosmith's rise to success, at the time, Maxanne's championing of the band did not get the support of all.

"She kept playing the same song over and over by this Boston group, that local group. They had that song she kept playing over and over — that same, 'Dream on, dream on, dream on!'" recalls Charles Laquidara. "I'd say:

'Max, find another song.'

'But this group is going to be huge, Charles!'

'Yeah, but you don't have to keep playing it.'

And of course, she broke Aerosmith, broke them in the world."

Another band that owes its success to Maxanne Sartori and WBCN is the Cars. At the band's 2018 induction into the Rock & Roll Hall of Fame, lead guitarist Elliot Easton paid tribute to Maxanne and WBCN with this story, which illustrates the impact the station could have on a local group:

> **In our very early days, we had an angel. Her name is Maxanne Sartori. A top DJ at WBCN in Boston, the city's biggest FM rock station, Maxanne did an amazing thing: she started playing our demo tape in heavy rotation alongside all the biggest records of the day. The spins got reported in the radio tip sheets. So it would say, "the Cars, 'Just What I Needed,'" and then in the column where the record label would normally be listed, it said, "TAPE!!!" A&R reps for major labels started flying to Boston to check out this local band, the Cars, whose demo tape got so much airplay that it was being reported on a national level. Maxanne did that. We are forever indebted.**

Another band that is identified and launched by Maxanne is Queen.

"Queen broke out of Boston," recalls Norm Winer. "Maxanne was one of the first people to hear the record, the first album — an unlabeled slab of vinyl, that's what they played it for us on. And it knocked her socks off — or whatever it was she was wearing on her feet — maybe her flip flops. And she was invariably right."

"Maxanne rocked harder than any of the rest of us. It's not like girls are wimpy musicians. Maxanne was out there pounding it out, and she became one of the stars because of it," recalls announcer Jim Parry.

The impact of having three female announcers on the air was significant, according to Marsha Steinberg, who was working in the WBCN news department: "It was a rock-and-roll station. That was the part that made it so radical — that they accepted [Bread and Roses'] demand, and then all of a sudden, you know, you had these women disc jockeys. Not just in the news department, but on the air, picking the music and interacting with the musicians in the way that disc jockeys do. It was transformative."

However, it's fair to say not everyone is sympathetic to the presence or the cause of the women on WBCN, who had to face ongoing ridicule and discrimination not only from the public but even from other broadcasting professionals.

WBCN agrees to Bread and Rose's demand that the station hire a full-time female announcer. WBCN hires Maxanne Sartori from Seattle, Washington, and Dinah Vaprin, and promotes Debbie Ullman, who has been selling ads and filling in on-air, seen here on the radio with Abbie Hoffman. *Sources: United Electrical, Radio, and Machine Workers of America (UE) Records; Tommy Hadges Collection, Special Collections and University Archives, UMass Amherst Libraries; Jeff Albertson Photograph Collection, Special Collections and University Archives, UMass Amherst Libraries.*

The Second Wave

Maxanne's playing of Aerosmith's first album, according to fellow announcer Charles Laquidara, "broke them in the world." *Source: Fin Costello, Getty Images.*

Maxanne's "ears were impeccable. Maxanne heard bands that none of us heard," says WBCN program director Norm Winer. Maxanne (left) in the WBCN record library with announcer Charles Laquidara. *Source: Boston Phoenix Collection, Northeastern University Library.*

Below
Maxanne's playing of a tape of the Cars on the air led to the band's record deal and success. *The Cars seen here at WBCN studios. Source: Eli Sherer.*

Maxanne poses with Queen and Paula the Penguin (on loan from the New England Aquarium). (Left to right) John Deacon; Kurt Nerlinger, Elektra Records; Brian May; Ric Aliberte, Electra Records; Maxanne Sartori; Freddie Mercury; and Roger Taylor, 1974.
Source: Ron Pownall.

Ron Wood and Maxanne at WBCN studios, circa 1974.
Source: Maxanne Sartori.

Maxanne in the WBCN production studio at 312 Stuart Street, circa 1972. *Source: Peter Simon Collection, Special Collections and University Archives, UMass Amherst Libraries.*

Maxanne at an outdoor concert, circa 1973. *Source: Steve Nelson.*

Jerry Williams is credited with being one of the originators of the radio talk show format, working on major stations up and down the East Coast. In 1970, he is on WBZ-AM, a Boston powerhouse station with a 50,000-watt clear channel signal that reaches all of New England during the day and listeners as far as South Carolina at night.

"I remember one night I am listening to BCN. I'm at home, and someone called me up and said, 'You ought to turn on Jerry Williams,'" recalls Tim Montgomery. "So I tuned in, and I hear he's talking about WBCN, and I am listening to these outrageous things he is saying about the station."

Williams began his on-air attack on WBCN by making fun of the announcing staff: "The free of form I like, but that business of freaks announcing – like everybody is sitting around smoking pot."

"Then he goes on and on about women," says Montgomery. "And how women want to sound like men, and they really don't belong on the radio, and so on and so forth. I mean, this is an extraordinary statement by this guy."

"Radio is just a voice," says Williams to his WBZ listeners. "Sometimes women's voices – because of the high frequency of those voices, sometimes they turn some people off." Williams begins to describe for listeners what he particularly dislikes about hearing women on the radio, including women seeking to be taken as seriously as male broadcast journalists: "You know what turns me off about women on the air? They are trying to be men. If they would try to be women – be themselves, be female. But some of the women I know on the air are trying to be male-ish. Some women fall into that trap of saying, 'Hi, there, Sally Krautfloid, from Los Angeles, California, bringing you the news.' You know, they're on that male kick. Be yourself. Be like you are."

Williams is then seconded by a female caller, who tells him: "I think that a lot of other women listening would feel the same way. As one man said, 'The radio is a woman's companion during the day,' and I think I would certainly, as a woman, rather listen to a man than listen to a woman rattle on and on. I could call up any of my friends and talk."

Williams then closes the segment by ridiculing the WBCN announcers: "There is a place in broadcasting for women but not the ones I heard on BCN. They are really straight on. They are all like – I can't even tell the guys from the girls over there. For that matter, when they are walking down the street, I can't tell them apart either."

While Jerry Williams reflects a broadly held view at the time that the place for women was in the home and not on the airwaves, things were about to change quickly.

"You know, you look back and you think – it's like looking back at what women used to wear in the 1920s – you go, like, 'My god, this can't be real. Did someone really say that? Did someone really believe that?'" reflects WBCN announcer Dinah Vaprin. "But all you can kind of do is look back on it and think, as a result of that, there was an impetus to change even more quickly. WBCN took that situation and helped change itself but also helped contribute to what was going on at that particular time."

Meanwhile, the female activists involved with Bread and Roses, emboldened by the success of their WBCN protest, plan several other high-profile radical actions, including the 1971 takeover of an unoccupied building owned by Harvard University at 888 Memorial Drive in Cambridge, which they demand be turned into a women's center. They are able to remain in the building for ten days before being removed by the university, but during their occupation, WBCN broadcasts their demands and requests for food and blankets – and listeners respond. In the end, the action is transformative for the women involved, who raise the funds for a down payment on a house at 46 Pleasant Street in Cambridge, which continues to operate a half century later as the Cambridge Women's Center, serving a wide variety of women's needs, from a safe space to a studio for creative arts.

Jerry Williams is a Boston radio host and one of the originators of talk radio, and he doesn't believe women belong on WBCN or radio generally. *Source: Associated Press.*

Bread and Roses activists speak at a rally at Soldiers Field by Harvard Stadium, May 8, 1970. *Source: Jeff Albertson Photograph Collection, Special Collections and University Archives, UMass Amherst Libraries.*

Women from organizations including Bread and Roses, the *Old Mole* Women's Caucus, and Gay Women's Liberation occupy an unused Harvard building at 888 Memorial Drive in Cambridge beginning March 6, 1971, to demand low-income housing and the creation of a permanent women's center. WBCN supports the ten-day takeover with requests on the air for food and other necessities.
Source: Jeff Albertson Photograph Collection, Special Collections and University Archives, UMass Amherst Libraries.

The Second Wave

The Lavender Hour:
Gender Freedom in the Air

13

The Lavender Hour: Gender Freedom in the Air

13

In 1972, journalist Andy Kopkind, who had covered politics for major national magazines, and his partner, John Scagliotti, join WBCN's growing news department. The following year, John and Andy begin producing *The Lavender Hour* — the first regularly scheduled broadcast of music, news, and public affairs of interest to the gay and lesbian community — which airs on WBCN.

"WBCN was one of the first places where diversity took off in a much greater way," says Scagliotti. "I think the idea that we found ourselves in the middle of an experiment where [everyone, including] gay people, black people, women were all working together. Andy and I were gay, so that changed the dynamics of WBCN. There were two gay guys there."

Andy Kopkind began his journalism career at the *Washington Post*, and then following graduate studies at London School of Economics, he was hired by *Time* magazine.

As John Scagliotti recalls:

You know, he was on his way. He was going to be the next editor of *Time* magazine. Then he got arrested for being gay, in Griffith Park in Los Angeles, and that ended it. And then he went to work for the *New Republic*, and he embraced the civil rights movement and all these other things that he grew up with and felt but now was able to work on them in a much more real way. But he was very talented and was a good writer.

John and Andy cover a variety of gay-related stories in their news and public affairs reporting for WBCN, including the 1973 Gay Pride Parade in New York City, featuring a performance by Bette Midler. Meanwhile, WBCN's program director, Norm Winer, is seeking to plug holes in the station's Sunday night schedule.

Scagliotti remembers:

Sunday nights were never a big time for the station, so Norm came up with this cockamamie idea, of "Potluck," which would be that anybody in our staff could sign up for "Potluck" and be on the radio. So it was our chance — Andy and my chance — to actually be DJs. Because we were doing the news and all of this, but we just wanted to play records. We loved playing music. We had the greatest gay parties in town on Newbury Street. We figured we could just be DJs, so we decided to do the first *Lavender Hour*. . . . We called it that because of lavender being half-pink, half-blue. You mix those two colors together, you come up with lavender.

Andy Kopkind (left) and John Scagliotti (right) join the WBCN news department in 1972. "WBCN was one of the first places where diversity took off in a much greater way," says Scagliotti. *Source: John Scagliotti.*

Danny Schechter (left) and John Scagliotti (right) at the WBCN studios. *Source: United Electrical, Radio, and Machine Workers of America (UE) Records.*

"*The Lavender Hour* was a very important addition to what was going on," recalls announcer Tommy Hadges. "No one was doing anything like that on the radio in those days. That was really pioneering stuff."

"It was the first time that people could actually come out," says WBCN announcer Andy Beaubien.

One person for whom the material being broadcast on *The Lavender Hour* had personal importance is former U.S. Representative Barney Frank, who in 1987 became the first member of the U.S. Congress to voluntarily come out as gay.

"I was the mayoral assistant in 1971," says Frank, referring to his work as chief assistant to Boston's newly elected mayor, Kevin White, following Frank's graduation from Harvard. Frank then successfully ran for the Massachusetts House of Representatives, where he sponsored the state's first gay rights bill.

Frank cites the importance of *The Lavender Hour* in giving voice to and connecting gay and lesbian people who, for too long, lived in the shadows due to prejudice against their sexual orientation and preference: "It was very important that people got to know each other. Most important to gay people back then was to get to know other gay people. We knew there were others, in theory, but we didn't know who they were or what they were like or what their diversity was . . . so that was important for people learning about each other and communicating."

"On the show," recalls Scagliotti, "we would play music and then mix in poetry, and we were discovering that gay people were doing such great stuff. It gave a voice to openly gay people on the radio. It was really powerful."

The Lavender Hour helps connect Boston's gay and lesbian community and spreads the word about news and events. *Source: Nick DeWolf Photo Archive.*

The Charles Street Meetinghouse hosts the area's first non-bar gay dances in the early 1970s that welcome everyone, not just those of drinking age or older. *Source: Nick DeWolf Photo Archive.*

The Lavender Hour

Scagliotti explains that the focus and presentation of the program reflected the approach of WBCN, with its focus on politics and social change as well as the culture, especially music. "We covered gay culture and life and what people were thinking and feeling and funny little jokes and montages I would create."

As an example of the kind of groundbreaking discussions heard on *The Lavender Hour*, Scagliotti recalls the time he went to interview David Bowie and ended up having "a fight with David Bowie at a press conference about why he was just going to be a bisexual – why wasn't he coming out all the way – and he would yell at me, and then we would play 'Changes.'"

David Bowie and his band, the Spiders from Mars, arrive in New York at the end of his first Ziggy Stardust tour of the United States and hold a press conference in Studio C of the RCA Studios in Manhattan on December 11, 1972. John Scagliotti is there and asks him about the issue of gender in his songs:

David Bowie and the Spiders from Mars during a press conference at the RCA Studios in New York City, December 11, 1972. *Source: Bob Gruen.*

David Bowie press conference, December 11, 1972. *Source: Bob Gruen.*

John Scagliotti: What made you start writing gay songs?

David Bowie: What made me start writing gay songs?

John Scagliotti: Well, let me put it this way. It is not something that would be normally be acceptable on the Top 40 market or any rock market before you started writing.

David Bowie: You see, it is acceptable to people that I've wrote and play for. It always has been.... Who doesn't like gay people?... There's no antagonism at all...

Reporter: You seriously believe that gay people are not suffering from oppression in this world? Are you crazy?

David Bowie: No, I —

Reporter: It doesn't happen anywhere? Gay people never have any trouble with their being gay?

David Bowie: I didn't say — I said I find no hostility...

John Scagliotti: Okay. Well, I am not trying to be hostile. You have done some openly gay stuff, which I was very glad to hear coming from a singer. I mean, you must have had some process of forethought before you actually started writing material.

David Bowie: I was inspired. (Laughter).

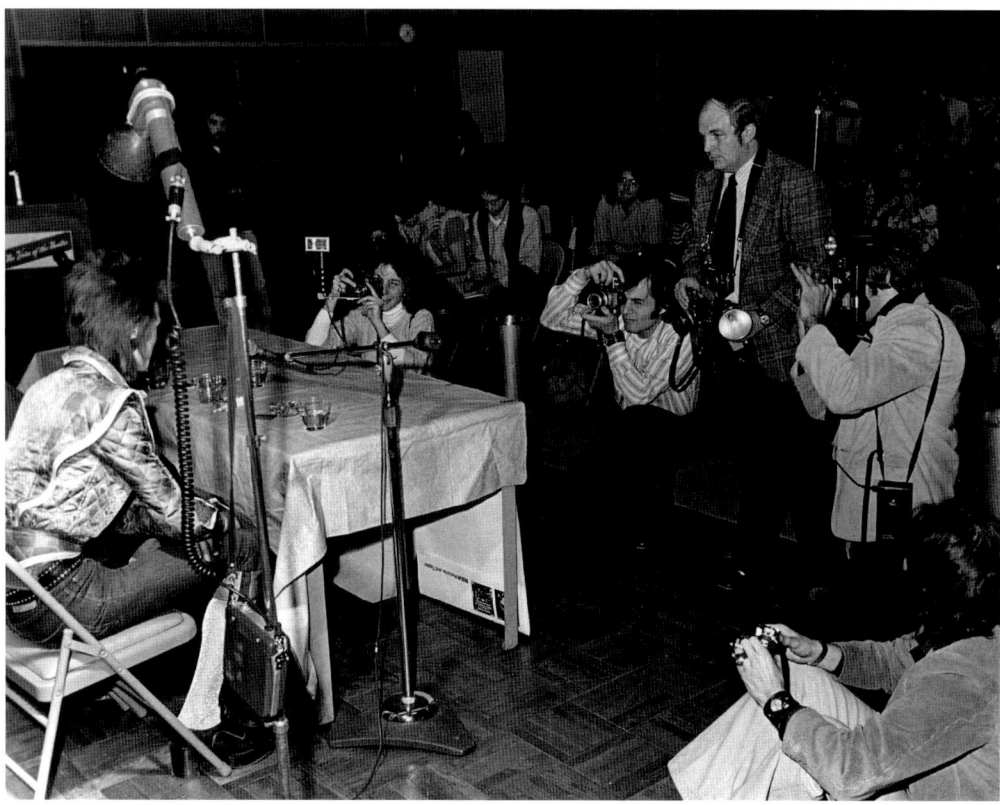

David Bowie press conference, December 11, 1972.
Source: Michael Fremer.

| Chapter 13

While *The Lavender Hour* begins as an opportunity for John Scagliotti and Andy Kopkind to share with radio listeners cultural and political matters of interest to them, its impact is significant and far-reaching. As Scagliotti recalls:

> I thought it was just me: this is my life. I was in a little bubble, you know – this gay bubble, where it wasn't a big deal. And the people I worked with didn't find it a big deal. But guess what? The radio station is fifty thousand or a million watts. I don't know – huge watts. And so there were people who were listening to us in New Hampshire and way out in Western Massachusetts. All of a sudden, there's this gay thing on the radio! The first time on commercial radio that a gay program had ever been on. We didn't know that, but now we do. But we didn't know that then.

This voice of – and for – gay and lesbian people was a significant event for those who had not come out publicly with regard to their same-gender preferences.

"There was a need to let each other and the rest of the world know that there was a significant number of gay people," adds Barney Frank. "That was the difference with the gay movement. Black people didn't need to announce they were black. No black teenager ever had to worry about coming out as black. So letting others and the rest of the world know our numbers was absolutely important."

As Scagliotti recalls:

> I was having a great time being a DJ and doing *The Lavender Hour*. Meanwhile, we started getting letters from kids who were sixteen that would say, "I was thinking of committing suicide, and your show saved me." It was a lifeline for them. They would write, *"I snuck up to my room because your show was on and put the earphones on, and I even kept it low even with the earphones because I didn't want my folks to hear it, but it just saved me."* And all of a sudden I realized, "My God. I'm having a great time being a DJ, doing *The Lavender Hour*, but people were actually seeing this as a life-saving experience." The idea that somehow this little moment of ours was turning into such a massive moment for their lives was pretty incredible. It changed my life completely.... You know, I dedicated my life to those sixteen-year-olds from then on.

WBCN's groundbreaking support for gay and lesbian issues goes beyond the broadcast of *The Lavender Hour*. A union contract between WBCN's staff and management becomes the first labor agreement to protect workers against discrimination based on their sexual preference, and it becomes a model for future union contracts nationwide.

According to Scagliotti:

> We thought it was important as workers to have a union. And in one of our first union negotiation meetings – Andy and I were there – they asked, "What would you like in your union contract?" And we said, "Oh, we'd like nondiscrimination for sexual preference." Well, everybody kind of looked as us, you know, like "What's that?" And Andy said, "So they can't fire us because we're gay." "Oh!" they said. "Yeah, we'll put that in." And it went up to management, and it was accepted. It turned out to be the first time anywhere in the country a union contract protected workers against discrimination for sexual preference. Pretty amazing.

Gay Liberation rally on the Cambridge Common, 1970. *Source: Jeff Albertson Photograph Collection, Special Collections and University Archives, UMass Amherst Libraries.*

Gay activists on Boston Common at an antiwar rally, 1970. *Source: Nick DeWolf Photo Archive.*

AGREEMENT
between
WBCN, INC.
and
UNITED ELECTRICAL, RADIO AND
MACHINE WORKERS OF AMERICA

ARTICLE I.   Recognition   page 1

ARTICLE II.   No Discrimination   page 2

ARTICLE III.   Union Membership   page 3

ARTICLE IV.   Safety and Health   page 4

ARTICLE II.   No Discrimination

2.01 There shall be no discrimination in interviewing or hiring applicants for employment and no discrimination against employees during and after their trial period of employment because of Union membership or activities, color, race, national origin, sex, sexual preference, marital status, age, or religious or political beliefs.

WBCN's contract with the United Electrical, Radio, and Machine Workers of America (UE) provides that staff members are protected against discrimination in the workplace for their sexual preference (detail).
Source: United Electrical, Radio, and Machine Workers of America (UE) Records.

14

Lock-Up

14

The widely held view of the WBCN staff, which reflects the views of a large number of the station's listeners, is that many people who are incarcerated in state correctional and federal prison facilities are, in fact, political prisoners.

This results from seeing many people who are being locked up due to political activities related to the civil rights or the antidraft and antiwar movements, oppressive drug laws where even small amounts of marijuana can result in jail time, and an unfair economic and racially skewed justice system.

Even inmates whose crimes are less political in nature are seen as fellow citizens who, in many cases, will be living back in the community again.

"Because of the nature of law enforcement in 1970s, with so many of our peers somehow becoming criminals – despite the fact that their so-called crimes didn't really match up with what we had been brought up to believe are genuine crimes – we became much more aware of the penal system and the criminal justice system in Massachusetts," observes Norm Winer. "And there were an awful lot of people who became aware of WBCN while they were behind bars."

In order to reach and support those confined to prisons and jails, WBCN and a group of local prisoner rights activists create and produce *Lock-Up*, an unprecedented weekly program of musical requests, dedications, and news relevant to those living behind bars. The show is hosted by Marsha Steinberg of the WBCN news department, whose on-air name is "Jamaica Plain Jane" (after the then working-class Boston neighborhood of Jamaica Plain where she worked as a community organizer). Marsha Steinberg is a former member of the Weathermen, who served jail time herself for her role in the "Days of Rage," a series of radical street protests that took place in Chicago in 1969 at the time of the Chicago 8 conspiracy trial as an effort to "bring the war home."

As Marsha Steinberg explains:

Lock-Up grew out of the fact that there was a rebellion in a prison in Attica, New York [in September 1971]. It was transformative in the whole prison culture throughout the U.S. The inmates at Attica took control of the prison for four days and made their demands, and authorities agreed to some of their demands. Unfortunately, it was a very deadly uprising, with many inmates and correctional officers killed in the end.

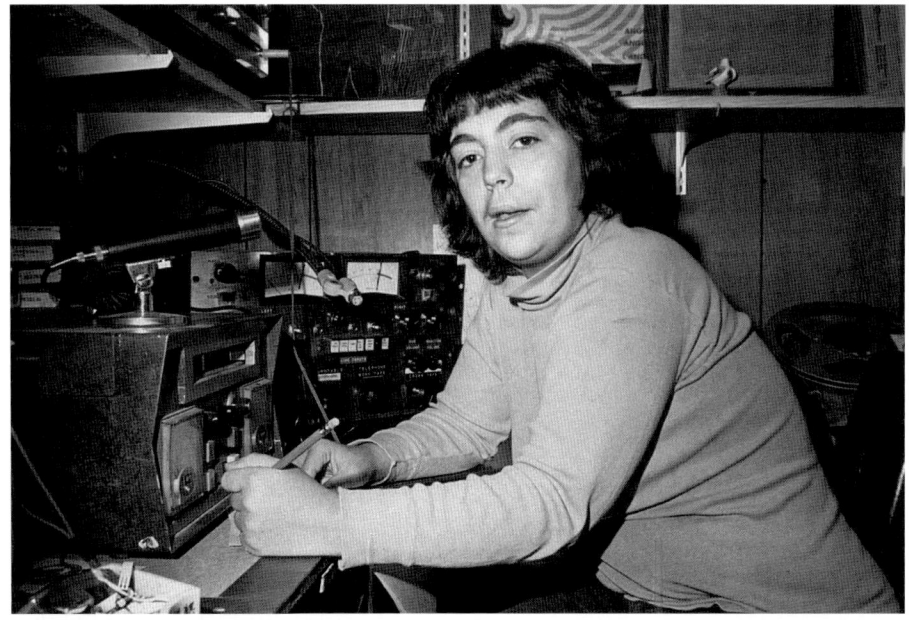

Marsha Steinberg of the WBCN news department hosts *Lock-Up*, the weekly program of prison news and requests, as "Jamaica Plain Jane." *Source: United Electrical, Radio, and Machine Workers of America (UE) Records.*

Following the uprising, there were radicals who came forward in local prisons in Massachusetts — in particular, in the highest-security prison in Walpole, Massachusetts. There was a group of prisoners there who were radicalized, and they supported those actions, and it created an atmosphere where people made demands such as to not be treated like animals and be subjected to brutality. They also insisted on some educational programs. BCN created *Lock-Up* to give voice to those prisoners and to act as a facilitator with their families.

As Norm Winer recalls:

All of the music on *Lock-Up* came from requests from the inmates. The show's hosts spoke over the radio to their friends, family, and loved ones by speaking to the public. It was a show that was on for several years and really made an impact. It's safe to say that this community [including inmates and their families] hadn't been represented prior to that on the airwaves.... It was nice to reach the people behind the walls of those institutions to let them know we are out there. Let them know we are thinking of them. Let them know we are waiting for them to come out.

The show represented an ongoing collaboration between the friends and families of inmates at Walpole and other correctional institutions who worked with Steinberg on the show. As she recalls:

It was a combination of news and music requests from inmates that had sexual innuendo, political innuendo, drug innuendo in them, as well as love songs and "power to the people" kind of music. Among the most requested songs on the weekly show were "Heroin" by the Velvet Underground, "The Pusher" by Steppenwolf, and "We Gotta Get Out of This Place" by the Animals.

Everybody was listening to it. It had a transformative effect of creating a political context for which to understand these guys in Walpole. BCN was a facilitator of integration of prisoners in the movement in the post-Attica period, and a lot of people liked it. It went on for a couple of years. I feel very proud of it. I was able to give a voice and let people speak for themselves. It was a very respected program.

In order to ensure the program can be heard by prisoners, WBCN raises funds on-air to buy radios for inmates.

"We tried to raise money to get radios for prisoners," recalls General Manager Al Perry. "A lot of inmates would write into the station and say something like, 'I've got to listen to Eddie's radio — and he's three cells down.'"

"We raised some money, and we drove to prisons around the Commonwealth and dropped off little table-top radios so that inmates would be exposed to what was going on on the outside," recalls Norm Winer. "The only thing we asked was that when an inmate was released, that they leave the radio behind in the cell for the next person."

To raise funds to pay for radios for prisoners, Al Perry says he was appointed the ambassador to approach Frank Zappa, whose film *200 Motels* was coming out, and to ask Zappa if the station could do a premiere of the film and use the money raised to buy radios for inmates.

"I did ask him. And Frank said, 'Yes!' It was a lot of fun," recalls Perry.

"Everyone at WBCN was passionate about *Lock-Up*," Perry adds. "We took a little heat from it, you know: 'Why are you playing songs for guys who are locked up?' But it's like, 'Wait a minute. How are we supposed to hope that when they come out, they can fit back into society?'"

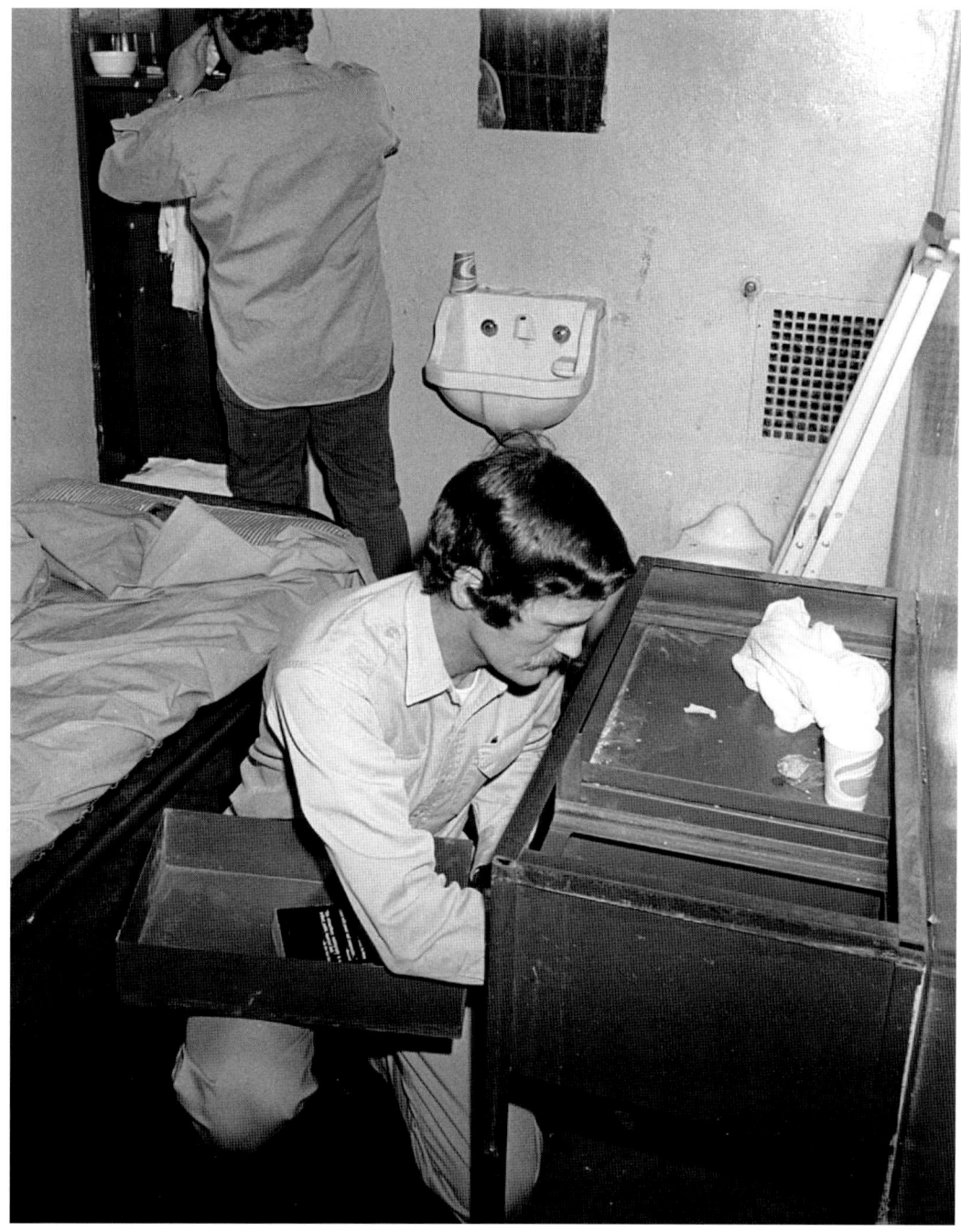

Lock-Up's weekly broadcast reaches prisoners including at the Middlesex Jail & House of Correction in Billerica, Massachusetts. In order to facilitate listenership, WBCN raises funds to buy radios for prisoners. *Source: Jeff Albertson Photograph Collection, Special Collections and University Archives, UMass Amherst Libraries.*

15

We've Got to Get Rid of Nixon

We've Got to Get Rid of Nixon

15

Increasingly, for both young people and even older Americans growing weary of Nixon's war in Vietnam and repressive activities at home, it can be said that no matter what you're doing — studying for an exam, shopping for dinner, or making love — somewhere in the back of your mind, you're always thinking, "We've got to get rid of Nixon."

An article in June 1972 by Ralph Gleason, the pioneering rock critic at the San Francisco Chronicle, who was also a founding editor of Rolling Stone magazine, underscores this point. In "We Gotta Get Rid of Nixon," Gleason depicts Vietnam as Nixon's "imperial war" that has gone over the edge, fueled by a propaganda machine that Gleason compares to George Orwell's 1984. His conclusion: the United States has to get Nixon out of office "before he kill[s] us all."

WBCN listener Steven Wayne recalls Nixon's April 30, 1970, televised announcement of the U.S. invasion of Cambodia:

> WBCN was on, and they said, "Turn on the television. The president's going to talk." So we turned on the TV. And there's Nixon pointing to a map, telling us that the United States was going to do incursions into Cambodia and Laos, and they are bombing Cambodia. . . . From May 1st to May 4th, there were giant protests across the country because we had had it. It's like, "They're invading another Asian country!"

President Richard Nixon goes on national TV on April 30, 1970, to announce his invasion of Cambodia. *Source: National Archives.*

Two years have gone by since Nixon's election as president after running on a claim that he had a secret plan to end the Vietnam War. And yet the undeclared — and in the eyes of many, the illegal — conflict in Southeast Asia not only continues, but now, with the announcement of the U.S. invasion of Cambodia, a neutral country that shares more than seven hundred miles of border with Vietnam, the war is spreading into other countries. To make matters worse, it is later learned that Nixon's orders — sending the U.S. military into Cambodia, purportedly to root out North Vietnamese forces that are allegedly using the neighboring country to mount attacks on American troops in South Vietnam — were issued on April 28, 1970, without Nixon telling either Secretary of State William Rogers or Secretary of Defense Melvin Laird, who both learned of the invasion only when it was publicly announced on April 30, 1970.

During the first week of May 1970, students on college campuses across the country, along with a growing number of high school and junior high school students, respond by walking out of classes and turning their focus to the war — both to learn more about it and how they can oppose or stop it. Classes are suspended, teach-ins are held on campuses that facilitate discussions with students and faculty, and protests are organized against the war as well as against the complicity of universities and other institutions with the conflict.

Nixon's invasion of Cambodia meets opposition on college and high school campuses throughout the country, where many students trade classes for teach-ins on the war and others organize mass protests. *Source: Nick DeWolf Photo Archive.*

Jennifer Thomas, age sixteen, becomes an enduring image of protest during this period when Peter Simon takes this photo of her that ends up in *Rolling Stone* magazine. Thomas's father was killed in Vietnam, but when she wears the flag that draped his coffin as a protest, she is arrested and says she was beaten by Boston police officers. *Source: Peter Simon Collection, Special Collections and University Archives, UMass Amherst Libraries.*

Kent State University student protester Alan Canfora, standing 225 feet away from members of the Ohio National Guard, ten minutes before the May 4, 1970, Kent State massacre. During the shooting, Canfora is wounded in his right wrist. *Source: Howard Ruffner.*

As at other schools across the country, student demonstrations erupt on the campus of Kent State University, in Kent, Ohio, on May 1, 1970. The Kent State protests escalate over the following three days and include the burning of the campus Reserve Officers' Training Corps (ROTC) building. In response, on Saturday, May 3, at 10 p.m., nearly a thousand Ohio National Guard troops arrive on the scene, sent by Governor James Rhodes to maintain order.

By Monday, May 4, classes resume at Kent State with a rally scheduled for noon on the school's Commons. University officials try to quell the situation by banning the gathering – but few students pay attention.

As approximately five hundred student protesters gather along with a few thousand onlookers, National Guard troops first fire tear gas at the demonstrators. When that fails to disperse them, according to the official Kent State University account, "28 of the more than 70 Guardsmen turned suddenly and fired their rifles and pistols. Many guardsmen fired into the air or the ground. However, a small portion fired directly into the crowd. Altogether between 61 and 67 shots were fired in a 13-second period."

Members of the Ohio National Guard shortly before they begin to fire on antiwar demonstrators and students at Kent State University, Kent, Ohio, May 4, 1970. *Source: Howard Ruffner.*

When the firing ends, four students, including two onlookers who are not participants in the demonstration, are fatally shot. Three of them—Allison Beth Krause, age nineteen, an honor student; Jeffrey Glenn Miller, age twenty, a psychology student from Plainview, New York; and Sandra Lee Scheuer, age twenty, an honors student in speech therapy walking across campus with one of her student trainees—die at the scene. William Knox Schroeder, age nineteen, an honor student who is enrolled as an army cadet in the school's ROTC program, is pronounced dead at a nearby hospital shortly thereafter. As one observer later states, "They were just gunned down in cold blood."

Norm Winer, who was working as news director at WBCN that day, recalls getting news of the shootings:

> When students were shot by the National Guard in Ohio, and they were students on a campus, and they didn't have weapons, it was such a shock. It was such a crime. I don't think anyone anticipated that sort of response from the authorities, and the consequences were irreparable.
>
> No one could have seen this coming. Kent State was the event that really took things to another level.
>
> I don't remember how, but I found somebody on the [Kent State] campus who was willing to talk.... I found an eyewitness to the events—a student who came on the phone with me and spoke to me for at least twenty minutes.
>
> Whether because there was no need for it or because I didn't have time [to edit it], I simply aired that interview verbatim in its entirety as soon as we concluded the conversation. I think I told the DJ, "Okay, we are going on in ten minutes."
>
> The fact that we were able to get it and provide it to [our listeners] so quickly was remarkable, so they could basically judge the events of that day for themselves and for years as the story continued to be retold.

Mary Ann Vecchio kneels over the body of Jeffrey Miller, who is killed by gunfire from the National Guard at Kent State University, May 4, 1970. *Source: Howard Ruffner.*

We've Got to Get Rid of Nixon

The following week, local police in Jackson, Mississippi, open fire, hitting fourteen students during an antiwar protest at Jackson State College, a historically Black university, killing two students, Phillip Lafayette Gibbs, a twenty-one-year-old college junior and father of an eighteen-month-old, and James Earl Green, a seventeen-year-old high school senior and star of the track team.

In the wake of the Kent State and then the Jackson State shootings, there is an uproar on college campuses everywhere, especially in the colleges and universities throughout the Boston area.

"WBCN was an integral part of every protest and demonstration we were in," recalls Steven Wayne. "That's how we were learning what was going on. Not only did WBCN news tell us about the event. They told us when they heard rumors that the tactical police were going to be deployed. They gave us information that we could use, and they were with us fighting the good fight. It was amazing."

Following Nixon's invasion of Cambodia and the shootings at Kent State University, students protest on college and high school campuses across the country, including at twenty universities that remain closed for the school year, **May 5, 1970.** *Source: Peter Simon Collection, Special Collections and University Archives, UMass Amherst Libraries.*

A crowd gathers on Boston Common in front of the Massachusetts State House to protest the invasion of Cambodia and the Kent State University shootings, **May 5, 1970.** *Source: Spencer Grant Collection, Boston Public Library.*

The Grateful Dead arrive in Boston for a scheduled concert at MIT on May 7, 1970. *Source: LCMedia Productions.*

With students not attending classes in the wake of the Kent State shootings, the Grateful Dead, in town for a concert the following evening, offer an impromptu performance at MIT's student center, which serves to calm tensions. *Source: Courtesy of the MIT Museum.*

The Grateful Dead, who had remained apolitical over the years, shows its support for students striking in response to the Kent State shootings by displaying a clenched fist image on Mickey Hart's bass drum during an impromptu free concert at MIT. *Source: Peter Simon Collection, Special Collections and University Archives, UMass Amherst Libraries.*

The student-run National Strike Information Center at Brandeis University, just outside Boston in Waltham, serves as the coordinating hub of all campus antiwar activity across the country. According to the center, whose records are preserved by the University of Washington's Mapping American Social Movements Project, "more than 883 campuses involving more than a million students [were involved in protest activities].... Authorities suspended classes on 97 campuses and 20 remained closed for the remainder of school year," including Boston-area schools such as Brandeis, Boston University, Tufts, and the University of Massachusetts along with Brown University in Providence.

At MIT in Cambridge, classes are cancelled at the same time that the Grateful Dead is arriving in town two days following the Kent State shootings to play a scheduled concert at the school's DuPont Gymnasium on May 7.

With classes called off and students milling around the campus, the band appears at the school in the afternoon a day early, on May 6, to play a free, impromptu concert on the steps of MIT's student center at Kresge Plaza to help calm tensions at the school.

The appearance, cut short by a rainstorm, marks a clear change for the band, whose members only a few years earlier professed their lack of interest in politics and social causes in an interview with Harry Reasoner for the 1967 CBS News special report "The Hippie Temptation," during which the Grateful Dead's Jerry Garcia says, "What we're thinking about is a peaceful planet. We're not thinking about anything else. We're not thinking about any kind of power. We're not thinking about any of those kinds of struggles. We're not thinking about revolution or war or any of that." However, when the band appears at MIT, on the front of Grateful Dead drummer Mickey Hart's bass drum is silkscreened a large, red, clenched fist in protest of the Kent State shootings.

During this period, WBCN is part of a broader effort in the Boston area to uncover and expose the actions of the Nixon administration and to inform people about what is going on in Vietnam and elsewhere.

"There was a war going on, and it wasn't just the war in Vietnam," says WBCN's News Dissector, Danny Schechter. "It was a war at home. There was a war covering up the war in Vietnam — all the abuse and war crimes that were taking place there. There was a culture in Boston that was supportive of actually informing people of what was really going on, and BCN was part of it."

The Pentagon Papers (officially titled the *Report of the Office of the Secretary of Defense Vietnam Task Force*), the confidential study of U.S. involvement in Vietnam from 1945 to 1967, was released to the press by researcher Daniel Ellsberg in 1971. "[They] were really a document about the history of how the United States got involved in Vietnam," says Schechter.

"It was Daniel Ellsberg in Cambridge who was copying these documents in Harvard Square. On BCN, we covered the Pentagon Papers, and we interviewed Ellsberg," says Schechter, who can be seen standing, mike in hand, next to Ellsberg on the steps of the federal court house in Boston the day Ellsberg turns himself in to federal authorities on charges stemming from his release of the Pentagon Papers. Other activists, like Howard Zinn at Boston University and Noam Chomsky at MIT, continue to reveal and challenge hidden government excesses and wrongdoings and to put them into a broader context on the air as regular commentators on WBCN.

WBCN is also one of several media outlets to receive copies of confidential files that were stolen by antiwar activists who call themselves "The Citizens' Commission to Investigate the FBI" during a break-in at the FBI's Media, Pennsylvania, office in March 1971.

224

Chapter 15

"There was an activist group that found an FBI office in Media, Pennsylvania, of all things — that name is fascinating — and they were able to, as we would say, 'liberate these documents' and try to make them public," says Schechter. "And so BCN was certainly interested in this information. It was about infiltration and surveillance — the ways in which the government was spying on us as opposed to informing us or serving us. And of course, the government didn't want this known, and we did want it known."

The top-secret documents for the first time publicly reveal the existence of the FBI's "Counterintelligence" program (code-named "COINTELPRO"), an illegal campaign of surveillance and harassment of American citizens for legally protected speech and political activities. As the federal government scrambles in an ultimately unsuccessful effort through the federal courts to prevent the *New York Times* and the *Washington Post* from publishing the documents, WBCN's Danny Schechter reads sections of them live on the air to get them into the public record.

Left
Daniel Ellsberg, the military analyst who releases to the press the confidential documents that become known as the Pentagon Papers. Among other things, the Pentagon Papers reveal that the White House systematically lied, not only to the public but also to Congress, about the war. *Source: Boston Phoenix Collection, Northeastern University Library.*

Daniel Ellsberg, working at the time as a senior research fellow at MIT, speaks to reporters on his way to surrender to federal authorities in Boston on June 28, 1971, for his role in leaking the Pentagon Papers. WBCN's Danny Schechter (with hat and tape recorder) stands next to Ellsberg. *Source: Getty Images.*

Danny Schechter (standing) with Charles Laquidara in WBCN's production studio where the confidential documents obtained by WBCN are read on the air. *Source: Jeff Albertson Photograph Collection, Special Collections and University Archives, UMass Amherst Libraries.*

According to a report in the March 26, 1971, *Harvard Crimson*, "the 12 documents were anonymously mailed on March 18 to 'Resist' – a national peace organization in Cambridge including among its members Noam Chomsky of MIT which subsequently gave the papers to the *New York Times*, the *Washington Post*, the *Los Angeles Times*, the *[Harvard] Crimson*, and to Senator George S. McGovern (D-SD) and Rep. Parren J. Mitchell (D-MD)." The *Crimson*, reportedly, sends copies of the documents to WBCN, and only the *Washington Post* and WBCN initially release the contents of the documents after "Attorney General John N. Mitchell asked late Tuesday night that the documents not be published on grounds that 'disclosure of this information could endanger the lives or cause serious harm to persons engaged in investigative activities on behalf of the United States,'" according to the *Crimson*.

The *Crimson* also reports that "Mitchell had originally considered seeking a court order to restrain the media from publishing the documents but decided instead to make a personal request for 'those who have received copies of the material not to further circulate it or publish it.'"

Marsha Steinberg was a member of the WBCN news department and recalls Danny Schechter's decision to begin reading the highly confidential documents live over the public airwaves: "They started reading them on the air. All that spying – all that kind of, you know, COINTELPRO stuff – became public, and that undermined any possibility that would ever be secret, and they couldn't stop it. Danny did a really good job at, like, 'Just read it, read it, on the air.' I mean, what it says about BCN and particularly about, like, Al Perry, who was the general manager at that time: it's, like, he didn't try and shut that down."

Schechter's actions – ignoring U.S. Attorney General John Mitchell's request and broadcasting material from the confidential documents on the public airwaves ahead of any government injunction – were endorsed by Al Perry, the station's general manager.

The *Harvard Crimson* on March 25, 1971, reports on WBCN's airing of the stolen FBI documents on the air "in order to thwart an injunction against their dissemination that Attorney General John N. Mitchell will seek later this morning in Washington." *Source: Harvard Crimson.*

The Harvard Crimson

PAGE FIVE

WBCN Broadcasts Stolen FBI Memos

Radio station WBCN-FM broadcast two excerpts from a package of stolen FBI documents this morning at about 12:20 a.m. The group of documents concerned surveilance of suspicious organizations and individuals and the rewarding of FBI informants.

The Citizens Commission to Investigate the FBI allegedly took the documents from the FBI's Media, Penn. office. WBCN reported that it was broadcasting the documents immediately in order to thwart an injunction against their dissemination that Attorney General John N. Mitchell will seek later this morning in Washington.

The first memo, a December, 1970 directive from FBI Director J. Edgar Hoover, called for increased surveillance of black student unions and other black groups on campuses. The other memo, entitled "New Left Notes —Philadelphia—Edition One" concerned the travel and fees of student informers.

WBCN general manager Al Perry (left) with Danny Schechter "the News Dissector" (right). Perry allows the broadcast of the stolen FBI documents on the air, later saying "there is a time when you have to take a stance, and maybe in a lot of ways that's what WBCN was about." *Source: Boston Phoenix Collection, Northeastern University Library.*

The *Washington Post* publishes the stolen documents in a March 24, 1971 front-page story. *Source: Washington Post.*

The Washington Post

WEDNESDAY, MARCH 24, 1971

Stolen Documents Describe FBI Surveillance Activities

By Betty Medsger and Ken W Clawson
Washington Post Staff Writers

Copies of stolen FBI records sent to The Washington Post described the bureau's surveillance of campus and black activist organizations at one college as involving the local police chief, the postmaster, letter carriers, campus security officer and a switchboard operator

One of the documents encourages agents to step up interviews with dissenters "for plenty of reasons, chief of which are it will enhance the paranoia endemic in these circles and will further serve to get the point across there is an FBI agent behind every mailbox.

"In addition," continues the Sept. 16, 1970, document, "some will be overcome by the overwhelming personalities of the contacting agent and volunteer to tell all—perhaps on a continuing basis."

Late yesterday, Attorney General John N. Mitchell asked that the documents not be published on grounds that "disclosure of this information could endanger the lives or cause other serious harm to persons engaged in investigative activities on behalf of the United States."

Copies of the stolen records were received Monday by Sen. George McGovern (D-S.D.) and Rep. Parren J. Mitchell (D.-Md.). McGovern and Rep. Mitchell gave the FBI the documents, believed to be identical to those received by The Washington Post.

Justice Department sources said yesterday there is no question that the documents are copies of files stolen in a burglary of the FBI's Media, Pa., office on March 8.

See FBI, A11, Col. 1

"I remember this," recalls Al Perry. "Look, what's the issue here? Danny didn't steal them. They were made available to him. So, yeah, if you don't do this, they are in control, complete control, and you can't — there is a time when you have to take a stance, and maybe in a lot of ways that's what WBCN was about in that respect. There was a time when you have to say, 'Hey, we are stopping it right here.'"

"It was during this period that BCN was becoming a voice that was quite unique and courageous, and it made a huge difference," recalls Noam Chomsky.

By 1972, after the killing of the students at Kent State and Jackson State and during the continued escalation of the Vietnam War with no end in sight, the deep divide in the country increases as Richard Nixon runs for a second term, even as the war he promises to end rages on.

Leading up to the 1972 presidential election, WBCN interweaves its music and news programming with a decided focus on Nixon, including his failed efforts to end the war in Vietnam and oppressive policies at home. With the July 1971 passage of the 26th Amendment to the Constitution, 1972 is the first national election in which eighteen-year-olds can participate, and WBCN conducts a widespread effort to register new, young voters from among the hundreds of thousands of college students and other young people living in Massachusetts.

Additionally, following the June 17, 1972, break-in at the offices of the Democratic National Committee, located in the Watergate apartment and office complex in Washington, DC, and arrest of five men caught wiretapping phones and stealing documents, the WBCN news department devotes significant time and resources to reporting and covering the details of the Watergate scandal, including the White House cover-up and its subsequent unraveling.

"There was so much media material about Watergate once the story started surfacing. It was extremely appealing to us," recalls Norm Winer. "It was something that our audience was clamoring for. It was like a soap opera that we weren't writing, but it surpassed our expectations with every new episode, and it just kept getting better and better."

In November 1972, with Watergate still only a tangle of loose, unconnected leads in the eyes of many voters, Nixon is reelected in a landslide victory over Democratic peace candidate, Senator George McGovern of South Dakota, as Nixon wins forty-nine states. But for WBCN, there is one redeeming aspect of the election results: even with the disheartening reality of Nixon's decisive reelection and fears that the Vietnam War could therefore continue for another four years, there is a feeling of victory that, following WBCN's intensive voter registration efforts and coverage of the election, Massachusetts is the only state that didn't go for Nixon. This is reflected in the title of a station public affairs documentary called *Nixon 49, America 1*, which is later seen as a slogan on buttons and bumper stickers throughout the region.

The role played by Massachusetts in avoiding a Nixon sweep is saluted by McGovern after the votes are counted: "We want to give a special note of thanks to the people of Massachusetts. It isn't just an accident that the American experiment began in Massachusetts and that we're carrying it on in the nation's capital. We're going to keep doing that for a great many years to come."

"Whether we can legitimately, as the BCNers at that time, take credit for enlightening enough Massachusetts people to alter the results here in Massachusetts, I don't know," reflects WBCN's Sam Kopper. "But it is certainly symbolic of the consciousness-raising we were trying to do and the effect it could have."

The Watergate Office Building in Washington, DC, where the headquarters of the Democratic National Committee are burglarized in 1972. Subsequent events, including the cover-up of the burglary by the White House, leads to the resignation of President Richard M. Nixon. *Source: Library of Congress.*

The five Watergate burglars, arrested during the break-in of the Democratic National Committee office on June 17, 1972, as they seek to photograph campaign documents and wiretap the phone lines. *Source: David Bieber Archives.*

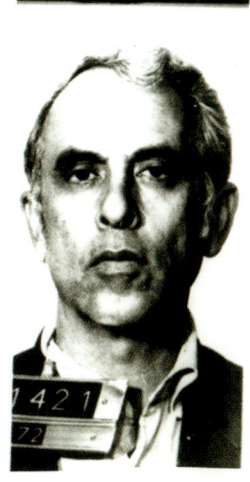
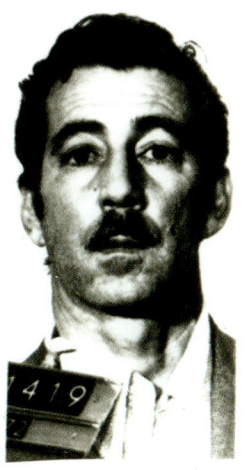
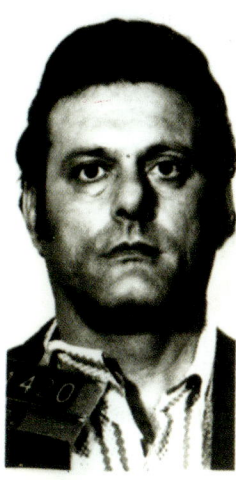

We've Got to Get Rid of Nixon

In the wake of Nixon's reelection, WBCN continues its focus on Watergate. Actress and antiwar activist Jane Fonda calls in a report for WBCN news from the Senate Watergate hearings in Washington in June 1973. Fonda reports a confidential memo links Charles Colson, special counsel to President Nixon, to the CIA as the White House was seeking to distance itself from the Watergate burglars and their CIA ties.

WBCN also produces a one-hour documentary, *The Watergate Primer*, which airs in May 1973 and connects the dots on Nixon's role in Watergate and its cover-up at a time when many news organizations are ignoring the evolving presidential scandal.

WBCN's in-depth reporting on Watergate wins it national journalism awards, while the station's focus on other local, national, and global issues, including apartheid and the oil industry, provides listeners with critical news and commentary not heard elsewhere.

Massachusetts is the only state to vote for Senator George McGovern over President Richard Nixon in the 1972 election, and this inspires the name of a WBCN documentary — *Nixon 49, America 1*. The phrase is seen on buttons and bumper stickers throughout the state. *Source: LCMedia Productions.*

Senator George McGovern in Boston as he wins the Massachusetts presidential primary, April 25, 1972. *Source: Spencer Grant Collection, Boston Public Library.*

Chapter 15

WBCN's coverage of Watergate includes a report
from Jane Fonda, who attends the Senate hearings.
Source: Allen Green.

We've Got to Get Rid of Nixon

Rock and Roll Future

16

Rock and Roll Future

16

From its humble beginnings as an underground radio station broadcasting live from the dressing room of the Boston Tea Party rock club, WBCN's on-air programming was intertwined with live musical guests and performances. This results from Ray Riepen, creator of both the Boston Tea Party and WBCN, installing a makeshift studio in the backroom of his dance hall, after the staff of the failing classical music station—whose airwaves Riepen and his underground radio announcers use in the late-night hours—let it be known that they don't want the long-haired college kids that Ray hired coming into their offices at night to broadcast.

"T. Mitchell Hastings was very leery of having long-haired hippies going into the studios of his classical music station, which was on Newbury Street in the Back Bay—kind of an upscale shopping area with a lot of ad agencies there. It seems he didn't want to be associated with these people even though he was maybe thinking he'd be happy to take their money," recalls Steve Nelson, the manager of the Boston Tea Party.

From the beginning, broadcasting from the dressing room of the Boston Tea Party as bands performed on stage, WBCN's legacy is intertwined with live music performance. *Source: David Bieber Archives.*

Top
The Who performs *Tommy* at the Boston Tea Party in May and November 1969. *Source: Eric Engstrom.*

Right
Roger Daltry and Pete Townshend perform *Tommy* at the Boston Tea Party in May 1969. While in town, the band discusses the meaning of the rock opera on the air with WBCN's Steven Segal and Charles Laquidara. *Source: James Kozlowski, photographer. Collection of John Visnaskas.*

Ray Riepen's solution was to move the announcers to the back room of the Boston Tea Party where, as WBCN's Tommy Hadges recalls, "we were often doing radio programs as bands were playing on stage. Somebody brought up the point that it was going to be kind of noisy when we turned on the mic, and [Ray Riepen] was like, 'Who gives a shit? It's going to sound fantastic. Let it go.'"

And what could be better for an underground rock radio station than broadcasting live as Led Zeppelin, the Who, the Velvet Underground, and other bands and musicians are walking past while coming and going from the stage or waiting around for a sound check and can be grabbed for a quick interview?

In May 1969, the Who's long-awaited two-record album containing the groundbreaking rock opera *Tommy* is released in the United States. *Tommy* is the brainchild of the Who guitarist Pete Townshend, and it tells the story of the fictitious Tommy Walker, whose early life trauma leaves him "deaf, dumb and blind" and yet with amazing pinball skills. According to Townshend, the story of *Tommy* is inspired by the life of Meher Baba, the Indian spiritual master whose mystical transformation started at age nineteen in the early part of the twentieth century and who was later credited with originating the phrase "Don't worry, be happy."

While in town, the band – including lead singer Roger Daltrey, guitarist Pete Townshend, bass guitarist John Entwistle, and drummer Keith Moon – huddle around the microphone to chat about their new rock opera with WBCN announcer Steven "the Seagull" Segal along with the station's Joe Rogers and Charles Laquidara:

Steven Segal: It's immensely exciting. . . . Stand by for *Tommy the Pinball Wizard*, the Who's new double album set released in the stores today on Decca and some words of wisdom from the Who. . . .

Seeking to untangle the opera's meaning, Charles Laquidara asks the band about the dramatic climax of the story:

Charles Laquidara: Okay. Now, Tommy goes through this whole thing where he finally gets cured. The last track, "Tommy's Holiday Camp" or "We're Not Going to Take It": it's like everybody's saying, "We're not going to take your cure. We're not going to take your cure," and all of a sudden they all say, you know, like, "We know what you mean."

Pete Townshend: You kind of got it screwed up there. What happens is that Tommy gets cured, right? But with the cure comes a whole lot of other things – a kind of a saintly aspect and a divine aspect. But then he goes through a thing where he's incredibly famous, and all the people around him want to be like him, and they demand a religion from him. And Uncle Ernie institutes the Holiday Camp to cash in on the – you know, "The kids want a religion, so we'll give it to them, and they can pay the price." And Tommy is just a pawn in this game. And eventually Tommy realizes that in order to break the whole materialistic farce of the thing, he's going to have to get tough, and so he starts to lay down rules, which he knows they're not going to like, so that they'll get back to their own trips. And they don't like it. So they revolt against him and break the whole place up – the whole Holiday Camp and everything and Uncle Ernie with it – and they run off into the night, and he's left kind of in a very kind of poignant atmosphere.

It's like despite the fact that he's cured and he's a divine figure and he's universally conscious and all this other stuff, that he's still basically deaf, dumb, and blind, you know, and still just as far away and remote from those people as he was before. And that's why at the end he sings, "See me, feel me . . ." and then you get into that devotional song. I think when you look at the book and you see who's saying what, it helps a little bit.

By 1971, Ray Riepen closes the Boston Tea Party, but WBCN remains committed to supporting emerging Boston-based artists as well as up-and-coming bands from other cities. *Source: Jeff Albertson Photograph Collection, Special Collections and University Archives, UMass Amherst Libraries.*

While today this kind of interaction between musicians and a radio announcer is commonplace on the air—with artists discussing their new album, the meaning of their songs and lyrics, and their upcoming plans for performance or recording—it had really never happened on the radio before, where musicians or bands would drop by a radio station for a chat live on the air.

"[Pete Townshend] was really patient in outlining the story, the sequence of events, and telling about Meher Baba," says Norm Winer, recalling several visits Townshend made to WBCN to discuss the *Tommy* project. "He had such great rapport. It was riveting, compelling, and absolutely unheard of. It was a fabulous conversation which you would hear on NPR now—perhaps that kind of attention and the length of the interview and which was really a conversation."

By the end of 1970, the Boston Tea Party closes its doors, due to the increasing popularity of the performers who play there—which is reflected in their fees—making it no longer economically possible to present major musical artists in a small club that holds only 550 people. Led Zeppelin, for example, was paid only $4,000 total for the band's three-night appearance at the Boston Tea Party in 1969. Just a couple of years later, their concerts move to a larger venue, the Boston Garden, which holds nearly sixteen thousand people, and like other major bands, they receive significantly larger fees. Still, for WBCN, even after it moves its air studio from the back stage of the Boston Tea Party to offices on the third floor at 312 Stuart Street in downtown Boston, having live music on the air continues to be a staple of its broadcasts as the station continues to serve as a musical incubator for local and emerging artists. In the words of announcer Joe Rogers, "We wanted local bands to be successful. Why wouldn't we?"

For up-and-coming musicians and bands, this means a combination of performing at dozens of local clubs to develop their acts and skills and to attract a fan following while getting exposure on WBCN, which plays their music on the air often even before they have record deals, sometimes from tapes right out of the recording studio—or even made in someone's basement. At the same time, the stream of musical artists in and out of WBCN's studios, where they are interviewed and perform live on the air, is nonstop.

In early 1971, full-scale live performances on WBCN start with a broadcast featuring the Youngbloods, whose iconic song "Get Together" and its signature line—"Come on, people now / Smile on your brother / Everybody get together / Try to love one another right now"—is at the time as much an anthem of the counterculture as any tune. On a cold winter night, the four-member group, including lead singer and guitarist Jesse Colin Young, crowd into the radio station's front office while staff members sit cross-legged on the floor around the band. Although NPR today has what it calls "Tiny Desk Concerts," where musicians come by and play in its offices, the Youngbloods' appearance at WBCN, which involves moving desks out of the way in the impossibly cramped reception area to make room for the band and its equipment, could easily be called a Tiny, Tiny Desk Concert.

The broadcast is a success for the station with listeners, but it raises the question about where else, outside of the station's reception area, live performances can happen. The station tries broadcasting live from a local recording studio, Intermedia, at 331 Newbury Street, inviting Canned Heat to perform on February 22, 1972, for which members of the J. Geils Band drop in to play. And Little Richard is rumored to be flying in from New Orleans to sit in on what becomes a late-night jam. On later dates, Jerry Garcia and Howard Wales, Loggins and Messina, and the New York Rock Ensemble perform live on WBCN from the studio.

During 1972, WBCN begins airing weekly live broadcasts from a host of small clubs across Boston, including from the adjoined Paul's Mall and the Jazz Workshop on Boylston Street.

"Jazz Workshop, run by Fred Taylor, was one of the great jazz clubs in the world," recalls Norm Winer. "Next door, you walked down the stairs, and to the left is Paul's Mall owned by the same guy, booked by the same guy — Fred Taylor."

In these intimate live broadcasts, WBCN's listeners are introduced to artists, many at the beginnings of their careers — including Bob Marley and the Wailers, Randy Newman, Little Feat, Taj Mahal, and Aerosmith — as well as seasoned blues and jazz greats like B.B. King, Muddy Waters, Miles Davis, Charles Mingus, Chick Corea, and Keith Jarrett, among many others.

"[Paul's Mall and the Jazz Workshop] were dingy, underground clubs very, very constrained in terms of space," remembers Tommy Hadges. "You know, if Randy Newman was performing at Paul's Mall, the front row was six feet away from him, and that was it."

Perhaps the greatest champion of new artists and music at WBCN is Maxanne Sartori, one of the female announcers hired in the wake of the 1970 Bread and Roses women's protest at the station. Maxanne arrives at WBCN soon after she turns twenty-three, and over the next seven years she discovers and champions such bands as Aerosmith (at the time, a local group playing area bars and church basements), Queen, the Cars, Billy Squier, the New York Dolls, Jonathan Richman and the Modern Lovers, and many others.

But perhaps WBCN's two areas of greatest impact on music during the era involve reggae and Bruce Springsteen.

"In 1973, WBCN pretty much introduced reggae not just to Boston but to the whole country," recalls Norm Winer.

Fred Taylor (right) outside his adjoining clubs, Paul's Mall and the Jazz Workshop, on Boylston Street in Boston, where starting in 1972 WBCN begins weekly live broadcasts. *Source: Courtesy of the Boston Globe Collection, Northeastern University Archives and Special Collections.*

Fred Taylor in his office at Paul's Mall and the Jazz Workshop. *Source: Courtesy of the Boston Globe Collection, Northeastern University Archives and Special Collections.*

Among those who perform at Paul's Mall and the Jazz Workshop are Linda Ronstadt, Herbie Hancock, Jesse Colin Young, and Thelonious Monk (left) and Charlie Rouse (right). *Sources: Jeff Albertson Photograph Collection, Special Collections and University Archives, UMass Amherst Libraries (Ronstadt, Hancock, and Young); Bernard Moss Collection, UMass Amherst Special Collections and University Archives (Monk and Rouse).*

Rock and Roll Future

Maxanne Sartori in the WBCN air studio at 312 Stuart Street, circa 1972. *Source: Tommy Hadges Collection, Special Collections and University Archives, UMass Amherst Libraries.*

Backstage at Paul's Mall during live broadcast of Maria Muldaur on WBCN. Left to right: Paul Wennik, Maxanne Sartori, Maria Muldaur, Carolyn Cook, Charlie McKenzie, Bill Lichtenstein, circa 1973. *Source: LCMedia Productions.*

Backstage at live broadcast on WBCN of Bob Marley and the Wailers from Paul's Mall on June 26, 1975. Left to right: Bill Lichtenstein, Tracy Roach, and Bob Marley. Signed "Rasta lives, Bob Marley." *Source: LCMedia Productions.*

In fact, the introduction and launch of reggae in the United States comes after a chance trip to Jamaica by WBCN announcer John Brodey, who was seeking an inexpensive and warm place for an overdue vacation. As Brodey recalls:

> We had a client who had a travel agency that advertised [on the radio station]. I told him, "I got $300 for a great warm vacation. Where can I go?" He tells me, "Jamaica" and sent me down to Ocho Rios at the time when the North Shore was just a little backwater town.
>
> I happened into a place called the Superstar Record Shack because the reggae was just blaring out in front. I figured that's where I've got to be. So I walked in, and there was this guy, Rudy McFarland, who was a big magnanimous guy. We started talking and smoking, and I was there all day, and he said, "Tomorrow night we're going to the movies." So the next night, we went to this theater, and on comes *The Harder They Come* with Jimmy Cliff. A great movie with this amazing soundtrack . . . It was life-changing for me. I was, like, "This is the kind of thing that can change a music scene." It's such a powerful vehicle.

The Harder They Come is the first-ever reggae music movie, starring Jamaican singer Jimmy Cliff as a reggae performer turned outlaw turned national hero. The film features the music of leading reggae artists at the time, including Cliff, Toots and the Maytals, and Desmond Dekker. Following a warm reception at the 1972 Venice Film Festival, *The Harder They Come* was acquired by Roger Corman's New World Pictures but has little success beyond a run at a few theaters in New York City in 1973.

WBCN announcer John Brodey's vacation in Jamaica ends up helping bring reggae to America.
Source: Anthony Wermuth.

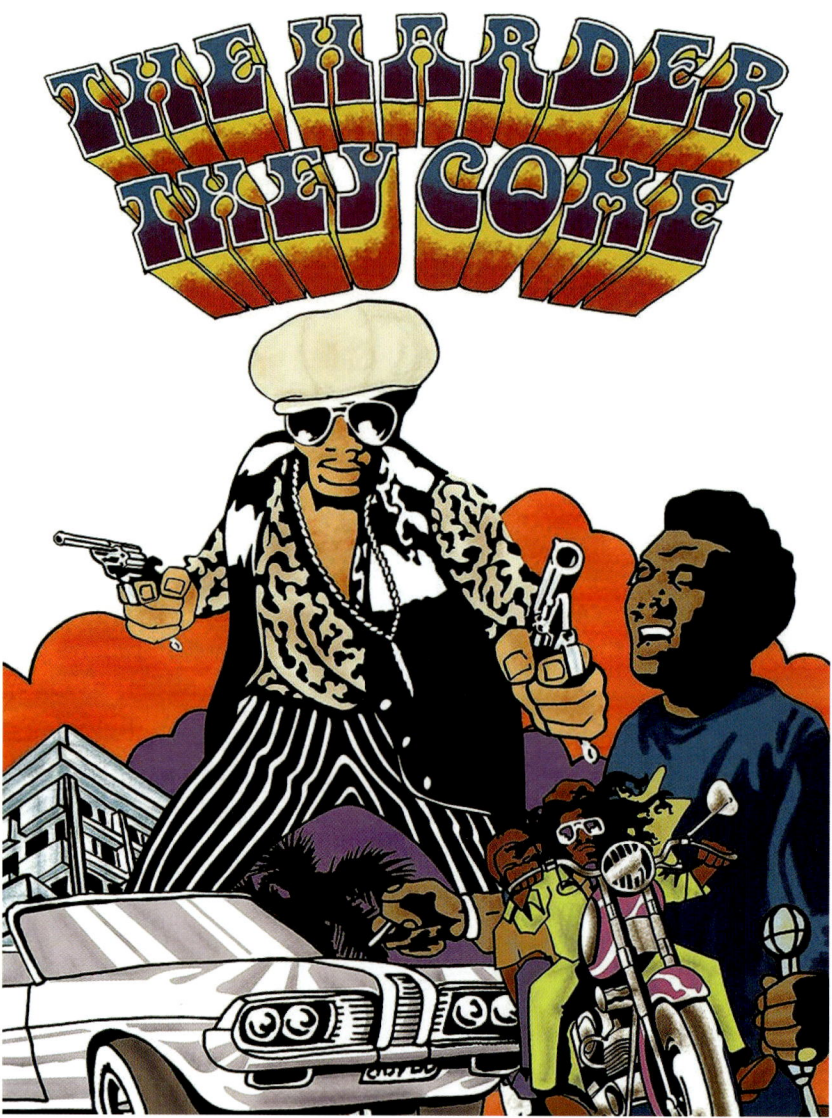

The Harder They Come is shown at the Orson Welles Cinema in Cambridge for more than seven years, helping introduce and popularize reggae in America.
Source: LCMedia Productions.

Chapter 16

But according to John Brodey, he knows the people who run the Orson Welles Cinema in Cambridge because they advertise on WBCN. When he speaks with them, they tell him they are aware of the film and are planning to show it, but are struggling with how to promote it. Brodey recalls:

> So I got on the radio, and I said, "If you're going to do anything this weekend, you better go to the Orson Welles." There are about twenty people there the first night. But the second night, it was half full, and then I said, "Look, this is going to keep growing." So they continued to show it, and it was sold out from then on. It was the second-longest run of any movie ever other than *The Rocky Horror Picture Show* for those midnight screenings. It made the audience aware of reggae.

Orson Welles Cinema's manager at the time, Larry Jackson, says that WBCN's championing of the film and at the same time playing the soundtrack album and other reggae music on the air was "instrumental" to the film's overwhelming and enduring success.

In a 1974 article titled "Films That Refuse to Fade Away," *New York Times* critic Vincent Canby notes the movie's popularity as a midnight attraction. As reported by Canby, "*The Harder They Come* ran for 26 weeks at the Orson Welles Cinema in Cambridge, MA," where it then remained for another seven years.

The success of the movie in Boston and the airing of the soundtrack on WBCN leads to Bob Marley and the Wailers' first U.S. appearance in July 1973. Performing at Paul's Mall, their stay in Boston includes a live broadcast and interview on WBCN, paving the way for the Jamaican sound to reach the rest of America as other radio stations around the country, particularly in New York and Los Angeles, follow the lead of WBCN by playing reggae from the soundtrack album from *The Harder They Come* and bands like the Wailers.

In fact, in a *Rolling Stone* article, *Boston Phoenix* writer James Isaacs observes: "Who would have imagined that Boston-Cambridge, with its thousands of middle-class, white college students, comparatively small (10%) black population, and penchant for folkie music, would at this moment be the North American hotbed of reggae?"

Another musical breakthrough in Boston came in January 1973 when a twenty-three-year-old musician from New Jersey came by to perform live in the studios of WBCN.

"This was someone who had never played live on the radio before. And he and his band came in with acoustic instruments and played on Maxanne's show," recalls Norm Winer. "If I remember correctly, they even had a tuba," adds Charles Laquidara.

The artist was Bruce Springsteen and the members of what would come to be called his E Street Band.

"It was very touching and very cool, very spontaneous," recalls Norm Winer. "You could hear how nervous he sounded. You could tell how young he was. You could hear the voice quivering."

Maxanne: Hello, Bruce Springsteen!

Bruce Springsteen: We're on the air?

Maxanne: Yeah, we're on the air.

Bruce Springsteen: Aw-right! . . . This is my very first time on the radio, and I want to say hello to my mother who lives in California. Hi, mom!

244

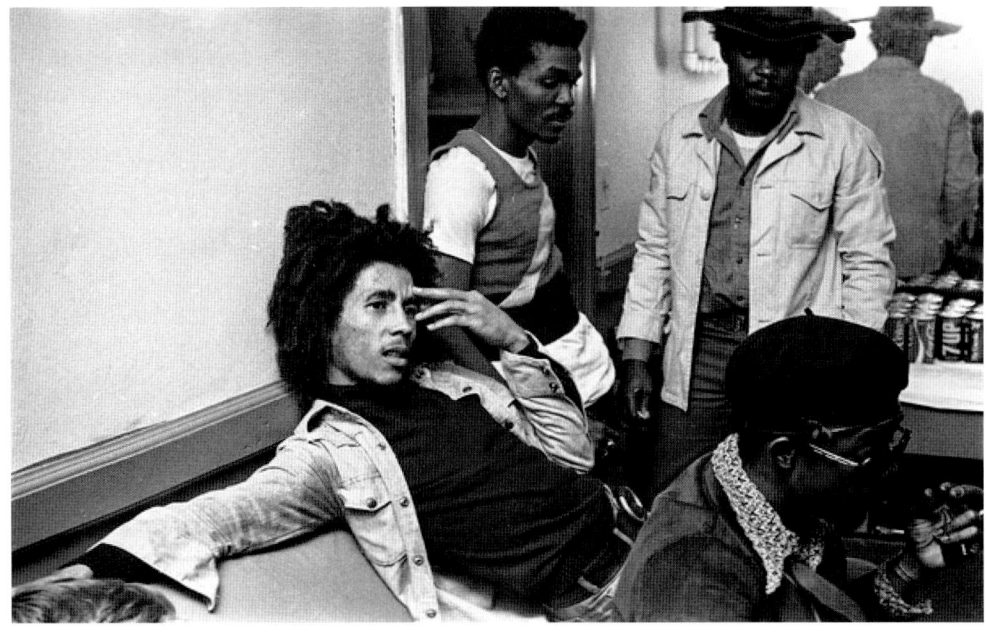

Chapter 16

"Coming from New Jersey, New York was not a problem, but spreading out from there was really tough for them at the time," explains Tommy Hadges. "He just showed up in the studio and brought a few other people and they set up the microphones. It was not just one or two songs. He was on the air for more than a half an hour playing. And no one would interrupt him naturally because that was not what BCN did. It was really a magical moment."

Maxanne: Don't you want to say a word or two about Asbury Park, New Jersey?
Bruce Springsteen: Uh, I have been trying to get out of there for twenty years (laughter). . . .
But I do want to thank WBCN and Maxanne because when we first came here — we first came to Boston — we played at Oliver's to about ten or twenty people. And now — there must be fifty people in the place. [laughter].
Maxanne: It's the power of media.
Bruce Springsteen: I just want to thank you. I really do.

In 1973, Bruce Springsteen and his band are regular performers — often as the opening act — in small clubs throughout Boston. Springsteen works to break through his bar band success on the Jersey Shore to reach a wider audience by playing songs of his own composition at Boston clubs like Joe's Place and Oliver's.

Left
The Wailers featuring Bob Marley make their first visit to America in July 1973 starting with four nights at Paul's Mall, which includes a live broadcast on WBCN. Bob Marley seen here backstage and performing.
Sources: Jeff Albertson Photograph Collection, Special Collections and University Archives, UMass Amherst Libraries; Clif Garboden Collection, Special Collections and University Archives, UMass Amherst Libraries.

James Isaacs in *Rolling Stone* chronicles the arrival of reggae in America via Boston. *Source: Rolling Stone.*

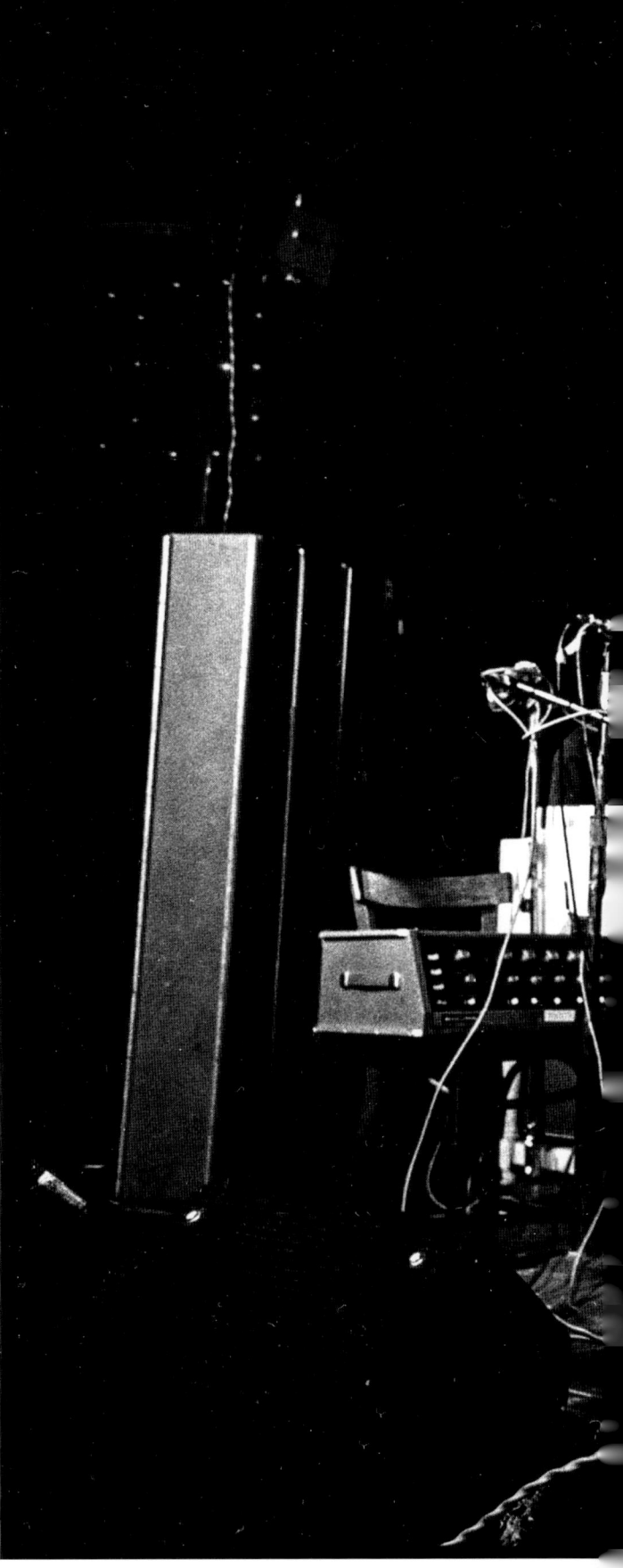

Top
Bruce Springsteen works to attract a following in Boston by playing bars like Joe's Place, in Inman Square, Cambridge. *Source: LCMedia Productions.*

Bruce Springsteen and band perform at Joe's Place, Cambridge, January 1974. *Source: Jeff Albertson Photograph Collection, Special Collections and University Archives, UMass Amherst Libraries.*

Chapter 16

Rock and Roll Future

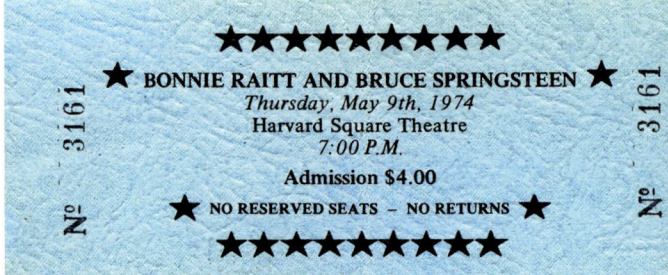

Bruce Springsteen and band open for Bonnie Raitt at the Harvard Square Theatre, May 9, 1974. *Source: LCMedia Productions.*

Bruce Springsteen and Bonnie Raitt backstage at the Harvard Square Theatre, May 9, 1974. *Source: Jeff Albertson Photograph Collection, Special Collections and University Archives, UMass Amherst Libraries.*

Bruce Springsteen and band backstage preparing to perform at the Harvard Square Theatre, May 9, 1974. *Source: Jeff Albertson Photograph Collection, Special Collections and University Archives, UMass Amherst Libraries.*

"He didn't just play in one or two venues. He played in all these crummy bars," recalls WBCN's Bob Slavin. "Then he was playing a theater, Harvard Square Theatre. That's like a real theater. That's a big deal." Springsteen and his band get their career-altering break when they are asked to perform on May 9, 1974, as the opening act for Bonnie Raitt at the Harvard Square Theatre in Cambridge.

Photographer Barry Schneier was in the audience and still remembers the moment. "[Bruce Springsteen] took the stage, and within minutes people knew that there was something going on here that was extremely extraordinary and extremely incredible."

"Opening up his set was 'New York City Serenade,' which starts with a classical piano introduction by David Sancious," recalls Schneier. "That's unheard off. A band hits the stage, you hit it hard: the horns blare, the guitar blares. He comes out there, and he starts with this beautiful melodic piano, and people are going, 'What is this?'"

Schneier recalls the sense he had at that moment, which he captured in one particular photo he took of Bruce Springsteen that night: "This one photo — the way his back is arched, the way his hands are extended out on the keyboards. It's just — something is about to happen, and that's the feeling you get from it."

In fact, Barry Schneier couldn't have known how right he was. In the audience that night is Jon Landau, a local writer and music critic for the *Real Paper*, an independent publication started by the staff of the *Cambridge Phoenix*. Landau's review of Springsteen's performance, headlined "Growing Young with Rock and Roll," appears on May 22, 1974, and includes the now iconic passage: "Last Thursday, at the Harvard Square theatre, I saw my rock'n'roll past flash before my eyes. And I saw something else: I saw rock and roll future and its name is Bruce Springsteen."

"It wasn't until later on that I had learned that that was the show that Jon Landau was at," recalls Barry Schneier. "And as he said, 'I have seen the future of rock and roll, his name is Bruce Springsteen.' That date is always called out. Bruce Springsteen opens for Bonnie Raitt. Jon Landau declares him the future of rock and roll."

The Landau review not only lights a fire under Springsteen's career, culminating in cover stories in *Time* and *Newsweek* in the next year, but also, in the views of many, it helps save rock and roll itself from its precarious drift into soft rock, as the era was seeing such *Billboard* number one hits as "Kung Fu Fighting" (Carl Douglas), "Love Will Keep Us Together" (Captain & Tennille), and "Mandy" (Barry Manilow). Springsteen's rise and success — piloted by Landau, who goes on to become his manager — is credited with breathing new life into rock and roll, including its roots, its authenticity, and its power of redemption and social conscience, as personified by Bruce Springsteen himself, and his music.

As Tommy Hadges recalls:

Bruce took such a different approach to a lot of what was going on in pop and rock music of the time. Popular music, including rock, was getting more synthesized and more producer-based and getting away from the traditions of rock and roll. It wasn't as much about singer-songwriters. [Bruce] really brought the singer-songwriter into rock and really rocked his ass off, and the band rocked their asses off. It was really a blues-based individual sound. A very honest sound.

The band got such a good review from Landau after their performance at Harvard Square Theatre. It really gave everyone more energy to rock and roll. He inspired a lot of bands to actually move more in that direction. It was quite a seminal moment in time.

•••

Rock and Roll Future

Left

Bruce Springsteen opens his performance at the Harvard Square Theatre with "New York City Serenade," which begins with a haunting, stark piano solo by David Sancious. *Source: Jeff Albertson Photograph Collection, Special Collections and University Archives, UMass Amherst Libraries.*

Barry Schneier's photograph captures a moment during the Harvard Square Theatre concert that he says looks like "something is about to happen." *Source: Barry Schneier.*

Jon Landau's review of the concert for the *Real Paper*, which includes the line "I saw rock and roll future and its name is Bruce Springsteen," adds rocket fuel to Springsteen's career. *Source: Real Paper.*

Jon Landau (left) with Bruce Springsteen (right). Following Landau's *Real Paper* review, he works as Springsteen's manager and producer. *Source: Jeff Albertson Photograph Collection, Special Collections and University Archives, UMass Amherst Libraries.*

But tonight there is someone I can write of the way I used to write, without reservations of any kind. Last Thursday, at the Harvard Square theatre, I saw my rock'n'roll past flash before my eyes. And I saw something else: I saw rock and roll future and its name is Bruce Springsteen. And on a night when I needed to feel young, he made me feel like I was hearing music for the very first time.

When his two-hour set ended I could only think, can anyone really be this good; can anyone say this much to me, can rock'n'roll still speak with this kind of power and glory? And then I felt the sores on my thighs where I had been pounding my hands in time for the entire concert and knew that the answer was yes.

"Absolutely one of the highlights of WBCN's live broadcasts was from the Jazz Workshop on Boylston Street with Patti Smith – the Patti Smith Group," says Norm Winer, at the time, WBCN's program director. "They had just come out with their debut album the year before. Patti Smith – the writer, the cultural figure, and so on – and she had distinguished herself. Not exactly as a mass appeal artist, but our cult loved her."

As the broadcast of the Patti Smith Group was about to begin, Maxanne, who was live on the radio from the Jazz Workshop, and Joe "Mississippi" Rogers, who was back at the studio, have a conversation on the air to set the scene:

Joe Rogers (on air): Maxanne, so what's happening down there?
Maxanne: They have been turning away people by droves. It's standing room only. I couldn't believe it. There's a line of people down the street . . . . Patti's like a professional boxer. She's, like, warming up. Dancing around, pacing around.

Says Norm Winer:

It was Friday night, and we broadcasted her set in its entirety. And because she was on a major record label at the time, the record executive, a kind of a blustery fellow, took her backstage before she began and said to her, "Listen, on the radio you can't use any questionable language. The FCC really frowns on that. Please, Patti, we know you are a poet. We know you have this conversation all the time. Please watch your language. Don't use any bad words." But he was kind of heavy-handed in the way that he conveyed this to her. It wasn't diplomatic and charming.

So Patti came on stage. And the band was rocking, and they played a few songs, and she was kind of measured in her remarks to the audience. And I was sitting with my boss, the general manager of WBCN at the time, Al Perry, and we were enjoying the show. And at a certain point she stopped, and she did a little monologue about the importance of radio, and it was very heartfelt and very sincere:

Patti Smith: You know what *radio* has in it – R-A-Y-dash-D-I-O and *dio* is "god," and so radio is like "ray of god." That's its highest possibility.

Continues Winer:

And the show moved on. And at a certain point, she stopped dead in the midst of a song and admitted to the audience that she felt very intimidated by the limitations being placed on her to say what was on her mind:

Patti Smith: We shouldn't worry about slang terminology on a rock and roll station. I mean, you should be able to express yourself in America. We have, like, one of the most colorful languages, which is, like, integrated with our art. The art of this generation is rock and roll.

And according to Winer:

She just started blurting out in the form of a poem – she started blurting out obscenity after obscenity. A stream of obscenities:

Patti Smith, frustrated by the limits on her language since her performance is being broadcast live on WBCN from the Jazz Workshop, lets loose with a string of obscenities after issuing a warning to her radio audience: "if you don't want to hear it uncensored, cut me off." *Source: Barry Schneier.*

Rock and Roll Future

| Chapter 16

Patti Smith: If you don't want to hear it uncensored, cut me off. I can't even read my fucking poem. It doesn't even interest me anymore. It's not to fear *fuck*. **It's only a word –** *fuck*, *shit*, *piss*. **They're just words that we invented. Like, we are not afraid of machines, we will not be afraid of words. Oh, please . . .**

Joe Rogers, who is back at the studio and is the engineer signed on the air with his FCC license, recalls it was a difficult decision to make: "There was the Patti Smith broadcast, and my assignment was to be back at the studio, with my hand on the on/off switch, which basically controlled whether or not that broadcast would proceed. There was a difficult decision there because as the obscenities came out, I had to decide whether to let them go or to cut them off. And I guess at the time, it seemed to me the better idea to let them go and we should continue with the broadcast, and that's what we did."

In fact, nearly 50 years later, station staff, like Tommy Hadges, are neither shocked nor opposed to her on-air transgressions: "I think she went out of her way because she was singing it to kind of alert the station of the fact 'I am going to sing this song to the club. If you don't want to hear these words broadcast, turn me off right now,' and it would have been an option," recalls Tommy Hadges. "Well, it didn't happen, obviously, but, you know: that's radio. If that doesn't quintessentially sort of package up BCN's true essence, stuff like that on the radio – wow. Amazing. Amazing. Never happen again. Never happen again."

Hadges is seconded by announcer Dinah Vaprin:

Patti was an artist. She was a poet. She was able to encapsulate in just those five or six sentences what the mindset was at that time. When she said, "This is rock and roll radio, and we should be able to say what we think or say what we feel" – you feel like you could do that at WBCN. You could say what you think and feel. . . . That's what radio represented to people at that time. A swear word here and there, but I think the swear words were the least of it. It was really about being able to say what you thought and doing it in rough, honest language. Radio was so much of that. It provided that form at that time. It was meaningful. That's why people listened to the radio. That's why people listen to BCN.

Joe Rogers agrees as well: "I endorse everything that she said there. There were rules against it, and those have to be addressed, but I want her to be free. It's better to be able to express. It's something that's so fundamental that it's hard to express itself."

"She was saying that we must control the airwaves – that we have to keep good radio on the airwaves," says Norm Winer. "And the fact is that, really, BCN was one of the few stations in America that played the music of Patti Smith. It was not traditionally, commercially viable, you know. She would push the limit. She pushed the envelope artistically. And these are the kind of artists that we wanted to support."

In the end, likely due to the late hour and the fact that her obscenity barrage came in the middle of her concert, there were no complaints to the FCC.

"Maybe no one heard it," jokes general manager Al Perry. "And I don't think anyone did because I don't recall hearing about that. One of the few."

17

Fifty Stories above Boston

Fifty Stories above Boston

17

In 1973, T. Mitchell Hastings (who continues to own WBCN until 1979) realizes a personal dream to move his radio station from its cramped offices at 312 Stuart Street in downtown Boston, just upstairs from Flash's Snack and Soda Shop, to an ultramodern suite of offices on the fiftieth floor of the Prudential Building in Boston, which since its opening in 1964, has been the tallest building in New England.

WBCN's offices and studios atop "the Prudential Tower" are surrounded on all sides by the Skywalk Observatory, a popular observation deck where tourists, families, and others pay to get a spectacular view of the Boston area. The location of WBCN's offices, with exclusive access to the Skywalk in the evenings and mornings, when it is closed to the public, likely makes it at the time the most expensive real estate per square foot in the Boston area. It's an unexpected home for what remains a radical, underground radio station, albeit one that is starting to feel the strains of its commercial success.

"You know, we were beginning to get ratings. Adults were listening to us. The station was making more and more money, and symbolically, moving to the top of the Prudential Tower — I guess there is some symbolism in that," remarks WBCN announcer Sam Kopper.

"The move to the Prudential was the dramatic one because that was the plushest, the most amazing, modern, sterile, mainstream, corporate USA place you could imagine moving into. That place should have been the home of *The Today Show*," says Tommy Hadges.

"The station's move to the Prudential Building was a big deal because the Stuart Street offices were like a clubhouse. They were a mess and unhealthy on so many levels, but we loved it," recalls John Brodey. "And then we get onto the fiftieth floor of the Prudential, and it felt as though the day of reckoning was coming. It was coming as radio became a bigger and bigger business. Being up there was a daily reminder of just how much value the station held just on a business level. I think we kept resisting going along as best we could, but there was a certain realization inside that this is not going to last forever. Our days are numbered."

Particularly bizarre to the staff is that they suddenly find themselves working in a virtual fishbowl, where visitors to the Skywalk observation deck can look through large picture windows and see the offices of the radio station and its staff while at work and on the air.

"People would pay to come up to the fiftieth floor to walk around the top of the Prudential Building to look at the environment. They would pay and then, 'Oh, by the way, there is BCN,'" recalls Tommy Hadges.

In 1973, T. Mitchell Hastings moves WBCN with its offices and studios to the fiftieth floor of the Prudential Building, at the time the tallest building in New England (on left). *Source: Spencer Grant Collection, Boston Public Library.*

T. Mitchell Hastings, WBCN owner, atop the Prudential Building. *Source: Sam Kopper.*

WBCN's Tommy Hadges on the air at WBCN in the main studio on the fiftieth floor of the Prudential Building in Boston, where visitors to the Skywalk Observatory deck can look into the station and see radio staffers at work. *Source: Don Sanford.*

"You know, BCN was considered alternative media but at the same time mainstream media," says Danny Schechter. "It was a commercial station with offices at the top of the Prudential Tower, the highest and most prestigious address in the entire area. I would go to work at 6 in the mornings and walk around the Skywalk and look at Boston waking up and looking at the beauty of this whole area — and BCN was on top of it."

Despite the obvious culture clash of a long-haired, radical radio station staff occupying one of the most visible and exclusive addresses in New England, Danny Schechter notes that the station sitting on top of the Prudential Tower — which can be seen from virtually every neighborhood in the Boston area and is the building to which people look as a navigational marker the way New Yorkers in midtown Manhattan look for the Empire State Building to orient themselves — is part of what makes WBCN so powerful as a community radio station:

> Part of what gave BCN its standing is that, while it's an underground station, it wasn't hidden away in some church basement. It was at the top of the Prudential Building, where the station could be seen from everywhere in the city. People knew we were there and that we were there to give people a voice.

From WBCN's offices atop the Prudential Building, one can see a hundred miles away. *Source: Spencer Grant Collection, Boston Public Library.*

"The station could be seen from everywhere in the city. People knew we were there and that we were there to give people a voice," says Danny Schechter.
Source: Jeff Albertson Photograph Collection, Special Collections and University Archives, UMass Amherst Libraries.

| **Chapter 17**

> [The station] was treated with respect and support by a lot of institutions that might not support an underground newspaper but would support BCN because it had ratings, it had an audience, and it also had an impact. It was a money-making radio station, and at the same time it was a consciousness-raising radio station that was willing to tackle controversial issues. It was willing to put people on the air who offered all kinds of dissenting perspectives, but it also paid the bills with commercials, including a lot of support from the music industry because they were selling records and concert tickets.

In fact, WBCN's move to the Prudential in 1973 was still three years away from Tom Wolfe's game-changing cover story for *New York* magazine that announced America's "Third Great Awakening" as the "We Decade" of the 1960s and early 1970s was to become the "Me Decade" of the mid- to late 1970s — but the early signs of the coming cultural transformation are evident among the station and its listeners, as WBCN finds itself rising to new heights in numerous ways.

The station's listenership and ratings are at an all-time high, with a broad audience that includes Harvard students, working-class kids from South Boston and Roxbury, politicians such as future Massachusetts governor and Democratic presidential nominee Michael Dukakis, and Red Sox players like pitcher Bill "Spaceman" Lee. Even Cheech Marin and Tommy Chong drop by to visit.

At the same time, the increased rent for the plush offices atop the Prudential and the related costs put pressure on the station to sell more ads. As Tommy Hadges recalls: "There was a tension growing between the demands of paying bills and what we all wanted. We all wanted to be faithful to the original concept of WBCN and the mission of BCN. Personally, for me, it was a challenge. It was the difficulty of being sure we could maintain our honesty, and the fact that we weren't selling out. 'Ugly Radio Is Dead' was just as important when we moved into the Prudential in the mid-1970s as it was when the station launched in 1968."

Tim Montgomery, who not only sells but writes and produces ads, recalls one particular incident where the need for ad revenue ran smack into the station's tradition of not taking national or corporate advertising:

WBCN's Sam Kopper on the roof of the Prudential Building overlooking Boston. *Source: Sam Kopper.*

Comedians Cheech Marin (on right) and Tommy Chong (on left) in front of the Prudential Tower, 1972. *Source: Jeff Albertson Photograph Collection, Special Collections and University Archives, UMass Amherst Libraries.*

Chapter 17

As things changed and the pressures grew and particularly after the radio station moved to the Prudential Tower, there was a tension growing between the demands of paying the bills and what we all wanted. We all wanted to be faithful to the original concept of WBCN, the mission of WBCN, and the purity of WBCN. Demands were greater, and we were trying to reach out to palatable advertisers who could help us pay the bills, but there was always a tradeoff.

We were starting to sell national advertising. And I became responsible for national ads. I'll never forget the first time I went to New York with our national rep and made my first call. I put on a tie, and I went to this huge agency, McCann Erikson. I walk in, and the media buyer, a rather imposing woman, stood up behind her desk and cursed me out. She then threw me out because, apparently, they had sent the station a tape reel — all the ads came to the station on eight-inch audio tape reels — and the production manager from WBCN at the time had written "F- You" on the box and mailed it back to the agency. [Laughs.] I had a lot of those experiences.

Tim Montgomery wears a tie to his meeting with McCann Erikson in New York. *Source: Dan Beach.*

18

Nixon's Resignation and the End of the Revolution

Nixon's Resignation and the End of the Revolution

18

By the summer of 1974, it has been only a little over six years (roughly three hundred weeks) since WBCN's "the American Revolution" first went on the air in March 1968 with long-haired college student announcers who got stoned and stayed up all night to play music on the air from their personal record collections while taking calls from listeners who asked them what to do about a draft notice or a roommate who was on a bad LSD trip.

At its core, WBCN remains the radical, iconoclastic radio station that is run more like a collective than a business, with its views about the counterculture, President Richard M. Nixon, and the war in Vietnam still worn on its sleeve. But now, the station has also become one of the most successful commercial rock stations in the country, sitting atop Boston's landmark skyscraper, with a vast listening audience throughout New England and top-priced advertising rates.

As Steve Nelson recalls:

> **I remember getting jumped while on the street at night in 1967 by some guys, you know, yelling at me "hippie" or something like that. By 1974, the length of your hair was completely unnoteworthy. There was also a tremendous change in people's attitudes about African Americans and about women. I mean, a lot of issues are still not resolved yet but really changed hugely during that relatively short period of time. We are not talking about decades or generations here. We are talking about a lot of attitude changes becoming part of the mainstream, when they were really out on the fringe just a few years before.**

The times are changing, and they are changing in Washington, DC, as well, where Nixon's lies and the cover-up surrounding the Watergate break-in and related affairs lead to a growing sense among Americans — young and old, in college towns and in the heartland, Democrats and Republicans — that Nixon is responsible for the criminal activities that took place in and around the White House and should therefore leave office and even face criminal charges. Nixon coasts into a second term in 1972, and in January 1973, the month of his second inauguration, he has an impressive 68 percent Gallup Poll approval rating among all voters, according to Pew Research Center. However, as details about Watergate continue to be uncovered, public concerns grow. According to Pew, following the vote by the House of Representatives to recommend Nixon's impeachment in July 1974, the majority of Americans, 57 percent, tell Gallup polls they believe the president should be removed from office.

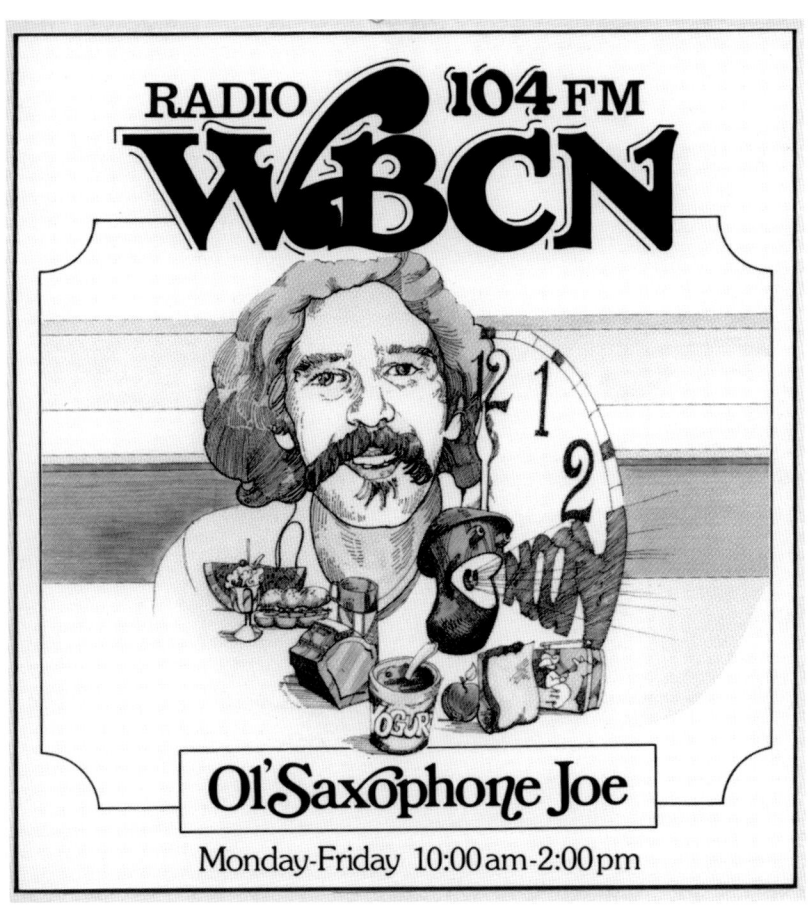

Ol' Saxophone Joe
Monday-Friday 10:00am-2:00pm

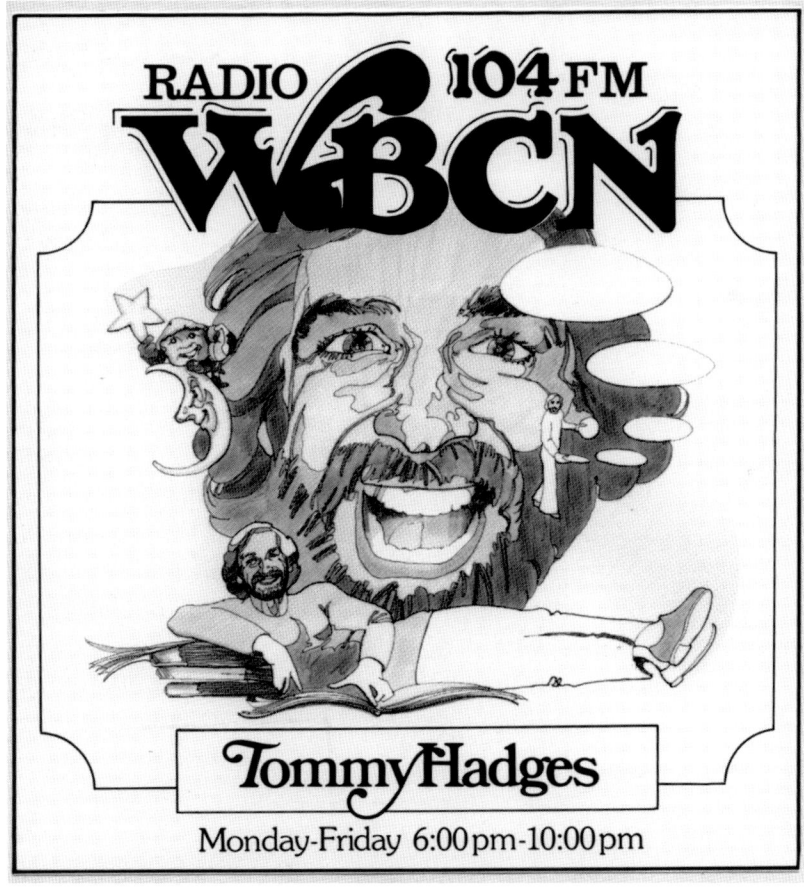

Tommy Hadges
Monday-Friday 6:00pm-10:00pm

Maxanne
Monday-Friday 2:00pm-6:00pm

John Brodey John Brodey
Monday-Friday 10:00pm-2:00am

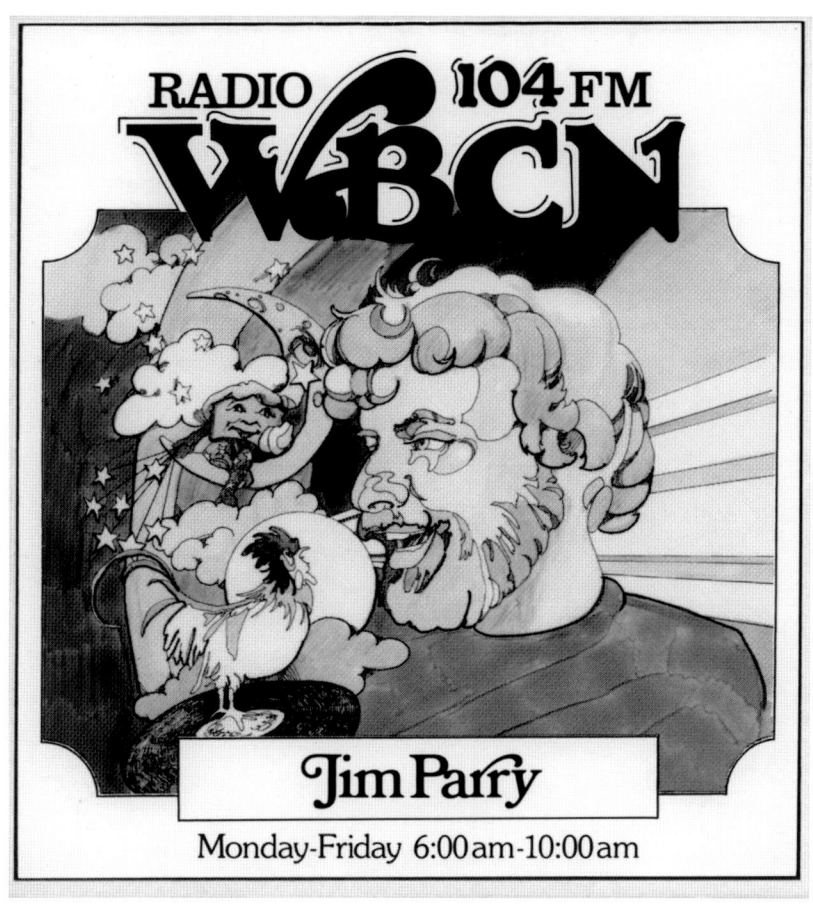

In the 1970s, WBCN promotes its announcers with this ad campaign, which stands in contrast to the "Ugly Radio Is Dead" posters that launched the station in 1968. *Source: Tommy Hadges Collection, Special Collections and University Archives, UMass Amherst Libraries.*

The 1970s bring a new look for WBCN, including contemporary designed bumper stickers, posters, and even business cards. *Sources: Tommy Hadges Collection, Special Collections and University Archives, UMass Amherst Libraries (two posters); Danny Schechter (business card).*

Abbie Hoffman remains a frequent guest at the station, but in 1974, he goes underground for several years following a drug bust – and is in touch with the station during that time. *Sources: Jeff Albertson Photograph Collection, Special Collections and University Archives, UMass Amherst Libraries; Tommy Hadges Collection, Special Collections and University Archives, UMass Amherst Libraries.*

Nixon's Resignation and the End of the Revolution

Chapter 18

"You know, people talk about the 1960s as being the hippie era, the golden era, depending on what your perspective is," says Charles Laquidara. "But the sixties really went past the 1960s because, if I had to say when the sixties, when that golden era ended and when FM radio started going in the other direction of being capitalistic and not underground anymore, it was after Nixon resigned."

It is on August 8, 1974, that Nixon addresses the nation on television to announce his resignation (the only American president to have done so), in the face of almost certain impeachment and removal from office. The network television cameras begin recording minutes before Nixon's live address and reveal a talkative, almost giddy Nixon sitting in the Oval Office as he prepares to end his term as president. When the moment comes, he announces and explains it with the following: "I have never been a quitter. To leave office before my term is completed is abhorrent to every instinct in my body. But as president, I must put the interest of America first. . . . Therefore, I shall resign the presidency effective at noon tomorrow. Vice President Ford will be sworn in as president at that hour in this office."

"The fact that it ended with Nixon's upper lip perspiring profusely, that was a good ending," recalls Norm Winer. "I remember sitting there in my home with my three-year-old daughter and forcing her to watch it and telling her that I just want her to remember these images — even vaguely because she was just little. But eventually I would talk to her about the significance of this, and it was something she could tell her grandchildren about. It was a great day."

WBCN's Sam Kopper recalls feeling "overjoyed and vindicated and sad that we had to have put up with everything that we had, you know, in the interim. . . . It was elation and celebration and but also sadness that it had to come all the way to this to get this gargoyle out of running our country."

Photographer Barry Schneier recalls "There was that moment of 'We did it! We ended a war, and we got that guy out of office.'"

Then, just before 12 noon on the day following the televised announcement, Nixon officially ends his term as the thirty-seventh president of the United States by delivering, as provided by federal law, a letter to the secretary of state, in this case Henry Kissinger. The seventeen-word signed note, dated August 9, 1974, reads as follows:

Dear Mr. Secretary:
I hereby resign the Office of President of the United States.
Sincerely,
Richard Nixon

Secretary Kissinger initialed the note as having been read at 11:35 a.m.

Before departing with his family in a helicopter from the White House lawn, Nixon smiles and gives his signature "V" for victory salute to the applause of White House staff. Shortly thereafter, Vice President Gerald R. Ford is sworn in as the thirty-eighth president of the United States in the East Room of the White House.

For many, including Mitchell Kertzman, who was one of the original WBCN announcers in 1968 but by 1974 is running his own tech company, the country is at an important "transition point":

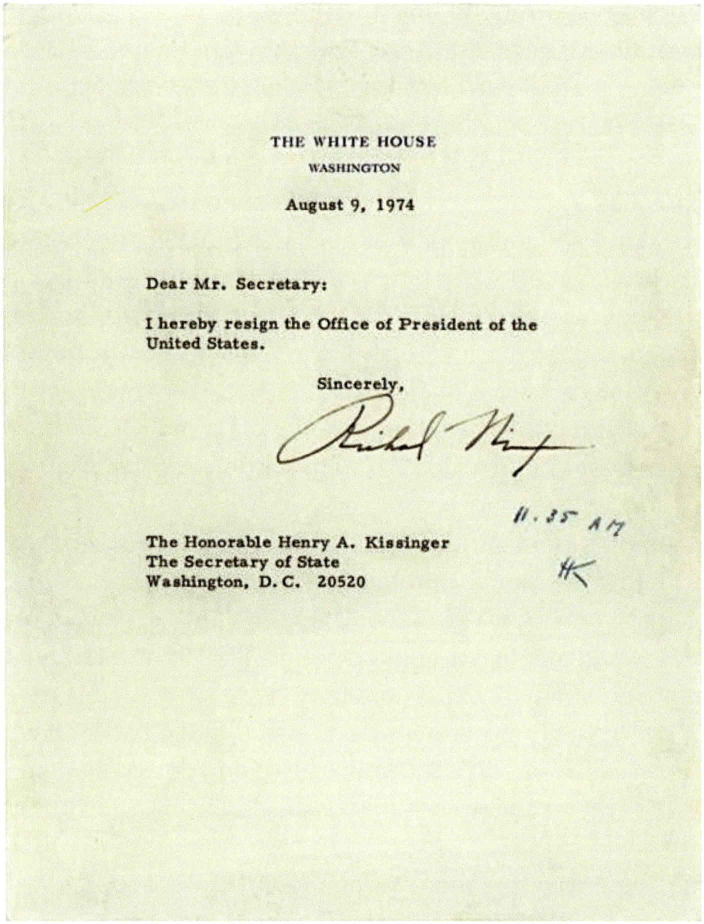

> THE WHITE HOUSE
> WASHINGTON
>
> August 9, 1974
>
> Dear Mr. Secretary:
>
> I hereby resign the Office of President of the United States.
>
> Sincerely,
>
> *Richard Nixon*
>
> The Honorable Henry A. Kissinger
> The Secretary of State
> Washington, D.C. 20520

With the presidential resignation letter dated **August 9, 1974, the Nixon era comes to an end.** *Source: Richard Nixon Presidential Library and Museum.*

You couldn't be angry and at war for that many years without wanting to have a relief and maybe get on with your life. I was nineteen years old in 1968 when Bobby Kennedy was assassinated, you know. By 1974, I was twenty-five years old. I had a real job. I started my first company by then, and I was ready to let go of the day-to-day battles. It was pretty hard to have the kind of anger at Gerald Ford that you had about Richard Nixon. I think the whole country took a deep breath after Nixon was gone.

Nixon's departure and the end of America's involvement with the Vietnam War puts an exhausted end to the intense political and countercultural excitement and uproar that fueled WBCN's early days. While the station continues, the era of the American Revolution is coming to a comparatively quiet conclusion – partially due to the sheer fatigue from all that has happened.

President Gerald Ford seeks to heal the divisions of the nation, with his calming style and perhaps most importantly, his decision to give Richard Nixon a full and unconditional pardon for any crimes that he might have committed against the United States as president. In particular, the pardon covers Nixon's actions during the Watergate scandal.

But the majority of Americans are not ready to forgive and forget. In September 1974, *Time* magazine finds 58 percent of Americans polled say Nixon should be tried for possible criminal charges. Ford's pardon of Nixon precedes a decline in Ford's own poll numbers and is a factor in his loss to Democrat Jimmy Carter in the next presidential election.

The *Boston Globe* announces the departure of President Nixon. *Source: Boston Globe.*

"By 1974, the acts that played the [Boston] Tea Party are now playing big halls and get tons of money as prices are going up," says former Boston Tea Party manager Steve Nelson. Creedence Clearwater Revival concert at the Boston Garden, circa 1971. *Source: Jeff Albertson Photograph Collection, Special Collections and University Archives, UMass Amherst Libraries.*

Chapter 18

Steve Nelson recalls the evolution and mainstreaming of the countercultural scene in Boston and America, including the changes to popular music and radio:

> By '74, it's not only that Nixon resigned. He was such a convenient target of all of our wrath. But it was — everything was becoming in a way more institutionalized, more commercialized. It all started out more as an underground cultural phenomenon and really became big business. I mean, by 1974, the acts that played the [Boston] Tea Party are now playing big halls and get tons of money as prices are going up. Records are selling hugely, and there are a lot of stations all over the country now doing what BCN was doing, pretty much — not as well and not as political, but playing the kind of album cuts and all that. So it really was becoming much more institutionalized and just part of the regular American culture.

"Everything had changed. We thought we had won the war, but that was just the beginning," says Charles Laquidara, who by 1972 becomes WBCN's most prominent and successful announcer as host of *The Big Mattress* morning show, a top-rated mix of rock and roll, alternative news, surprise wake-up calls, weather, traffic, and an ever-growing cast of outrageous characters. "Maybe all the people that were hippies and were going to share and everything decide they had families now and they had to take care of their own families and they had to make sure they could support themselves and get that car that they wanted. Everything just started changing."

Finally, WBCN listener Steven Wayne speaks for many of the station's listeners when he says he saw the era overseen by Richard Nixon and WBCN's first six years as a time of "us versus them."

> It was lies versus truth. We were being lied to, and people were dying because of it. We were being lied to, and poor people were having violence committed against them, especially Black people in this country, and we wanted the truth, and we wanted to change it. And [Noam] Chomsky and Danny [Schechter] were main sources to help us to do that. I mean, at the end of it, my parents were against me, my long hair, everything from the beginning. They said, "It's those drugs. Steven, get off those drugs!" But at the end, they sat down, and my father had tears in his eyes, and he said to me, "You were right," he said. "You were right. They've been lying to us."

19

Lessons Learned

Lessons Learned

19

And so the era comes to a sudden end with Richard Nixon's departure from the White House as he winds his way home to San Clemente, and with the arrival of his successor, Gerald Ford, who oversees the end of the Vietnam War on April 30, 1975, with the fall of Saigon. Protest music is widely replaced with disco as the "We Generation" morphs into the "Me Generation." WBCN continues on the air until 2009 as just another tremendously successful commercial rock and roll radio station, going on to break such bands as U2 and bringing punk and new wave music to the radio airwaves, while championing such social causes as the struggle to end Apartheid, but like much of the rest of the countercultural movement of the late 1960s and early '70s, its sharply radical, subversive, and transformative years would be behind it.

For those who worked at and listened to the early days of WBCN, the station left an indelible mark on how people looked at virtually all aspects of American society, including war and peace, education, racial disparities and relations, drugs, gender and sexual preferences, music, fashion, and perhaps most importantly, what had been called the American Dream. Here are some of them:

Little did we know, you know. Little did we know that we would be involved in something that would be as much fun and so meaningful to so many people.
Al Perry

We figured out a way to connect with the audience by not taking yourself too seriously, by remembering the importance of the people we were speaking to, by treating them with respect — consistently and constantly in everything we did — and by holding up our end as a vital part of the community. I mean, for WBCN to have succeeded for as long as it did was really a matter of the — I hesitate to say — the perspicacity, but maybe perspicacity and just the relentless spirit and blind ideas, blind idealism of the people that worked there.

We believed in the unthinkable, and we tried to make that come true. And to a certain extent, we did, more so than many other media outlets did. And if it had not been in Boston and if all those conditions had not been at play at the same time, it might have all been impossible.

I think that we can learn from that experience. I think that we can agree that setting your sights — too reasonably, without ambition — will get you what you deserve. But I think a bunch of wild-eyed idealists can accomplish the things they dream of sometimes — if their motives are pure and if they are in the right circumstances. But it was a lot of fun to do it. And there was an awful lot of hard work and heartbreak and a lot of giggling going on, too — but ultimately more rewarding than anything else that I could imagine doing.
Norm Winer

The best thing about it was we were doing it ourselves. We were making it up as we went along. We were developing friendships. We were putting up with each other. We were trying to create something that had not existed before. You do not get that opportunity much in broadcasting. You go to work for somebody, and you are told what to do. We actually created something new and something important, and the audience really responded to it. So it was that challenge. It was that excitement of being part of something that could make a difference, and it did make a difference.
Danny Schechter

I think one of the things I would like to see people remember WBCN for was what it stood for – independence, having people make up their own minds as what to play, what to say.
Charles Laquidara

I think that the unique thing about the station was that it was an assemblage of young people who were just people – smart people, passionate – who saw all that was going on in American life at that time – saw all of these truly revolutionary changes taking place in civil rights and the women's movement, in the music, and of course, standing up to the government when it came to the war in Vietnam. But I think people should appreciate that WBCN took that responsibility very seriously. And I think we comported ourselves appropriately and helped a lot of people through what was, in retrospect, a very difficult time.
Tim Montgomery

The FCC rules broadcasting in America and has forever. The actual license that people would apply for – and the process has changed dramatically – but the license that enables you to broadcast on a radio station in America, clearly states that you are there for the sake of the community.

But it's something that – in the passage of time, deregulation has taken news off the air throughout America, and FM stations alike have lessened their responsibility to the community, lessened the number of public service messages that need to be run. It's all about finding room for more commercials in the world of commercial radio. And the fact is that the responsibility that we took at WBCN in the early days and right through the 1970s was really a matter of the responsibility that all broadcasters were obligated to take. But we took that literally. We were very loose with certain other rules that were applied to us. But that was something that we took to heart. And it really was the most important thing that we needed to do. We were a part of the community in a lot of respects. But in terms of providing people with the information and the tale and the truth, that was one of the most significant things we did.
Norm Winer

I see this period in Boston – of all these actions that had the benefit of having their voice amplified by BCN. That was what was really rare. It was not that those same actions in bits and pieces did not happen in other places because they certainly did. There were bombings, there were protests and takeovers, but not with this radio station, to which we had tremendous access and which gave voice to all these movements and let them speak for themselves. That was the difference. That was the power of BCN. And that was what was not, at least to my knowledge, available anywhere else.

That is why it happened. And all this stuff happened in Boston. But that was the unique thing – to have that radio station give voice to all these movements and be available to allow people to speak in their own voice and give them presence on the air. That was the magic of it. And you can only say that was WBCN.
Marsha Steinberg

We were dealing with the draft. We were dealing with those civil rights issues and how we were going to relate to those who were different than us. And WBCN was talking to us. It was saying "We know what you are talking about. We know what you are thinking about here. Listen to what we have to say about this with our music."
Eric Jackson

Radio, politics, rock and roll were inseparable back in those days. When I look at today, I do not think that music is as entwined with the politics as it was back then. So today you don't have something like Neil Young's "Ohio" as a song about an event in the era that itself was influential of the politics and the events in the era. And so I think that time, that radio station, those politics, that war, that music were inseparable. And that's why BCN is so important.
Mitchell Kertzman

We were truth seekers in the sixties. And that is one of the reasons why BCN came about, I believe – was because when you listen to WBCN, you got authenticity, you got the golden age of music. You got authenticity in the most free music that was made – you know, that had the least corporate control over it. That was the music that BCN played in the sixties. And you had the news people – Danny Schechter and the other people. They had integrity. And they were the people that you trusted to give you the information so that we could make the important decisions.
Steven Wayne

There was no way we knew what we wanted as the counterculture. But we knew what we didn't want. We did not want what they had. We did not want war. We did not want discrimination. We did not want the idea of 2.2 children and a husband or wife for the rest of our lives – that whole nuclear family thing. We did not want to work in an office all our lives. And that whole world – we did not want that. Only what we did want – that was a little difficult. I think that is the problem – that we never came up with what the alternative was. But we really did not have the power. And we did not have the money.

There was no way to organize a whole attack on this system, which had started in the industrial revolution and had just changed America so dramatically and turned it into, you know, a military state. We were up against the military industrial complex. In many ways, in Boston, we were also up against the educational industrial complex, which was a big complex, making a lot of money, and they weren't about ready to give that up. And the health industrial complex, which was not as big then, but it's big now. All those things were big bucks. We were up against a lot of money, and it created a world that with it came stability, and the way in which the world would see Americans and what was called the American dream. We knew we did not want that.

But we were not in a position to have a revolution and get rid of it. We could not in any way take over. But we were right. And so we called them out on it.

And yet we were not in a position to change things. But we were in a position to change ourselves. And we did that. There is no question about it that many people were transformed from WBCN. And that battle continues. It is not over. It is not like, "Oh, I give up." I do not think we ever gave up. We discovered what was wrong. And we had new ways of changing things, and radio was a big new way for us. And the sounds and the things that we did were new, but it was all part of a big struggle that has been going on and still goes on.

John Scagliotti

It was an environment where people were really learning from each other, changing, seeing the world around them, moving forward in terms of their attitudes about women, about how they were going to live their lives. And you know, BCN allowed that change to happen for people working there to recognize how each other can really, you know, affect them. There was always – no one was ever malicious or unkind, everybody really cared about each other, even if they didn't agree with each other. And that was – that allowed you to really be able to do what you wanted to do and be your own person. Everybody there was their own person, you know. And everybody changed, you know, radically over the course of even those four or five years. So it was a different time. It was different. It was challenging but very exciting – a very exciting time, for all of us.

Dinah Vaprin

Well, I think there are some hopeful lessons. Young people can change the country. I love that young people are on the march today. It just is heartwarming to me. They are the future. Young people have to fight and make their future. They can't let old people stop it – which is what I think is going on in the country today, which is old white men are trying desperately to stop the future to hang on to their power. Personally, sexually, economically, politically, young women and men: if you want the future that you deserve, you have to fight for it. This period shows it's possible.

There are also good lessons about what *not* to do, which is that sometimes you start, as we did, and you're in the minority, and you're trying to create space for dissent, and you're trying to expose lies, and then over time you are no longer in the minority. And at that point, you have to change what you're doing. To lead the majority is very different than to be the prophetic minority, and we didn't understand that, and we weren't able to go from the prophetic minority, the protesters – however effective we might have been – to the leaders of the majority.

I'm looking at people today who are entering politics – the women of the #MeToo movement, the high school students who are walking out of classes. They seem to be, frankly, far more advanced than we were, and it gives me great faith because you can be a prophetic minority. But when the country turns, you have to be prepared to lead and lead the majority and to be embracing that – and to be welcoming new people who only a little while ago were opposed to you. We were not as good as we should've been on that.

Michael Ansara

You know, I have thought a lot about that period. And one thing I realized is that the Weathermen was exactly the wrong thing for SDS to do. It became more radical. It took the movement into a radical, violent direction. And in fact, the movement should have gone in the other direction. It should have been much more mainstream because the whole country was turning against the Vietnam War at that point. And so this and these ideas about revolution were romantic fantasies. And people did not really think about what they were saying. And you

know, in the end, some people died. And they paid a stiff price for that. For what reason? No good reason that I can think of. And I hope it does not happen again.
Bo Burlingham

We have learned a lot since the seventies around what inclusion means and how damaging exclusion is and about tribal mentality. And some of what we have learned is that we are actually all on the same planet here in the process of suffering some of the same consequences of our neglecting to recognize our shared humanity. But at that point, we were learning how to share our humanity in concrete and personable ways.
Debbie Ullman

Very simply, you know, if you love something, don't give it up. Follow your instincts. It is, like — it is real clichéd. But do not give up on a dream, you know, if you think that it is worthwhile and you think it has substance to it. You know, do not just stop doing it because it is hard. You know, do it until the energy is sucked out of you, and then try to come back and do it some more.
Steven Segal

Of course, the question that everyone's asking, is if this can happen again?
Richard Barna

To say it could not happen again, it cannot happen again, in the way that it did. But the fact is everyone can be a communicator. Pick up your smartphone; shoot a video. If it is important, it will get seen by a lot of people. And it can create social change — no question about that.
Tommy Hadges

Abbie Hoffman, the godfather of the Yippies, was from Worcester, Mass., and he became a sort of occasional correspondent for WBCN and was on the air. And you know, when he was asked to summarize the legacy of his work, he said basically, "We were young, we were sometimes crazy, we made mistakes, but we were right." I think that could be said of WBCN.
Danny Schechter

Acknowledgments

The work on this book began more than fifty years ago, in 1970, when I began volunteering at WBCN, and witnessed events at the radio station and elsewhere that, even to me as a fourteen-year-old, clearly had historic importance. I began to preserve bits of audio and visual archival materials, tapes, photos, buttons, newspapers, and magazines, which might have some importance someday. I was not alone; in fact, this book and the companion documentary film of the same name were made possible by a multitude of people who had also kept bits of history, including tapes of historic broadcasts, photos of musical performances and protests, and so on, and were willing to share them for this project.

WBCN family gathers for the Boston premiere of the *WBCN and The American Revolution* documentary film at the Independent Film Festival of Boston on April 27, 2019, at the Somerville Theatre. Back row (left to right): Joe Rogers, Jim Parry, George Wardwell, Tony Wermuth, Jay Rooney, Eric Jackson, Lesley Palmiter, Andy Beaubien, Dinah Vaprin, Amanda Sullivan, Bobi Adelman, Kate Curran Rooney, Bob Slavin, Pamela Alessandrelli, Charles "Master Blaster" Daniels, Tommy Hadges, Norm Winer, Sridar Tayur, Nancy Dieterich, Ray Riepen. Front row (left to right): Branka Rogers, Fred Taylor, Debbie Ullman, Sam Kopper, Bill Lichtenstein, Tina Armstrong-Levine, Lynn Perry, and Al Perry. *Source: Photograph by Ron Pownall.*

The acknowledgments and thank-yous need to begin with my mother and father, Bernice and Eddie, who somehow allowed a fourteen-year-old to go off and volunteer at a radical, underground radio station. As a parent myself, I now see that their support was remarkable, including on occasions when they would have to pick me up and drive me home when I got caught up editing tape or otherwise with my working there, and missed the midnight cutoff time for the MBTA subway home.

I want to thank Tri-School, the alternative educational program at Weeks Junior High School in Newton, Massachusetts, which had the bright idea to send ninth graders out one day a week to volunteer in the community, which led to my work at the radio station.

To my best friend since we first met in seventh grade — and the coolest kid I knew — Harry Goldman, who shared my interest and passion for the quickly changing social, political, and cultural world all around us, but gone far too soon from cancer.

To Kate Curran, who hired me as a volunteer to answer WBCN's then newly launched Listener Line (although to this day she swears I told her that I was sixteen, despite the fact that I was in the ninth grade!). And an enormous thank-you to Danny Schechter, WBCN's "News Dissector," for handing me his Sony cassette recorder that day in 1971 and asking me to run up the street to a demonstration in front of the old Boston Police Headquarters, and to ask those protesting the murder of Fred Hampton by the Chicago police "Why are you here?" and then for showing me how to edit the tape, thus launching my career in journalism for the next more than fifty years. To Al Perry and Norm Winer, for the completely unexpected idea to give me my own weekly radio show, and all of the WBCN staff and volunteers of that era, especially including announcers Charles Laquidara, Tommy Hadges, Joe Rogers, Steven Segal, Maxanne Sartori, Sam Kopper, Eric Jackson, John Brodey, Andy Beaubien, Dinah Vaprin, Ron Della Chiesa, Jim Parry, Debbie Ullman, Bob Slavin; WBCN News' Marsha Steinberg and John Scagliotti; and the sales and traffic department's Tim Montgomery, Amanda Sullivan, and Pam Alessandrelli; volunteers Arlene Brahm, Lori Goldman Silverman, Tony Wermuth, and Pam Mitchell; and finally, not to be forgotten Andy Kopkind, J. J. Jackson, Jack Kearney, Kenny Greenblatt, John Ragucci, "Little Walter" DeVenne, Carla Wallace, Lee Buckley, and Steve "Mono" Crowley (in memoriam).

I also want to thank the WBCN staffers who came after this era for supporting the book and film project even though it precedes their time at the station, and for their efforts to remain true to the spirit of WBCN: Oedipus, Bradley Jay, Albert O, Lisa Traxler, Tracy Roach, Eli Sherer, Carter Alan, Tank, Chachi Loprete, Tami Heidi, and Susan Sprecher.

And, of course, many thanks to the one person without whom WBCN — as well as the Boston Tea Party and the *Cambridge Phoenix* — would never have happened, Ray Riepen.

Thanks and deep appreciation to the others who shared their stories for the book and film, including Steve Nelson, Bill Zimmerman, Bill Lee, Bo Burlingham, Charles "Master Blaster" Daniels, David Hull, Michael Ansara, Noam Chomsky, Rochelle Ruthchild, and Steven Wayne.

Much appreciation to those who allowed their photographs to be used in the film, including Barry Schneier, Spencer Grant, Liane Brandon, Ron Pownall, Steven C. Borack, Charles Sawyer, Dan Beach, Howard Ruffner, Anthony Wermuth, Yale Joel, and Timothy Carlson; and enormous thanks to Peter Simon and Jeff Albertson (in memoriam).

A major thank-you to Aaron Rubinstein and the late Rob Cox, both from UMass Amherst's Special Collections and University Archives (SCUA), for being the generous and supportive partner on this project, and for helping manage the more than one hundred thousand images and hundreds of hours of audio material for the book and film, and for setting up a permanent online archive for the public. Thank you to Haley Wood and Mass Humanities for their support of the film and for suggesting I contact UMass Amherst SCUA for their archival assistance.

To James Montgomery, for help at every stage of the process, and for keeping the blues alive.

And to Katie Helke, the editor at the MIT Press who embraced the idea of the book at our first meeting over coffee and patiently shepherded the book through its stages. And deep appreciation to the amazing MIT Press team including Deborah Cantor-Adams and Laura Keeler for their help in organizing the hundreds of images and editing the thousands of words herein along with designer Marge Encomienda, production coordinator Jim Mitchell, art coordinator Mary Reilly, and publicist Molly Grote, who shared the vision of this book and helped realize it.

To the lawyers who donated their time to assist on the film and book who collectively amounted to the greatest legal Dream Team of intellectual property attorneys ever assembled, including: Peter Jaszi, along with Pat Aufderheide, American University; Sula R. Fiszman, David Johanson, and Peter G. Byrne at Morgan, Lewis & Bockius; Christopher T. Bavitz, Berkman Center for Internet and Society; Jay Fialkov, WGBH; Jerry Marr at WilmerHale; and Vanessa O'Connor along with student advocates Sarah Atkinson and Erika Pey at the Transactional Law Clinics of Harvard Law School.

Deep appreciation to the executive producers of the film who provided the launching pad and grist for the book: Jay Rooney, Mitchell Kertzman, Richard Barna, Robert Sennott, and Sridhar Tayur.

And thank you to all who helped make the documentary film possible through the sharing of archives, stories, and financial support.

Thanks to Charles Laquidara, Ty Burr, and Louis Menand for sharing your thoughts in the forewords.

And thank you to Peter Kupfer and Marc McGarry for reviewing the draft and to interns Molly Flanagan and Sydney Adams for their diligent assistance.

Thank you to the archivists who assisted the project, including Alex Rankin at Boston University Libraries, Tom Blake at the Boston Public Library, Natalie Sinclair at the MIT Museum, and Molly Brown at the Northeastern University Library.

And a great debt of gratitude to film publicist Chris Kelly, of Fifth House Public Relations, who is simply the best.

Much appreciation to Susi Walsh and Mira Simon of the Center for Independent Documentary, the 501(c)(3) fiscal sponsor of the project, for overseeing the finances.

And thank you to Elizabeth Gildersleeve, Brad Ruskin, Hugh McKay, Al Cacozza, Bob Goodman, Danny Warren, and Tom Watkins for your enduring encouragement and support.

And finally to my daughter, Rose Madeleine Elizabeth Lichtenstein, who carries the promise of the revolution into this next century and generation.

Index

Advertising, radio, 53–55, 181
Aerosmith, 83, 185, 238
Albertson, Jeff, 175
Allman, Duane, 139–140
Allman Brothers, the, 16, 20, 27, 33, 139
Alter, Jonathan, 172
Alternative Media Conference, 140, 149
Altman, Robert, 140
American Indian Movement, 172
AM radio, 35–36. *See also* WBCN
Ansara, Michael, 93, 112, 116, 136, 139
   on Danny Schechter, 169–170
   on lessons learned at WBCN, 280
   the Weathermen and, 151, 153–155, 159
Ansen, David, 175
Antidraft movement, 77
Associated Press, 149, 165
Autobiography of a World Saviour, 13
Avatar, 13, 80
Ayers, Bill, 155

Baba, Meher, 235, 237
Baez, Joan, 181
Baird, Bill, 140
Barna, Richard, 35, 39, 48, 281
Beatles, the, 26, 48, 61, 82–83, 179
Beaubien, Andy, 21, 39, 199
Beck, Jeff, 16
Before Stonewall, 165
Benton, Jessie, 13
Benton, Thomas Hart, 13
Berry, Chuck, 16
Best Rock Station in the East: WBCN, The, 55
Bieber, David, 47, 61, 71, 165, 171
Big Brother and the Holding Company, 181
Big Mattress, The, 275
Blumenthal, Sid, 171, 175
Bob Marley and the Wailers, 238
Bonzo Dog Band, 20
Boston
   anti-war movement in, 77
   counterculture in, 1967, 1–11
   Love-In in, 7
Boston Common, 7–11, 112, 116, 123
Boston Five, 77
Boston Globe, 7, 171, *183*
Boston Herald, 21
Boston Magazine, 47
Boston Phoenix, 171, 243
Boston Tea Party (music venue), 11, 13–20, 128, 175, 233, 235
   closing of, 237
Boudin, Kathy, 153
Bowie, David, 200–202
Bread and Roses, 181, 183, 185, 238
Brodey, John, 89, 241, 243
Brown, Ken, 26–27
Bruce, Lenny, 111
Burlingham, Robert "Bo," 151, 153–159, 280–281
Button ban, 3–4

Cactus, 140
Cambodia, 213
Cambridge City Council, 3–4
Cambridge Phoenix, *11*, 175, 249
Campus unrest, 91–109, 214
   draft lottery and, 91, 93
   Harvard University, 93–106
   Jackson State College, 220
   Kent State University, 217–219
   Massachusetts Institute of Technology, 101
   suspended classes due to, 223
Canby, Vincent, 243
Canned Heat, 237
Cars, the, 185, 238
Carter, Jimmy, 273
Cate, John, 33
Censorship, 5, 80–81
Chicago 8, 119, 165, 207
Chomsky, Noam, 111, 164, 165, 170–171, 223, 226
Chong, Tommy, 261
CIA and the Cult of Intelligence, The, 165
Civil Rights Act of 1964, 61, 67
Cliff, Jimmy, 241
Clinton, George, 21, 26
Clinton, Hillary Rodham, 171
Clinton, President William Jefferson, 171
Cocker, Joe, 16, 83
Coffin, William Sloane, Jr., 77
Cohen, Len, 183
Colbert, Stephen, 170, 171
Colson, Charles, 230
Conception Corporation, 111
Copyright laws, 82–83
Corea, Chick, 238
Corman, Roger, 241
Country Joe and the Fish, 20
Cox, Robert, 116
Cream, 16, 39, 48
Curran Rooney, Kate, 132

Daily Show, The, 170
Daley, Richard J., 67
Daltrey, Roger, 128, 235
Daniels, Charles "Master Blaster," 20, 50
Davis, Gary, 140
Davis, Miles, 16, 238
Davis, Stephen, 175
Della Chiesa, Ron, 35, 37, 39
Democratic Convention, 1968, 67, 119
Devlin, Bernadette, 139
Diddley, Bo, 16
Digital Millennium Copyright Act of 1998, 83
Dohrn, Bernardine, 155
Donovan, 48
Doors, the, 27
Draft lottery, 91, 93
Dr. John, 140
Dukakis, Michael, 261
Dylan, Bob, 140, 151

Easton, Elliot, 185
Ellsberg, Daniel, 223
Entwistle, John, 128, 235
Exploding Plastic Inevitable, 21

Federal Bureau of Investigation (FBI), 119, 140, 159, 172, 175, 225–229
Federal Communications Commission (FCC), 80, 129, 149, 255
Feedback, 147
Feminine Mystique, The, 181
Feminism. *See* Second-wave feminism
Film-Makers' Cooperative, 13
Firesign Theatre, 111
Fleetwood Mac, 16
FM radio, emergence of, 35–36. *See also* WBCN
Fonda, Jane, 139, 165, 230
Ford, Gerald, 271, 273
Ford Foundation, 13
Frank, Barney, 9, 199, 203
Franklin, Aretha, 181
Freak Brothers, 140
Friedan, Betty, 181
Frye, David, 111

Garcia, Jerry, 139–140, 223, 237
Gay and lesbian community, 197–205
Gibbs, Phillip Lafayette, 220
Ginsberg, Allen, 139
Gleason, Ralph, 213
Gold, Ted, 153
Gordon, Bob, 33
Graham, Bill, 9
Grant, Peter, 16
Grateful Dead, the, 16, 20, 139, 223
Great Society, 61
Green, James Earl, 220
Greenblatt, Kenny, 119
Grossman, Jerome, 112
Guy, Buddy, 16

Hadges, Tommy, 16, 53, 83, 86, 199
   on Bruce Springsteen, 245, 249
   on Danny Schechter, 175, 183
   on lessons learned at WBCN, 281
   on the Listener Line, 132
   on offices in the Prudential Tower, 257, 261
   on Patti Smith, 255
   on radio as relationship with listeners, 127
   on radio programs featuring live bands, 235
Harder They Come, The, 241, 243
Hart, Mickey, 223
Harvard Crimson, 5, 183, 226
Harvard Square Theatre, 249
Harvard University, student protests at, 93–106
Harvey, Cyrus I., 4
Hastings, T. Mitchell, 37, 233, 257
Hendrix, Jimi, 179
Henning, John, 9
Hoffman, Abbie, 119, 136, 139, 165, 269–270, 281
Hooker, John Lee, 16, 20
Hoover, J. Edgar, 119
Howlin' Wolf, 20
Hull, David, 83
Humphrey, Hubert H., 67, 71

Iannella, Christopher, 9
International Feminist Planning Conference, 134
In the Life, 165
Isaacs, James, 243
It's a Beautiful Day, 27

Jackson, Eric, 21, 81, 279
Jackson, J. J., 80
Jackson, Larry, 243
Jackson State College, 220
Jarrett, Keith, 238
Jaszi, Peter A., 5
Jazz Workshop, 238
Jefferson Airplane, 47, 48, 80, 111, 181
Jethro Tull, 26
J. Geils Band, 27, 140, 237
Jim Kweskin Jug Band, 13
John, Elton, 16
Johns, Glyn, 82
Johnson, Lyndon B., 61, 75, 77
Joplin, Janis, 181
Journalists, alternative, 140, 149, 165, 175. *See also* Schechter, Danny

Kennedy, John F., 61, 67
Kennedy, Robert F., 61, 67, 75, 273
Kent State University, 217–219
Kertzman, Mitchell, 8–9, 16, 35, 71, 75, 77, 128, 271, 279
King, B. B., 16, 20, 238
King, Martin Luther, Jr., 9, 47, 61, 67, 75
King Crimson, 26
Kinks, the, 16
Kirk, Rahsaan Roland, 16, 20
Kissinger, Henry, 99, 165, 271
Klein, Joe, 175
Kopkind, Andy, 165, 197, 203
Kopper, Sam, 61, 67, 75, 149, 228, 257, 271
Krackerjacks, 3–4
Krause, Allison Beth, 218

Laird, Melvin, 214
Landau, Jon, 175, 249
Laquidara, Charles, 48, 55, 139, 140, 151, 155, 179, 185, 243
   on Danny Schechter, 171
   on the hippie era, 271, 275
   on lessons learned at WBCN, 278
   Listener Line and, 129, 132
   second-wave feminism and, 181, 183
   on *Tommy*, 235
Larson, Kay, 175
Lavender Hour, The, 197–203
Led Zeppelin, 16, 21, 26, 235, 237
Lee, Bill "Spaceman," 261
Lee, Stan, 140
Lennon, John, 134–136, 165
Levy, Don, 3–4
Lichtenstein, Bill, 165, 169, 171
Life, 116
Little, Rich, 111
Little Feat, 238
Little Richard, 237
Lock-Up, 207–211
Loggins and Messina, 237
Los Angeles Times, 226
Love-In, 7
LSD, 21, 129
Lyman, Mel, 13

Maher, Bill, 170, 171
Mahoney, Thomas H. D., 3–4
Marchetti, Victor, 165
Marin, Cheech, 261
Marks, John D., 165
Marley, Bob, 238, 243
Marsh, Dave, 175
Maslin, Janet, 175

Massachusetts Institute of Technology, 101, 223
McCarthy, Eugene, 61, 112
McFarland, Rudy, 241
McGovern, George, 116, 226, 228
McNeil, Duncan S., 5
Media criticism, 170–172
Mekas, Jonas, 13
Melanie, 181
Midler, Bette, 197
Miles, Buddy, 83
Miller, Jeffrey Glenn, 218
Mingus, Charles, 238
Mitchell, John, 155, 226
Mitchell, Joni, 181
Mitchell, Parren J., 226
Montgomery, James, 50
Montgomery, Tim, 53, 91, 181, 192, 261, 263, 278
Moon, Keith, 128, 235
Morrison, Van, 16
Mother Jones, 159
Mothers of Invention, 39
Muldaur, Maria, 13

National Organization for Women, 134
National Public Radio, 127
Nelson, Steve, 15–16, 20–21, 26, 37, 48, 265, 275
Newman, Randy, 238
New Republic, 197
Newsweek, 172, 249
New York Dolls, 238
New York magazine, 261
New York Rock Ensemble, 237
New York Times, 225, 226, 243
1968, 61–75
1984, 213
Nisker, "Scoop," 169
Nixon, Richard, 71, 75, 81, 91, 111, 112, 151, 164. *See also* Vietnam War
  invasion of Cambodia and, 213–214
  public opposition to Vietnam War and, 213
  resignation of, 265–275
  Watergate and, 228–230, 265, 273
Nyro, Laura, 181

Occupy Movement, 99
Ochs, Phil, 111
Oh! Calcutta!, 5
Old Mole, 93, 101
Ono, Yoko, 134–136, 165
Orson Welles Cinema, 5–6, 48, 243
Orwell, George, 213
Oughton, Diana, 153

Parliament-Funkadelic, 21
Parry, Jim, 37, 43, 140, 147, 163, 185
Paul's Mall, 238, 243
Peace Corps, 67
Pentagon Papers, 223
Perry, Al, 81, 119, 123, 128–129, 183, 209
  on FBI documents read by Danny Schechter, 226, 228
  on the FCC, 255
  on lessons learned at WBCN, 277
Pink Floyd, 16
Project Place, 181

Psychedelia, 26–27
Pusey, Nathan M., 101

Queen, 185, 238
Quicksilver Messenger Service, 48

Radio. *See also* WBCN
  advertising on, 53–55, 181
  arrival of FM, 35
  censorship on, 80–81
  copyright laws and, 82–83
  gay and lesbian community and, 197–205
  talk show format on, 192
  top 40 AM, 35
Raitt, Bonnie, 249
Ram Dass, Baba, 140
Real Paper, 249
Reasoner, Harry, 223
Reed, Lou, 21
Reserve Officers' Training Corps (ROTC), 93, 99
Richman, Jonathan, 3, 238
Riepen, Ronald Ray, 127, 149, 155, 159, 175
  Boston Tea Party and, 11, 13–20, 27, 235
  WBCN radio and, 35–51, 53, 55, 233
Robbins, Terry, 153
Rogers, Joe, 39, 45, 77, 80, 140, 235, 252, 255
Rogers, William, 214
Rolling Stone, 140, 213
Rolling Stones, 80, 111, 179, 185
Rudd, Mark, 155
Ruthchild, Rochelle, 181, 183

Sancious, David, 249
San Francisco Chronicle, 213
Santana, 16
Sargent, Frank, 140
Sartori, Maxanne, 183, 185, 238, 243, 245, 252
Scagliotti, John, 165, 197, 200–203, 279–280
Schechter, Danny, 86, 93, 99, 101, 132, 134, 155, 159
  coverage of the Vietnam War, 165, 223, 225
  FBI interview of, 172, 175
  on lessons learned at WBCN, 278
  as news dissector, 161–177
  on offices in the Prudential Tower, 259
  reading of confidential government documents on air, 226–228
Scheuer, Sandra Lee, 218
Schneier, Barry, 48, 116, 249, 271
Schroeder, William Knox, 218
Sebastian, John, 140
Second-wave feminism, 179–195
  female artists and, 181
  John Lennon and Yoko Ono and, 134–136
Segal, Steven, 21, 35, 50, 67, 128, 235, 281
Segregation, 71
Shelton, Gilbert, 140
Silver, David, 7
Simon, Carly, 89
Simon, Peter, 89, 175
Slavin, Bob, 91, 165, 249

Slick, Grace, 181
Smith, Patti, 252–255
Solman, Paul, 175
Spock, Benjamin, 77
Springsteen, Bruce, 238, 243, 245–252
Squier, Billy, 238
Staples, Mavis, 181
Steinberg, Marsha, 101, 165, 185, 207, 226, 278–279
Steve Miller Band, 48
Stewart, John, 170, 171
Stewart, Rod, 16
Stone, Sly, 26
Student protests. *See* Campus unrest
Students for a Democratic Society (SDS), 93, 99, 101, 151, 280

Taj Mahal, 238
Taylor, Fred, 238
Taylor, James, 27
Time, 165, 197, 249
Timilty, Joseph F., 9
Today Show, The, 257
Tommy, 128, 235–237
Top 40 AM radio, 35
Townshend, Pete, 128, 235, 237
Traffic (band), 16

Ullman, Debbie, 183, 281
Underground journalists, 140
Unger, Craig, 175
United Press International, 149

Vanilla Fudge, 26
Van Ronk, Dave, 140
Vaprin, Dinah, 183, 255, 279
Velvet Underground, the, 16, 20, 21, 235
Vietnam War, 26, 61, 71, 75, 77, 149, 171. *See also* Nixon, Richard
  Boston Common Moratorium events against, 112–119, 123–125
  campus protests against, 91–109, 214, 217–220
  Danny Schechter's coverage of, 165, 223, 225
  draft lottery, 91, 93
  end of, 273
  FBI documents regarding, 225–229
  Pentagon Papers and, 223
  public opposition to, 111, 149–151, 161
  ROTC programs and, 93, 99
  WBCN opposition to, 111–112

Wailers, the, 238, 243
Wales, Howard, 237
Wallace, George, 71
Warhol, Andy, 13, 21, 27
Washington Post, 197, 225, 226
Watergate, 228–230, 265, 273
Watergate Primer, The, 230
Waters, Muddy, 16, 20, 21, 238
Wayne, Steven, 77, 119, 213, 220, 275, 279
WBCN
  advertising for, 267–268
  advertising on, 53–55, 181
  and the American Revolution, 77–89

  antiwar counterculture and, 77, 220, 223
  censorship and, 80–81
  change in music industry in the 1960s and, 48
  conflicts between classical and rock staff at, 40
  copyright laws and, 82–83
  Danny Schechter as news dissector at, 161–177
  deaths of Robert Kennedy and Martin Luther King, Jr., and, 67
  early announcers on, 35, 37, 48–51, 80
  Feedback program, 147
  as hub of the community and soundtrack of the city, 127–147
  Lavender Hour, 197–203
  lessons learned at, 277–281
  listener feedback for, 45–47
  Listener Line, 129, 132, 139, 165
  Lock-Up, 207–211
  news and public affairs reported by, 149–159
  opposition to the Vietnam War, 111–112
  Prudential Tower offices of, 257–263
  Richard Nixon and, 213–231, 265–275
  Riepen's change in format of, 39, 48, 53
  as rock and roll station, 233–255
  second-wave feminism and, 179–195
  as struggling classical music station, 37–39
  women hired by, 183, 185, 192–193
Weathermen, 101, 151–159, 280
What's Happening Mr. Silver?, 7
White, Kevin, 9, 199
Who, the, 16, 20, 128, 235–237
Wilkerson, Cathy, 153
Williams, Jerry, 192
Winer, Norm, 48, 93, 112, 123, 128, 132, 159, 163, 243
  on the criminal justice system, 207, 209
  on Jazz Workshop, 238
  John Scagliotti and, 197
  on the Kent State University shootings, 218
  on lessons learned at WBCN, 277, 278
  on Patti Smith, 252
  on resignation of Richard Nixon, 271
  as WBCN's first news director, 149–150
  on women hired by WBCN, 183, 185
Wolf, Peter, 50
Wolfe, Tom, 261

Yardbirds, the, 16
Youth International Party (Yippies), 119, 281
YouTube, 83

Zappa, Frank, 16, 209
Zimmerman, Bill, 101, 172
Zinn, Howard, 111, 165, 223
Zuckerman, Ed, 175